MICHAEL FOOT

BOARDING SCHOOL HOMOSEXUALITY

From Plato's Academy to the Princeton Rub

© 2016

Cover photo: an anonymous athlete, the pride of academies.

"The talk in the dormitories and studies was of the grossest character, with repulsive scenes of onanism, mutual masturbation and obscene orgies of naked boys in bed together. There was no refinement, just animal lust."
John Addington Symonds

"The horniness of teenagers is a force greater than sexual orientation."
"My looks by then had in any case declined to the point where only women would go to bed with me."
"Mutual and manual gratification is the rule."
Three quotes from Christopher Hitchens in his *Hitch-22*.

"Sex was always smoldering under the surface."
George Orwell

He had "dark hair, green eyes, and a classic head with the wistfulness of an angel in a Botticelli."
Cyril Connolly of an Eton boy, some of whom were gorgeous.

"He compelled me to agree to meet him in a public toilet in the cemetery on the outskirts of Shrewsbury, where he raped me. Oddly enough, much as I hated the experience, I think I had become so accustomed to systematic sexual abuse that I wasn't especially traumatized by the experience."
D.J. Peel

The first order that William Makepiece Thackeray received on his first day at school from a schoolmate was "Come & frig me," he wrote later.

DEDICATION

This book is dedicated to boarding schools, ateliers, lyceums, academies, dormitories and fraternities where boys can discover first love, among themselves, unhampered by the perverting interests of adults, free to experience a part of their sexuality that will help them choose the road they'll take later on, should it be heterosexual, homosexual or omnisexual.

The inspiration of my books dates from the French Revolution with its Declaration of the Rights of Man in 1789, the end of homophobia in 1791, followed by the right of each man to marry the boy of his choice in 2013, the whole confirmed, in the States, by the American Supreme Court. My books include: *Cellini, Caravaggio, Cesare Borgia, Renaissance Murders, TROY, ARGO, Greek Homosexuality, Roman Homosexuality, Renaissance Homosexuality, Alcibiades the Schoolboy, RENT BOYS, Henry III, Louis XIII, Buckingham, The Essence of Being Gay, Homoerotic Art (in full color), John (Jack) Nicholson, SPARTA,* and *Gay Genius*. I live in the South of France.

(http://www.amazon.com/author/mbhone)

INTRODUCTION

In writing this book I'm casting very large. Academies and Lyceums in Greece, home of the world's most beautiful ephebes, Spartan barracks, schools and sexuality in Rome and how they compared with those of Ancient Athens. Because so much information existed during the Renaissance, I'm limiting myself to the communal life in workshops and ateliers, which were Renaissance-style boarding schools where, because girls were protected with Brink's-like security, boys whiled away the nights in virile couplings and the days in lewd gestures and lewder jokes. The golden age of boarding-school homosexuality was England of the 1800s and 1900s (Oxford, Cambridge, Harrow, Eton and others are included in my definition of boarding schools), which spilled over, homoerotically, into the Apostles and the Bloomsbury Set that I've treated in fully-illustrated detail, as well as the eroticism in today's dormitories, the Princeton Rub an example. There is a full section on the erotic Greek and Roman texts professors used to excite the imaginations of the boys, justifying their sexual overtures. This study will take us into the lives of the most supremely powerful individuals to have ever lived: Plato, Aristotle, Alexander the Great, Lorenzo de' Medici, da Vinci, Cellini, Byron, Rupert Brooke, Duncan Grant, Maynard Keynes, T.E. Lawrence, Caravaggio, Michelangelo and many others--issued from various types of schools, men who have enriched us forever, men of genius who happened to have preferred other men.

I'm a boy of my times, one who prefers vocable like cock to weenie, fuck to liaison. This will be crude and offensive to some readers, but one has to be true to oneself, and today's liberties are to be cherished, even if those liberties have strict limits: a boy would be a fool to admit to his locker-room buddies that he prefers them to the chirping maidens in the showers next door.

For purists: I use numerals when I think a number is important--especially age milestones--because they stand out more clearly, no matter how big or small the number. And please forgive my personal interventions during the telling of the lives of these extraordinary men; I do try to keep them to a minimum.

CONTENTS

SCHOOLING IN GREECE

> **ATHENIAN SCHOOLING**
> Page 6
>
> **ALCIBIADES**
> Page 16
>
> *ALCIBIADES THE SCHOOLBOY*
> Page 22
>
> **SCHOOLING IN SPARTA**
> Page 29

SCHOOLING IN ROME

> **EDUCATION AND SEX IN ANCIENT ROME**
> Compared to Greek Love
> Page 35

SCHOOLING DURING THE RENAISSANCE

COSIMO DE' MEDICI
Page 44

DA VINCI
1452 – 1519
Page 45

MICHELANGELO
1475 – 1564
Page 51

CELLINI
1500 – 1571
Page 56

RAPHAEL
Page 65

CARAVAGGIO
1571 – 1610
Page 68

**CAPTAIN ROBERT JONES'S TRIAL, 1772,
THE RESULT OF BOARDING SCHOOL NOSTALGIA**
Page 78

ENGLISH BOARDING SCHOOLS (and one French example)

**OXFORD - CAMBRIDGE
HARROW – ETON – AND OTHERS**
Page 84

HOMOEROTIC GREEK AND ROMAN TEXTS
Page 97

FAGGING
Page 116

BYRON
1788 – 1824
Page 121

THE BLOOMSBURY SET
Page 131

AUDEN – ISHERWOOD – SPENDERS - KALLMAN
Page 146

RUPERT BROOKE
1887 – 1915
MAYNARD KEYNES – DENIS BROWNE
Page 157

LAWRENCE OF ARABIA
1888 – 1935
Damascus – 1918
Page 159

JACQUES D'ADELSWÄRD-FERSEN
Page 171

THE PRINCETON RUB (OR THE FIRST-YEAR-PRINCETON)

DEFINITION
Page 179

MORE ABOUT THE PRINCETON RUB
Page 181

TODAY
Page 182

SOURCES
Page 183

SCHOOLING IN GREECE

ATHENIAN SCHOOLING
(A complete biography of the sources for Greece and Rome

can be found in Sources.)

Before age 7 boys were taught at home, their education depending on the wealth of their parents. Boys from poor households were required to work in the fields and what they learned depended on the knowledge of their parents, which was minimal.

Wealthier families offered their boys pedagogues, who taught them how to read, write and do sums.

At age 7 rich families continued the education through tutors or through public schools, especially opened to the poor. Reading skills continued, as did learning the works of poets by heart.

At the same time boys entered gymnasiums whose purpose was threefold: to make boys' bodies beautiful, to prepare them for military service, and to conserve them for a healthful old age.

Secondary education began at age 14 and was often taught by philosophers. It consisted of rhetoric, biology, geometry, astrology and literature. Its purpose was to develop a lad's intelligence and character, the determinants of the person he would become. Those aspiring to emulate Pericles had to have a good secondary education.

At 18 one could go on to ephebe training, advanced military strategy and advanced academic schooling.

Solon saw to it that the poor were apprenticed in trades. Girls were taught at home by their mothers in order to, first, serve their fathers and, second, their future husbands.

Spartan education will be covered later.

There were two schools at the time of Aristotle's arrival in Athens, that of Isocrates and that of Plato. Later Aristotle would add his own college, the Lyceum. Isocrates' school was based on rhetoric, training for public speakers and lawyers, a sure guarantee of wealth. Speakers in Athens were highly praised and often elected to important positions. Every educated Greek was expected to speak convincingly, whatever the subject, and could win prizes of considerable value. Isocrates was rich thanks to his father who manufactured flutes and, like his father, he had a good head for business, charging his pupils 1,000 drachmae, a huge sum. The same curriculum held sway in Oxford and Cambridge too before the Middle Ages. As in Isocrates' school, only the aristocrats had the money to place their children there as students, but the rewards of a good education were bountiful, as Athenian speakers, in the role of advocates, were extremely well remunerated. Plato's school was more liberal, and it was there that Aristotle chose to go, perhaps in part because Plato accepted Macedonians more readily, a people that most Athenians found course and dominating. Courses were free for those who couldn't pay. Plato had been an accomplished athlete in his youth, trained in gymnastics. He gave up an athletic career when he heard

Socrates speak. Plato is known to have loved a certain Aster, meaning "star". He wrote, "You gaze at the stars, my Star; were I Heaven so that I could gaze at you with many eyes." He also loved Agathon, described as the handsomest boy in Athens: "When I kiss Agathon my soul is on my lips." Plato's classes took place in the Academy, land left to him by a man named Academus. It contained statues and sepulchers, plane trees and olive groves, and, eventually, Plato's tomb. The school would go on for 900 years. As to what went on in the dormitories, we have only brief etchings, ancient graffiti: Cleobis loves Biton, Agamedes can't take his eyes away from Trophonius, wondrous love shared by boys right up to Christian times.

Dion, 21, was a student of particular interest to Plato. He wrote this to the handsome lad: "O Dion who makes my heart mad with love for you." Dion came from Syracuse and convinced Plato to return home with him in order to establish his ideal republic by teaching its present dictator, Dionysius. When Dionysius proved to be immune to education in any form, Plato told him he was a fool and a tyrant. Dionysius retaliated by selling Plato into slavery! Luckily a friend bought and then freed him.

When Dionysius died, Dion asked him to return and tutor his heir and son, Dionysius II. Still mad about the boy, Plato agreed. Dionysius II proved teachable but highly influenced by his entourage that convinced him that Plato was going to turn Syracuse over to the Athenians, after having made Dion the new king. Dionysius reacted by banishing Dion to Italy and locking up Plato in his castle where he nevertheless continued on as Plato's student. A war broke out and Dionysius, perhaps fearing for Plato's life, freed him. When the war ended he wanted Plato back, but the philosopher naturally refused until Dionysius told him that in that case he would seize all of Dion's holdings in Syracuse, reducing the boy to poverty. Still in love, Plato took the first ship. But things soured between Plato and Dionysius, and Dion was again expulsed and Plato banished. Dion raised an army and invaded Sicily at the side of another of Plato's students, the Athenian general Callippus. Dionysius fled and Dion was installed as king. From his exile Dionysius paid a succession of assassins to infiltrate Dion's friends and murder them, one by one. He then bribed Callippus with enough money to run Dion through with his sword, which he did. But instead of relinquishing the throne for Dionysius as was planned, Callippus took it for himself. He took Dion's wife Arete too, but when he became suspicious that she was plotting with Dionysius, he had her jailed, where she gave birth to Callippus' child. Dionysius finally raised an army large enough to win back his throne. Callippus retreated to Italy. If this were not enough, Callippus decided to win back the throne and recuperate his newly born son. He raised an army of mercenaries that he treated so badly that one of them killed him, supposedly with the sword Callippus had used on Dion.

Despite his obvious love for Dion, Plato was nonetheless a kind of Athenian Tartuffe. He often asserted that he was disinterested in boys physically, from whence we have our word platonic. At any rate, he got an evident kick out of putting Socrates in the erotic situations that he himself certainly enjoyed. An example is his accompanying Socrates to a wrestling school where the handsome Critias entered naked amidst a group of friends with whom he was arguing. Socrates ''marveled at the boy's stature and beauty, and felt that everyone else in the room was in love with the boy,'' but Plato knew in advance that Socrates would never have access to such perfection. Plato often used Aristophanes to express his own opinions, as when he was supposed to have written these words for the playwright to use in a play: ''While they are boys they love men and like to lie with them and embrace them, and these are the best of the boys and youths. The evidence is that it's these boys, when they grow up, who become the best men in politics.''

Plato believed in person-to-person dialogue which could, by its own dynamics, lead to insight into the minds of the persons exchanging views, the outcome being the discovery of truth. Aristotle spent years as an observer rather than a participant. As with karate, in the Academia one had to work one's way up from white belt to black belt 9th dan, which was eventually the case for Aristotle, although compared to Socrates (9th dan) he was perhaps 7th. Aristotle developed a system that allowed him to completely dissect a subject, to see it from every possible angle, the end being, as stated above, the discovery of truth. The Roman Cicero praised Aristotle's works as ''rivers of gold.'' Alas, nearly nothing remains other than minute fragments.

In 343 B.C. Philip II invited Aristotle to his court to give instruction to Alexander, age 13, and his inseparable companion Hephaestion. Aristotle set up a school where Alexander, Hephaestion and their friends shared quarters. Ian Worthington, in his book *Philip II of Macedonia,* wrote that Philip sent Alexander to Mieza ''to be better able to concentrate on his studies, and hence sent him away to a 'boarding school'.'' Aristotle considered Hephaestion a far more assiduous student than Alexander and noted that Alexander shared all his secrets with the boy who was ''by far his dearest friend.'' As they were the same age they most probably shared each other's bodies in equal measure, neither one being predominantly the lover or the belovèd. Athenaeus says that Alexander ''had a boundless passion for beautiful boys.'' He, Hephaestion and their friends certainly practiced sex from the very onset of puberty, an act as prevalent and shared as boys pissing in each other's presence. In addition to early circle-jerk-like inquisitiveness, they moved on, as did all Greek boys in the total absence of girls, to sex that was largely intercrural, one of the boys lying on his stomach or leaning against a wall while the other entered his closed thighs from behind, kissing his ears and neck and reaching around to give pleasure to his friend's manhood, the origin of the Princeton Rub. All other forms of physical release were assuredly, at times, present. Their friendship was compared--by their friends--as resembling that between Achilles and Patroclus.

Philip turned over the shrine of the Nymphs at Mieza as a study room for the boys and their companions, and in thanks for Aristotle's services he rebuilt Aristotle's hometown of Stagira that he had previously destroyed when the town offered resistance to his army.

A moving story recounted by Aristotle concerns an uncontrollable horse that the boy Alexander managed to break in, the legendary Bucephalas. When he jumped down his father, an incredibly harsh man, went to him shedding tears, kissed him and told him to find a kingdom worthy of him, as Macedon was far too small. Aristotle taught him the art of medicine as he himself had been instructed before his father's early death, instruction that continued afterwards thanks to other members of his family who wanted to see Aristotle follow in his father's steps. Alexander always carried a copy of Homer's *Iliad* that he kept under his pillow with his dagger. Dionysius of Halicarnassus informs us that Alexander, Hephaestion and their companions were Aristotle's pupils for eight years. Because Plato had failed in reforming Dionysius II in Syracuse, it's possible that Aristotle hoped to succeed with Philip, especially as they were the same age. Aristotle may have lost prestige when, later, his nephew Callisthenes turned on Alexander and was executed. Plutarch seems to confirm this possibility, saying that when Aristotle arrived Alexander loved him as much as he did his own father, "for his father gave him life while Aristotle taught him how to live life." But then things changed and Alexander only remained with Aristotle because of his unquenchable thirst for knowledge. One has the impression that Alexander's mind was incredibly mobile, flashing from one philosophy to another, shifting from tutor to tutor, idea to idea, as he did sexually from boy to boy, although Hephaestion was most assuredly the love of his life, especially as Hephaestion was always, irrevocably, his staunchest pillar.

Alexander and Hephaestion formed a partnership during which Hephaestion commanded troops, built bridges, went on diplomatic missions, founded new settlements, as well as the incredible multitude of other tasks necessary when one rode with Alexander. During the siege of Tyre Alexander turned over the fleet to him, a difficult enterprise as the men he commanded had been conquered by Alexander's army and were thusly not the most responsive of allies.

When Hephaestion died from fever in Ecbatana at age 32, Alexander was prostrated with grief. He sent to the Oracle at Siwa to ask if he could deify his lover. The Oracle allowed him to make Hephaestion a divine hero, which seems to have satisfied him. At the time of his own death, a year later, Alexander was still making plans for the monuments, cities and shrines to be erected in his companion's honor.

Hephaestion had been sent to Athens to work out a reconciliation with Demosthenes, an orator of immense importance who had first opposed the military advances of Philip II, and then those of Alexander himself. Known for his love of boys, it's not impossible that this was a reason why Alexander dispatched the handsome Hephaestion. History's judgement of Demosthenes is unsavory. He had inherited great wealth and surrounded himself with youths, Aristion, Cnosion, Moschus, Aristarchus, to name a very few, whom he prostituted to augment his income. Demosthenes was thought to have been sexually passive, a highly disrespected role for a man in Athens where the act was reserved for boys, the penetrated always considered to be either a youth or someone unacceptably effeminate, which was most probably Demosthenes' case. To gain the favors of noble youths, Demosthenes did not hesitate to promise them ascendance over Athenians, thanks to the oratorical skills they would learn from him, an ancient casting couch. Once he gained control over a wealthy boy he would do what he could to despoil him.

Demosthenes was guilty of breaking two Athenian laws. The first stated that any Athenian who prostituted himself, and then made himself known in a public sense (speaking before the Assembly, for example) could be stoned to death. As Dover writes: "If an Athenian citizen made no secret of his prostitution, did not present himself for the allocation of offices by lot, declared his unfitness if through someone's inadvertence he was elected to office, and abstained from embarking on any of the procedures forbidden to him by the law, he was safe from prosecution and punishment." The second law had a similar penalty for those who showed hubris. As Dover says, "Hubris is a term applied to any kind of behavior in which one treats other people just as one pleases, with an arrogant confidence that one will escape paying any penalty for violating their rights and disobeying any law or moral rule accepted by society." Both Demosthenes and Alcibiades were multiple offenders of hubris. But, again, both were protected in high places. Dover had been to Cambridge and had been inculcated in histories of Greek love by his tutors. He later distanced himself from homosexuality by maintaining that he was happily married.

There was, however, an "amusing" quirk in the law against hubris. If a man did what he pleased with a woman, if he arrogantly used her, *raped* her, this was clearly hubris according to the Athenians. But he couldn't be accused of hubris if he did so because of uncontrollable, *unpremeditated*, sexual lust, then this was no longer hubris and he could get off scot-free (although he could, naturally, be brought to trial for having broken other laws forbidding rape.)

Surviving Greek amphorae, plates, bowls and twin-handled cups show boys playing sexual games and adult men fucking other adult men, but the practice was little spoken of as the passive partner was often, like Demosthenes, a subject of ridicule.

When Philip was assassinated, Demosthenes offered up public thanks to the gods and tried to convince Athenians to fight on the side of the countries who revolted when the death became known. But when the Athenians saw with what incredible rapidity and savagery his son Alexander the Great took things in hand, they sent a delegation to plead for his forgiveness, a plea that Alexander acquiesced to.

Shortly afterwards a boyhood friend of Alexander, Harpalus, asked for sanctuary in Athens after stealing a great deal of money. In fact, this was the third time he had fled from Macedon with funds that were not his own, but as Harpalus had been a close companion, Alexander had always forgiven him. The Athenians granted him asylum and the money he came to Athens with was put in Demosthenes' care. Of the 700 talents, a fabulous sum, 350 disappeared. While an enquiry went on Harpalus fled to Crete and Demosthenes fled to Aegina. Demosthenes was found guilty but the Athenians felt he was of such importance--thanks to his rhetorical skills-- that a ship was sent to bring him home.

It was at this moment that Hephaestion was sent to Athens to work out a settlement. Demosthenes' answer was to spread the rumor that Alexander, on campaign in Thrace, had been killed, as had his entire army. Hephaestion rushed to Thrace where he found his friend and his army intact. Furious, Alexander began to march towards Athens but an Athenian delegation caught up with him and, again, begged forgiveness. It was accorded but only if Demosthenes were turned over to him. Demosthenes preferred poison to being captured and executed by Alexander's men. Thusly ended the life of this repulsive personage, as later, in Rome, the equally detestable Caligula and Nero would meet their fates.

Hephaestion was appointed, along with Cleitus, joint commanders of Alexander's personal guard, the Companion Cavalry. Hephaestion was in agreement with his lover that the Macedonians and Persians should integrate. Indeed, he was Alexander's torchbearer, his best man, when Alexander married Roxana. Cleitus, and the older guard, were against Alexander's adoption of Persian ways. It was because Aristotle's nephew refused to kowtow to Alexander that he was now killed.

Just a word on Roxana. She bore Alexander's son, the future Alexander IV, posthumously. When word came of Alexander's death she had his second wife, Stateira, and his third wife, Parysatis, assassinated. She then put herself under the protection of Alexander's mother, Olympias. Alexander's friends, all former students of Aristotle, united and nominated one of them, Cassander, to take Alexander's place in Macedonia, and act as regent for his son Alexander IV. Instead, he had Roxana and Alexander, age 13, poisoned, along with a bastard son of Alexander, Heracles, whose mother was the daughter of the Persian satrap Artabazus. With these three dead he turned his attention to Alexander's mother, Olympias, whom he brought to trial, after promising her her freedom should she put herself in his hands peacefully. Instead, she was condemned to death and Cassander turned her over to the relatives of those she had killed--and they were legion. Her body was torn to pieces and she was thrown into the wild without last rites or a tomb. Cassander died from the swelling of his members, dropsy, in bed.

Back to Alexander and Hephaestion.

They crossed into India together at the head of hundreds of elephants; together they descended the Indus to the sea. Aristotle had described the two lovers as "One soul in two bodies." This proved to be the case when they both came to Troy, home--thanks to Homer--of the most famous battle in the history of mankind. They laid a wreath on the tomb of Achilles and Patroclus and it was at that moment that Alexander declared that his friendship with Hephaestus was in every point identical to the love between Achilles and Patroclus. They then ran a race, naked, in honor of the two heroes. Claudius Aelianus, the Roman author and teacher, states that "Alexander laid a garland on Achilles' tomb, Hephaestion on Patroclus'," meaning that it was Alexander, the lover, and Hephaestion the belovèd, signifying that Alexander inseminated Hephaestion--but most sources believe that Patroclus, older than Achilles, was the inseminator. Yet Alexander and Hephaestion were the same age, which certainly implies that they shared all the possibilities of love making without the slightest interest concerning what was customary and what wasn't. Alexander was Hephaestion's lover, friend, king and commander, but would this count in matters sexual? Plutarch tells us that in bed together, they would go through Alexander's correspondence. When there was a letter that Alexander wanted kept secret, he would touch his ring to his lover's lips, a wondrously moving example of love, spanning so many centuries, so incredibly numerous life spans, all thanks to Plutarch, certainly as stirred as the reader. And, lastly concerning their intimacy, we have the quote from Diogenes of Sinope who maintains that the only time Alexander was ever vanquished, was by the thighs of Hephaestion.

Another proof of love, some suggest, was Alexander's request that Hephaestion marry his second wife's sister and daughter of Darius. Up until then Hephaestion's name was never mentioned concerning either another man or a woman. Four months after Hephaestion's marriage he was dead, of fever, probably typhus, in Ecbatana. Alexander had been away and didn't arrive back in time to tell his friend goodbye. Plutarch says that his "grief was uncontrollable." Alexander had the tails and manes of all the horses shorn and banned music of any sort. One source states that he flung himself on the body and was only dragged away by force, another that "he lay stretched upon the corpse all day and the whole night."

In memory of Achilles and Patroclus he had the entire tribe of Cossaeans decimated. As for Achilles and Patroclus: "At the pyre, Achilles gave his eternal farewell to Patroclus. He did it simply, respecting even in death his lover's modesty. The corpse was lifted onto the platform. Below, into the gutters between the edge of the pit and the logs, the animals were sacrificed, the jars of food, oil and wine were emptied and the captured Trojans were condemned to die. Each of the twelve was on his knees facing the logs. Each had his hands roped behind his back. All waited their turn as Achilles himself passed behind, pushed his knee into their spines, pulled back their heads by the hair, and slit their throats with Patroclus' own dagger. Their lives, valiant manhood and beauty ebbed rapidly down their chests and formed puddles where they fell after being shoved into the pit." (1)

As mentioned, the Oracle at Siwa allowed Alexander to have the boy worshipped as a divine hero, but not as a god. Funeral games with 3,000 competitors took place. A pyre 180 feet high, with steps, was raised. It was decorated with ships and banners and figures of armed warriors, torches with snakes entwining them, golden wreaths and eagles, lions and bulls and weapons taken from the enemy. Diodorus recounts that Alexander had the sacred flame in the temple extinguished, an honor exclusively reserved for the deaths of the great Persian kings themselves.

As for Alexander, he died a year later, at age 33, also of fever, also typhus. Some say Aristotle was present. His body was placed in a gold sarcophagus and filled with honey. On its way to Macedon it was stolen by Ptolemy and taken to Memphis. His successor, Ptolemy II, transferred it to Alexandria where the sarcophagus was later replaced by one made of glass. There is lies today, under unknown sands.

As with Achilles and Patroclus, Alexander and Hestaestion represent the very best in a couple: loyalty, ambition, the quest for knowledge, the utter refusal of passivity. All four were united when they were young and beautiful, when their bodies could achieve the utmost in adventure and passion. They all died young too, a terrible sacrifice, indeed, but one that spared them the ravages of demeaning old age.

Back in Athens Aristotle opened his own school that was called the Lyceum, but also the Peripatetic, meaning "to walk around", due to his habit of strolling with his students while teaching them. According to antique historians Aristotle had love affairs with several of his adolescent students, among them the 'ravishing" Nicanor. Because of something he said, he was accused of heresy by Athenians who were thin-skinned on the subject. To avoid Socrates' fate he fled home to the Chalcidice where he died at age 62, extremely young when one considers that nearly all the philosophers at the time lived to their 80s or 90s, (a quirk that continues to this very day).

Plato introduces us to Alcibiades, the most beautiful, the most sought-after Athenian of his day. Alcibiades knew that Socrates could give him everything he needed to complete his rise to political power: knowledge, argumentation, rhetoric, dialectic, strategizing and worldliness. As for Alcibiades, he had only his physical perfection to offer in return. And so began the tradition of students homoerotically rewarding and corrupting their tutors. He thusly invited the philosopher to a dinner in which he deployed his every charm. His surprise was great when his guest, finding that Alcibiades had dismissed all his servants, did not immediately make clear, in one of the multiply forms that men employ to assuage their lust, his interest in the boy. In fact, after eating, Socrates rose to leave. Telling Socrates that the hour was late, Alcibiades suggested he remain the night. When he did so, Alcibiades crept into bed, beside him, and told Socrates that he knew of no man as deserving as he to gain access to his beauty, and it would be stupid if they didn't seek pleasure one with the other. "After all," continued the boy, "who better than you can make of me a better person through education?" Socrates agreed that it was indeed his aim to make him better, and so saying, he closed his eyes and man and boy spent the night ... platonically. The next morning Alcibiades recounts that it was as if he had slept with his father or brother, and then goes on to add, with all the modesty of those who are beautiful, that he was forced to admire the inner strength of Socrates, because he had resisted the body of the lad a full night! Xenophon goes on to confirm that Alcibiades needed Socrates because of the philosopher's immense "competence in discourses and in strategic action." He adds that Alcibiades may have known about Socrates' total control over his pulsations and was thusly certain to be able to offer himself without the slightest risk of being abused.

In Plato's *Banquet* he and Socrates felt they had to absolve man/boy relationships by finding a virtuous justification for them. This was apparently easy in man-to-woman attachments because the man and the woman worked in a virtuous tandem, in that he gave his sperm and she became physically pregnant with a child, this being the first virtue; the second virtue resided in the fact that, thanks to his progeny, a man became immortal. Man/boy relations could be virtuous when the players passed on to each other knowledge and wisdom (especially when the lover did so to his belovèd). The belovèd became pregnant in terms of his soul, and his child was the virtue his lover had implanted in him (knowledge/wisdom). Socrates claimed that without this kind of insemination the sex act was useless. Because Alcibiades was incapable of giving virtue, said Socrates, he was doomed to mortality. For Alcibiades things were far simpler: the eroticism of his inseminating a handsome youth was perfect fulfillment in itself. We don't know if these two philosophers succeeded in making the boy feel guilty, we don't know if they were even sincere in disseminating such nonsense. We do know that Alcibiades tried to seduce Socrates despite his age and ugliness, perhaps to show the philosopher that the philosopher really did care for the physical aspect of love, just like everyone else. (If Alcibiades were as handsome as the ancients say--and only half as wonderful as he thought himself to be--then the temptation must have been truly difficult for Socrates.) But we know for certain that when Alcibiades left the banquet he took a good breath of fresh air, and went straight to find a warm bed with a warm boy to fill it.

Alcibiades knew the truth of Theognis' words:

> I play, enjoying my youth. For I shall lie
> A long time under the earth, when life is gone.
> Deaf as a stone I'll leave forever the sun's warmth;
> Fine though I was, I shall see nothing more.

ALCIBIADES
450 – 404 B.C.

The world loves a rogue, and there is no better example than Alcibiades. He was all things to those who crossed his path: intelligent, courageous, ambitious, eloquent in speech, charm personified, so handsome that it's the first adjective employed by biographers and historians alike, sexually versatile, the ideal top to women, the perfect bottom to men; he was totally amoral, as depraved as a teenager, as corrupt as a cop, as streetwise as a delinquent, as pampered as the son of a wallstreeter, as sexy as Paul Newman; he was irreligious, treasonous, and the proof that the gods really do raise to dizzying heights those they wish to utterly destroy.

Today we have showmen, great orators, warriors and boys who are totally fearless. We have boys who are nearly superhuman in their beauty. There are arrogant boys, willful boys and, naturally, boys who's only interest is in themselves. There are lusty boys who live for sex, taking bodies and offering their own; boys who get off with girls, and boys who go with other boys or other boys and girls. But never have we had a combination of all these as we have in Alcibiades.

He sought ways to remain in the public eye, going so far as to cut off the tail of his dog, its most beautiful attribute. This caused the desired scandal among the Athenians to which he answered, ''Well, I got the attention I was looking for on the one hand, while taking their attention away from the really bad things I've been up to."

Alcibiades

Many men were thought to have slept with him as a boy. Once, when he disappeared for over a week, Pericles' friends suggested that an alarm should be raised in order to find him. Pericles had been named the boy's guardian since the death of his father when the boy was ten. He now answered that if the lad were dead a general alarm would only find him a little earlier than if there were no alarm at all; if he were alive, on the other hand, the discovery that he had run away would only harm his reputation. Left unsaid was the certainty that if he had run away it was certainly with some man, as no woman could supply him--or would dare supply him--with the luxuries to which he was accustomed. When Alcibiades found out that his guardian, the most respected man in Athens, had defended him, he knew that from then on he could do exactly as he wished. "For now on," he said to his companions, "the Athenians can kiss my royal ass." Pericles could provide private tutors for Alcibiades, as we will see in *Alcibiades the Schoolboy* that follows, a work of fiction but one that uses the Socratic form of seduction, and clearly mirrors the relations between Greek students and Greek tutors.

Anytus, a rich lad, invited Alcibiades to a meal among friends. Alcibiades arrived with companions but proceeded only to the dining room doorway from which he greeted Anytus and his guests, seated before a table with silver and gold tableware. Anytus was, asserts Athenaeus (who goes out of his way to do so), "Alcibiades' lover". Alcibiades ordered his companions to gather up half of the tableware, after which he bade Anytus a good evening. When Anytus' friends, scandalized, asked what Anytus was going to do about the theft Anytus answered that, on the contrary, Alcibiades had shown great tenderness in not taking it all. As hope springs eternal in the human breast, Anytus certainly expected that Alcibiades would show other forms of tenderness at another time.

Alcibiades received gifts (or took gifts, as he did at Anytus' dinner) in exchange for love, the penalty for which, at certain times in Athens, was death. Athenian citizens could sell their bodies to whom they wished, but in doing so they could no longer benefit from the rights accorded to citizens. They could no longer speak before the Assembly. They could no longer use the courts for reparation should they in anyway be maligned. If they attempted to do so, they were in real danger of being stoned to death. All that was needed was for someone, anyway, to prove that the person had, at any time in his life, sold himself. A foreigner, on the other hand, someone who was not an Athenian citizen, could prostitute himself/herself without any juridical consequences of any sort. Many foreigners did so and perhaps the totality of male Athenians took advantage of their services at one time or another. When the young Alcibiades left his bedroom at Pericles' home, it was to sleep with a man who had something to offer him, and the "something" in question was often money. Alcibiades, as a youth, was a high-class rent-boy who escaped punishment thanks to his guardian, Pericles.

Handsome lads were in great demand in Athens and as the competition to win their favors was fierce, it often cost their aspirants a small fortune, not to speak of the lengthy wooing. Life wasn't always easy for the boys either, as they couldn't show themselves as being too easy for fear of being treated as whores. Stringent laws tried to protect them, but it was clear that when boys wanted to amuse themselves, total surveillance was next to impossible. Foreigners and slaves could be put to death if they tried their hand at boy-love with Athenian citizens. Stringent punishment was reserved for teachers and trainers who had access to them in schools and gymnasiums, access forbidden to older boys over eighteen. Their fathers' male friends were especially carefully watched. If a guardian prostituted the boy he was supposed to protect, he could be stoned. If men couldn't get what they wanted from "nice" boys, there were always whorehouses. They flourished throughout Athens. The ones for boys had courts where the lads sunned themselves, naked, their wares in varying states of arousal. But whorehouses offered compensations. With "nice" boys, men often had to content themselves with intercrural sex, performed upright with the penis inserted between the thighs, while in whorehouses they could penetrate anally to their hearts' content. They could also get blown, otherwise a seemingly rare occurrence in antiquity. Of course, what took place in the schools and the school dormitories, and what took place between students and teachers in a hundred secret places, is what takes place to this very day in schools throughout the world, from adolescence on.

Cruising areas were the market place, back streets, in the martial arts schools, in cemeteries, along the quays of the Piraeus and in the Ciramicus, the potters' quarter, northwest of the Acropolis. Sex was mostly a hidden activity, although some amphorae and twin-handled cups show men fucking in full view of other men, leaving one to wonder just how private a matter sex was, under certain circumstances, in ancient times. Philemon tells us that the great lawgiver Solon, seeing that young men at times did very unlawful and foolish things due to their inability to find a sexual outlet, allowed prostitutes, male and female, to post themselves throughout Athens in front of their housing, totally naked so as not to fool the client. One paid one's obol and took one's pleasure.

Love between men has rarely been a long tranquil river. At times lovers fought, sword in hand, for the love of a boy. Plutarch tells us of Theron who chopped off his own thumb to show his love for his belovèd, and challenged a rival to do the same. Plutarch mentions, too, the case of Konon who killed himself, weary of the tasks imposed on him, and never rewarded, by a youth he wished to have as a belovèd.

Alcibiades had the image of Eros embossed on his shield that Athenaeus states was made of ivory and gold, leaving no doubt as to his amorous pretentions, to the loathing of virtuous Athenians. Having been brought up in the company of the likes of his guardian, Pericles, and Pericles' friends--actors, statesmen, philosophers, as well as the whores Pericles frequented--there was little that the boy didn't know and hadn't experienced from a very young age. The philosopher Bion suggests that he had indeed begun early on: ''Even as a child he made men unfaithful to their wives, and as a young man he made women unfaithful to their husbands.'' Aristophanes tells us in *The Frogs*, ''They love him and hate him, but cannot do without him.'' He wrote another play, lost, entitled *The Man with Three Dicks,* in which Alcibiades' erotic exploits were satirized. Alas, we know not in what way.

Statues of Hermes, god of travelers, were erected at crossroads. Their particularity was a fully engorged phallus with ample foreskin. As crossroads were places of encounter, the phalli took on erotic signification. Boys looking for adventure would stroke them for luck, girls searching for husbands did likewise, and women wanting children made pilgrimages to the sites--in fact, the phalli were polished to a luster. During the night preceding an expedition to capture Sicily, Hermes' phalli throughout Athens were vandalized, most probably by drunken pranksters, exactly the milieu frequented--and most often led--by Alcibiades, a youth known by all for his brilliant intellect and total absence of morality. As during our own times, in ancient Athens too people were unduly respectful of those of high birth and affluence, the reason they were reluctant to attack Alcibiades head-on. The destruction was also heresy, as Hermes was an Olympian god. And it was the worst possible omen prior to a military enterprise. But there was a strong possibility that Alcibiades would escape punishment thanks to his connection with Pericles and his immense wealth.

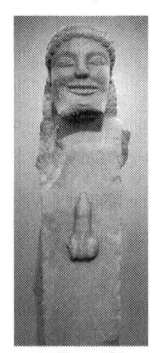

Hermes at the Crossroads

But in this case he was forced to flee to Sparta. A Spartan nurse had cared for Alcibiades and had instilled the love of Sparta in the child's heart. Also, his family had had traditional connections with Sparta. When a Spartan delegation came to Athens in search of a peace agreement in 421 Alcibiades, thanks to his family, enjoyed privileged access to the ephors. Alcibiades didn't waste time in seducing the Spartans. He wore their coarse clothes, bathed in cold water, ate their disgusting broths, drank their inferior wines, and fucked their women, one of whom was King Agis' wife who bore Alcibiades' son Leotychides. Alcibiades counted on Leotychides to found a new Spartan race of Alcibiadesian origin. It didn't help matters much when Agis' wife went around calling her baby Alcibiades, the name she preferred to Leotychides. Alcibiades could play the role of the perfect Spartan, Plutarch tells us, because he was the perfect chameleon--all things to all men, displaying virtue or vice as the occasion called. It must have been marvelous to observe his technique because men really liked and appreciated him, and being a man's man is not an easy task. Plutarch goes on to say that in Sparta he devoted himself to athletic exercises; in Ionia he enjoyed the luxury of the baths, oiled and perfumed, at ease with the fondling of both sexes; in Thrace he drank to the dregs among the dregs; in Thessaly he awed all with his horsemanship; and in Persia he exceeded even the Persians in magnificence. He was thusly accused of playing a double game, but men have been known to willfully march to more than just one tune without having treacherous motives.

Alcibiades had been sentenced to death in Athens, and now he was again sentenced to death, this time by the cuckolded Agis. It seems that Agis had no difficulty in believing the rumors of his wife's unfaithfulness simply because for a period of ten months that followed an earthquake--the magnitude of which had scared him out of his wits while copulating with her--he hadn't dared approach her again. Leotychides had been conceived during this time. Luckily Alcibiades was forewarned, giving him an opportunity to flee to his supreme enemy's camp: the Persian Tissaphernes.

Tissaphernes was the governor (called a satrap) of the western part of Phrygia, Lydia and Caria, a diplomat, a general and a key advisor to King Darius II. And he was right up Alcibiades' alley in the sense that he too was a lover of guile, an admirer of rogues, as well as being wonderfully subtle. He was also 40, an age during which a man especially appreciates a boy's beauty. And there was no one more beautiful and intelligent than Alcibiades, possessor of behavior so smooth it anesthetized the Persians into believing everything he said. In fact, Tissaphernes named his most beautiful garden, containing streams and meadows, pavilions and baths, Alcibiades Park, the name it was referred to ever after, a pleasure retreat both men shared during Alcibiades' sojourn. The situation was indeed remarkable as Tissaphernes loathed the Greeks for the disaster they wrought on Darius I and Xerxes. He was also, Plutarch says, psychopathic and perverse. Yet he ended up flattering Alcibiades even more than Alcibiades--an expert--flattered him.

He eventually moved on to the satrap Pharnabazus. Bewitched by Alcibiades who had lost none of his charm and little of his beauty, and who had known kings, princes, and generals, Pharnabazus offered him not only shelter but also the revenues from the town of Grynium. Believing he could do better, Alcibiades decided to see the great king himself, Artaxerxes II at Susa. He felt he could advise Artaxerxes on how to avoid mounting problems with Sparta. Perhaps fearing that Alcibiades would enthrall Artaxerxes as he did Pharnabazus himself, Pharnabazus refused to help Alcibiades in his quest to travel to Susa. The Athenian left anyway. The Spartan Lysander learned of his departure and informed Pharnabazus that if Alcibiades were not handed over alive or dead, Sparta would end all collaboration with Persia. Lysander, in turn, was being pressured by the oligarchy he had set up in Athens, men whose survival depended, they felt, on eliminating Alcibiades as a future menace to their very survival.

Alcibiades put in at a town along the way to Susa and, wanting company for the night, Cornelius Nepos tells us, took a young Arcadian, a loyal friend, to bed. Pharnabazus' men had followed him and very silently heaped brush around the habitation, which they then set on fire. Awoken by the light and crackling of the blaze, and guessing at its origin, Alcibiades flung his Spartan-style cloak around his left arm and took up his sword in his right hand. He and his friend threw as much clothing as possible on the blaze, making a narrow passage threw the flames. They leaped through a window and, naked, confronted men who immediately backed away. But they were outnumbered, and even from a distance many of their enemies' numerous spears and arrows hit their marks. Dead, Alcibiades was decapitated and his head bagged for Pharnabazus. His companion for a night, younger and faster, managed to escape.

Exactly like the Sparta he loved and admired, Alcibiades is one of the strangest, most original, most enigmatic creatures to have adorned the Earth. Lustful, intelligent and beautiful, even in boyhood his admirers had made him aware of every erogenous zone on his body, far in advance of the friends his age. He knew human nature and weaknesses thanks to his enlightened guardian Pericles, whose home and bed were replenished by his whore mistress, Aspasia, and whose salon was graced by the greatest philosophers and dramaturges the world has known. Just as importantly he allowed his body to serve, valiantly in battle, erotically in sex. Charm, class, a come-hither regard that could stagger, an orator capable of enthralling an assembly, a manliness that inspired other men, a self-confidence that won over diamond-in-the-rough Spartans and cynically jaded Orientals. People were truly fond of him, they genuinely liked to be around him, and so exquisite did he know himself to be that when Socrates chose *not* to lie with him, he honestly admired the philosopher's unfathomable restraint before such perfection. In the whole world I can only think of the Florentine Lorenzo *Il Magnifico* who comes close, minus Alcibiades' beauty and military expertise.

ALCIBIADES THE SCHOOLBOY
1630

Antonio Rocco (1586 – 1653) was a priest, a writer and an Aristotelian philosophy professor. He wrote *Alcibiades the Schoolboy* in 1630. In the story Philotime is modeled after Socrates and runs a school for boys. As far as the vocabulary goes, a boy's anus is referred to as his flower or garden, his cock is his bird and sperm is described as dew.

Here are some extracts. The full text as well as the complete life of Alcibiades can be found in my book *Alcibiades the Schoolboy* by Michael Hone.

Philotime's reputation was such that all Athens vied to place their sons under his instruction.

As for Alcibiades, the curls of his hair fell to his shoulders, so beautiful that the gold of the sun and the purple of his chiton felt themselves shamed before such perfection. His blue eyes were darts that went straight to the heart. His ruddy cheeks and coral lips opened on pearls of white in a delicate mouth, an invitation to be kissed. The long sculpted nose and flaring nostrils were promises of voluptuous, hidden treasures. His young hands promised dexterity in love and, later when more virile, strength in war.

Chiton

The parts hidden by his chiton were sanctuaries that certainly took their inspiration from his face: His chest resembled his forehead, his cheeks those two other cheeks, his cock his nose, his garden his mouth, his navel his chin, his feet his hands, his arms his thighs, and everywhere the same ruddy coloration. His voice was musical, his laughter a joy.

"Dear boy," began Philotime, "I promise to be even more affectionate with you than your father, and enter into your mind a dew so fertile and agreeable that it will seem supernatural. I won't use rough methods in instructing you, as is usual, but ways that you will find congenial. And so to begin with, let me offer you an affectionate kiss."

Docilely, the boy lent himself to the man's embrace. "That was not a kiss one gives a loyal friend, but one offers an enemy. To a friend one gives his tongue, which penetrates the mouth. The mouth is its true home. Please, let me fill you inside. Yes! Like that! I have it! I have it!"

The boy backed away but Philotime said, "Fear not, my son, the knowledge you seek in coming to me you will obtain when your tongue and mine are one!" And while caressing the boy's nipples, he interrupted each of his words with more kisses.

Philotime aspired for the sexual satisfaction he sought, knowing the road would be long and perilous with scandal and shame. So for the moment he contented the lad with gifts and when the occasion presented itself, he touched the secret parts of the young body, through the fine tissue of his chiton. The boy would frown, but even his knitted brows were an encouragement and a provocation, and at times the boy would allow Philotime to caress the cheeks within the tissue, two celestial apples.

As Alcibiades was infinitely more desirable than his other students, Philotime aspired to the day his longing would be fulfilled. And as the boy was often docile, one day he invited him to come to school earlier than the other students.

As for the other teachers, they were happy to see a boy so young apply himself to the teachings of his master, and they vaunted the merit of the said master, although a few had suspicions they kept to themselves for Philotime's reputation, in that way, was impeccable.

When Alcibiades arrived, Philotime took him into his room and as usual covered him with kisses, which Alcibiades was by now accustomed to. But then the master introduced his hand into the lad's hidden places, those destined for love and desire. Philotime panted and his hand trembled while foundling him. When the lad saw his master's cannon rise, ready for action and entry into his flower, his young eyes filled with tears of pain (*quand it vit son canon affûté prêt à batter la place, et à entrer par la brèche...*).

"How can you envisage something so shameful?" asked the lad, backing off. "How can a person of your standing dishonor a boy of good family? If a man of your age and stature commits such things, then there are no limits to the crimes youths such as I, whose blood is far hotter, can commit. Do you do this to other children? And if so, what do their parents think?"

Alcibiades said the words with displeasure but with enough respect for Philotime to not flee.

"Alcibiades, my beloved son, someone who loves you so deeply as I, does not merit your hatred. When Eros pierces a heart, age and the difference in sexes cease to exist. Your divine image has entered my soul and reigns there as an absolute sovereign. Love burns in my heart since the day I laid eyes on you. If you refuse to open your garden to me you will become an assassin, a parricide, for I love you like a father, with all the force of my soul, and I shall kill myself if not fulfilled. Don't repudiate me as a lover, for my standing as a teacher is equal to your royal blood. I bow low before you, awaiting your sentence of life or death."

"Dear master, I don't wish to dishonor you. Temper your desires, be discrete, take what I give you and will continue to give you, my kisses, my caresses, the permission to fondle my boyhood, but never will I allow you to go beyond that!"

Alcibiades left Philotime who gained courage with a plan to succeed later on. For the moment he took himself in hand, giving himself pleasure, all the while with the image of his adored angel before him, discharging into his fingers. (*Il se déchargea sur ses doigts du soin de le soulager, et ne cessa de se représenter à l'imagination, pendant la jouissance, l'image do son ange adoré.*)

When Alcibiades returned he reminded his master that not only was what he had in mind punishable by certain death, it was also against Nature.

"My adorable child, those who talk about what is against Nature are part of the nobility. They know that what is rare is valuable, so they want to make access to the flower rare, the pleasure of which is fit for only them. That is its unique object, blissful contentment. It's in recognition of pleasurable enjoyment that Sparta made laws binding boys to men. The man will appreciate a boy's garden until the flower has passed its time. The man will then seek a new flower and the boy, now a man, will seek a flower of his own.''

''If this is true, of what use are women?''

''My dear Alcibiades, man is guided by his instincts, the first of which is to reproduce himself so that he will continue on, from generation to generation. For this alone women must not be abandoned, nor enslaved, nor frustrated in the love that we owe them. We make children and at the same time we take our pleasure, and women achieve their greatest dignity. It is true that some men prefer women to boys, but Nature produced this affinity to ensure the survival of the species; others who shun boy-love are simply vulgar ninnies. And then, a boy's flower wilts rapidly, while that of a woman lasts far longer, happily for her. But it's because a boy's spring is so short that we give ourselves completely, and frequently and intensely in boy-love.''

''Tell me master, if one has such pleasure with boys, why do some turn to women?''

''Some find that the ultimate in erotic satisfaction is with women, that Nature has gifted them with secret, soft, warm parts that, when entered by the virile male member, facilitate coitus, enliven voluptuousness. And the voluptuousness, this quivering of two bodies, two epidermises, aided by ardent kissing, an act during which one loses oneself in another, in desire, is the only way to find true fulfillment. It is the essence of love. The tongues interlace, suck, breathe in the images of the other, the object of one's love. Both souls inhale into the heart, each in turn, the breath of Paradise. Both bodies interlace, like indissoluble vines. Both bodies form but one soul. Nothing is missing in their desire. The mystery of love is completed; nothing is lacking in the interminable orgasm.

''But a boy's flower, my dear Alcibiades, does it not enclose the very same Paradise? And even more, those two rounded cushions, lightly covered in down, conceived for the concavity of our lower abdomen, the rounded cheeks coinciding with our pubis. Is it not the height of felicity? And when one mounts a boy, one is bereaved neither of his kisses nor by the joy of his breath, perfumed by his amorous mouth. There too the union is complete, the intoxication shared. And the man can turn and take his belovèd face to face, his member in his garden, or gently play against the boy, according to his caprice. And when you take the lad's bird in your hands, feel it become inflamed, stand proud, stretch out fully, is that not the ultimate pleasure that inflames you, that invites you to attack harder, to multiply the strokes, to plunge deeper, fired by love?''

''But,'' asked Alcibiades, ''the form that a boy's bird takes, is it of importance to the pleasure between the lover and the belovèd?''

"Of course it must be well proportioned, neither too small nor too gross. Too small does not excite desire. Too big in only good when one reverses the roles. For me I like the member hard, rising from two small round balls, that will distill into my hands the wondrous dew. The bird is an instrument that gives and takes pleasure, nothing is more precious--as is yours, my belovèd."

While speaking Philotime had one arm around the boy's shoulder, while the other explored the depths of his secret parts.

"Before going further with me, my master, please satisfy my curiosity on other points. If one doesn't wish to go with women or boys, can one not assuage his ardors by himself with his own hands, without spending money, without fatigue, without submitting to anyone? Thanks to this means, for the least sensual itch we can have immediate and infallible remedy."

"Alcibiades my belovèd, jerking yourself with your own hands (*se pomper les humeurs avec ses propres mains*) is a miserable expedient which deprives us of our true being and kills our passion for the real thing. It's not only our semen that comes out, it's our very blood. It alters our features, makes us pale, and can even hasten death. Nature puts everything in the preparation of our dew, for it is that which regenerates our species. She makes it with the purest part of our blood, an enterprise that weakens our veins and saps the vital parts of our bodies. If we satisfy ourselves with our hands it becomes a habit thanks to the ease of doing so. The pleasure one has with the one one loves calms our spirit and contents our desire. Jerking leaves us unfulfilled and tires us out because, due to its facility, we do it so often."

"What is the best age, dear master, for pleasure with a boy?"

"From 9 to 18, but it depends. Some boys retain their freshness late, others fade early, and there are even infants that give you a hard-on when in their cribs," (*qui vous font bander dès le berceau*).

"But how can one so young be large enough to satisfy desires?"

"That's complex. Some are just naturally elastic enough, others become so through the habile efforts of their lovers. The secret is patience. Lovers must never impale their belovèds as do the barbarians. A good lover knows how to discreetly amuse his boy until he feels no pain, and by doing so the lover will increase the intensity of his own orgasm and make himself deeply desired by his boy, who takes more and more pleasure in the game of love."

"How does one go about it?"

"The boy must stretch out before the eyes of his lover, his cheeks raised and the passage into his garden always central. The boy keeps his bird half in and half out, as it were, giving himself pleasure with his stomach while the part out stimulates the ardor of the lover, the view of which is the first of the joys of love. And if the boy plays with himself or his lover takes his bird in hand, so much the better.''

"But, dear master, I don't see what the boy gets out of all this."'

"Surely you've already known some pleasure, Alcibiades, a boy as beautiful as you must have multiple suitors.''

"That is true, but I have been highly protected by my parents who have barred the route. I have had some exchanges with boys my age who did for me what I did for them, but the pleasure seemed in no way what you describe with men. So maybe I will try it.''

"As you wish," said Philotime, in full erection.

"But how can I know if it will please me?''

"Some boys have such pleasure when ridden that they become crazy with desire and they force their lovers to keep doing it. Other boys are calmer and do not admit to receiving pleasure. But I've never known a boy who can resist this form of bliss, and I know some so avid as to not support an interruption in the service of the cock (*pas d'interruption dans le service du vit*). They caress it, harpoon themselves on it!''

"Desire bids me to give myself to your wishes.'' So saying, Alcibiades removed his chiton.

The fortunate master fell to his knees and, kissing the boy on every part of his body, plunged his tongue into the most desired place, licking, sucking, drinking from his garden. He stopped just a moment and looked up at the boy, "You will be the Paradise of Athens, men without number will know your Heaven. You will make men's souls happy, and their bodies too.'' He continued to delight the boy, so much so that when Alcibiades no longer had the cock in his ass he forgot what bliss meant, and begged for the return of his perfect master.

So ends extracts from my own translation of *Alcibiade fanciullo a scula*, by Antonio Rocco.

To give the reader an idea of the dangers involved in boy abuse in Athens, consider the case of *Aeschines against Timarchus*, 346 B.C., a lesson in the haven of protection that schools and gymnasiums were meant to be for students who were nonetheless free to do as they wished among themselves, as sex was considered as normal a human function as eating and drinking, perhaps even more desirable, but no less a necessity.

An Athenian could do as he wished with a slave, a foreigner and a metic sexually, he could have sex with another Athenian, but he could not sell himself unless willing to give up all civil rights. If he became a rent-boy he could no longer appear before any assembly and plead or ask for aid for any cause. If he ever hid his having sold himself and then appeared before an assembly and was caught at it, he would be stoned to death.

Aeschines' father was a schoolteacher and Aeschines, born in Athens, tried teaching before distinguishing himself in the army, and finally becoming a government official. As such he went to conclude a treaty between Athens and Philip of Macedon. He was accused of selling himself to Philip by a certain Timarchus, an accusation of treason that Timarchus brought before the Assembly, the penalty for which was death. Aeschines struck back by bringing a counter-suit against Timarchus claiming that he had no right to speak before the Assembly as he had sold himself on the waterfront of the Piraeus when a boy. Timarchus was thusly forced to stand trial, giving us the first and only full account of male sexual relations in ancient Athens.

Aeschines began his speech by stating that Timarchus knew he had no right to appeal to the Assembly because "he knows that we live in a democracy, which means we live under the rule of law. Thanks to these laws a teacher cannot open a schoolroom or the gymnastic trainer the wrestling school before sunrise, and the law commands them to close the doors before sunset, for the law is suspicious of men being alone with a boy, or in the dark with him. No person who is older than the boys shall be permitted to enter a changing room while they are there. If anyone enters in violation of this prohibition, he shall be punished with death. The superintendents of the gymnasia shall under no conditions allow anyone who has reached the age of manhood to be alone with the boys. A teacher who permits this and fails to keep such a person out of the gymnasium will be liable to the penalties prescribed for the seduction of freeborn youths--death.

"If any boy is let out for hire as a prostitute, whether it be by father or brother or uncle or guardian, or by anyone else who has control of him, prosecution is not to be against the boy himself, but against the man who let him out for hire and the man who hired him. Moreover, the law frees a son, when he has become a man, from all obligation to support or to furnish a home to a father by whom he has been hired out for prostitution.

"As soon as the young man has been registered in the list of citizens, and knows the laws of the state, and is able to distinguish between right and wrong, he is responsible for his acts. If he then prostitutes himself, which is a reckless sin against his own body, and then seeks to address the Assembly or Senate, he shall be put to death.

"Now, a certain Misgolas got Timarchus into his own home and because Timarchus was well developed, young, lewd and in the very bloom of youth, Misgolas did what he wanted to do and Timarchus wanted to have done." Aeschines gives no detailed information as to what the sexual acts consisted of so as not to shame himself or the Assembly. Yet he gave a list of men who were shining, pious examples of how men should behave. Three of these men were Themistocles and Aristides who were fighting for the same boy, the outcome of which was Aristides' expulsion from Athens, while Solon wrote this:

> Blessed is the man sweaty from the gym,
> Having muscles, supple, strong and slim,
> Goes home where he may drink wine and play,
> With a fair boy on his chest all day.

Meaning that Aeschines was in no way speaking against male-male sexual couplings, but was referring exclusively to the law against a rent-boy later serving and addressing free Athenian citizens. He then goes on about Homer: "I will speak first of Homer, whom we rank among the oldest and wisest of the poets. Although he speaks in many places of Patroclus and Achilles, he hides their love and avoids giving a name to their friendship, thinking that the exceeding greatness of their affection is manifest to his hearers who are educated men. His lament following the death of Patrocles is proof of his love for him."

Aeschines goes on about beautiful boys who hadn't stooped to prostitution, going so far as to give a list of their names. The trial ends thusly:

"But your bestiality, Timarchus, is known to one and all. For just as we recognize the athlete, even without visiting the gymnasia, by looking at his bodily vigor, even so we recognize the prostitute, even without being present at his act, by his shamelessness, his effrontery, and his habits."

Aeschines finishes by reminding the Assembly that when they return home their young sons will ask them how the case the decided. "Does the Assembly want to tell them that it is now permitted for a boy to defile his body with the sins of a woman (being used as a woman)? Punish this one man. Do not wait until you have a multitude to punish."

Timarchus was indeed found guilty. He left his trial and hanged himself. (2)

SCHOOLING IN SPARTA

Spartan intellectual education was far less rigorous than that of Athenians. The schools were the barracks and Spartan boys learned only the rudiments of reading, writing, arithmetic and a smidgen of rhetoric.

Leonidas was co-king of Sparta at the time I choose to open this chapter, because it was he who tried to defend us all from Eastern barbarism, in the form of Xerxes, by forming a group of 300 men and lovers who all gave their lives at Thermopylae. There were always two kings in Sparta, one of whom had to remain home when the other left on military or diplomatic adventures. Kingship passed from father to son, but only to sons born after his father had been named king. The kings were priests who solemnized sacrifices, and supreme commanders of the army. In the field they had absolute power of life and death. The kings were aided by a council of 28, whose members were age 60 or over. It was an oligarchy chosen by the people but only from the ranks of the nobility. There was an assembly of citizens over age 30 who could only debate proposals offered by the kings or ephors, and voted by acclamation. The ephors, five in number, represented the people and made sure the kings protected the people's interests. Anyone could be elected ephor. In this way there were near-perfect checks and balances: the kings checked each other; the council represented the nobility, and the assembly the people; and the ephors maintained correct rapport between the kings and their citizens. In time, only the kings and the ephors would count. Later still, it was the ephors who detained power, perhaps because the kings, competing against each other, were often in deadlock. Two ephors always accompanied the king who took the field. It was also they who decided foreign policy.

All of Sparta was a giant military camp. When a child was born it was washed in wine in the belief that this would fortify it. It was then examined. If found wanting, it was exposed on Mount Taygetus, in a chasm known as the apothetae. It was more common for boys than girls to be killed in this way, as boys had to be perfect. Trials for babies included bathing them in cold river water and exposing them to the elements, insuring that only the strongest would survive and procreate.

From age seven the survivors were trained to endure pain and hardships through incredibly difficult discipline, making them invincible and totally dedicated to the state. From the age of twelve they were watched over by older men who were their lovers, with whom they assuaged their passion where they could, outside the barracks. The young boys were obliged to request this form of friendship, entering into it totally voluntarily.

The Spartans never hung around oil or perfume shops as did Alcibiades in Athens, but in their extremely limited lifespan, says Plutarch, ''They at times relaxed from the severity of their training or even, as at Thermopylae, during times of war. Then they beatified their hair and clothing, prancing around like horses, a true delight to the eyes.'' This was undoubtedly the great attraction for Alcibiades too.

An ephebe

The training center where the boys were enrolled at age seven was called the agoge (meaning "rearing"). They lived in groups called herds, under the authority of whip-bearing older boys known as boy-herders. They were given a red cloak and told to make their beds out of reeds, pulled up by hand as they were not allowed knives, from the nearby Eurotas River. They were underfed as an encouragement to go foraging--stealing--food to supplement their diet. There was no obesity under the Spartans, and thanks to this early training they could sustain hunger when on military campaigns. As said, they could enter a pedagogic relationship with older men at age twelve if they so chose. In these voluntary relationships the boys were sexually dominated, as older boys and men had to prove their strength and mastery in this practice (as they did in all others), a sexual bond that was both exceedingly intimate and yet known by all--there could be no secrets among companions who literally shared the same air. The boy was expected to endure the man's lust, although there were most probably moments of great tenderness among certain pairs. In exchange, the men made men of the boys, imparting that which was most precious to the boy, the men's knowledge and valor. They learned enough math and reading to get by, and besides their daily training and hunting expeditions, they played ballgames and took up singing and dancing, the latter an aid to their agility in silently approaching the enemy. At eighteen they became reserve members in the Spartan army and it was then that the best of them could join the Crypteia or secret police. At age twenty they were voted into one of the messes by their peers, but all had to agree to their entry, a requisite that must have been an enormous incentive for them to prove themselves strong and loyal comrades at all times. Incredibly, they were allowed ten years during which they could attempt to be admitted into a mess; if they failed to do so they were denied Spartan citizenship. At age thirty they could marry. Childbearing was certainly limited by the fact that they married late and then had to sneak into the women's quarters to do their duty. As boys had only a slight degree of literacy, they were encouraged to develop their reading and oratorical skills if they become diplomats or generals later on.

Belovèd and lover.

In Athens and Sparta one had to be very careful in how one treated a citizen boy. There was a code that had to be respected before a lover had sexual access to his belovèd. The lover had to show himself worthy, valiant, protective, a good teacher in terms of knowledge and the handling of arms. Gifts were appreciated: a new cloak, a chiton, a cup, a sword, a dagger, perhaps even body armor. While awaiting the moment for the boy to give himself completely, sex was mutual manipulation and intercrural (between the thighs). The boy was never treated brusquely if a lover wanted him to agree to be his belovèd. Things were totally different with women. They were bent over and entered from behind, vaginally and/or anally. They were also ordered on their knees while men thrust into their mouths, a scene on vases, but a scene not yet discovered concerning men and boys. In intercrural sex men were painted on vases as, says Dover, "bolt upright." An Athenian lost his manhood if he allowed himself to be entered. Men who fuck a great deal are supposed to feel the difference between the vagina of a virgin and that of a woman fully broken it, between a vagina that has not known child birth and one that has, the reason why many Greeks preferred anal sex with woman, as it was simply tighter. Men seemed to have found it degrading to go down on other men in ancient times, and they never went down on women.

The city-state was all-encompassing, and the people, as Plutarch says, "hadn't the time to live for themselves but like bees they slaved away for the benefit of the whole community.'' The Spartans' had thusly engineered, arguably, the most extreme militaristic society in recorded history.

Spartan women were trained like boys and were noted for their chastity, albeit a queen gave herself to Alcibiades. Because they had to defend the city-state when the men were away, they were, paradoxically, better educated and better fed than other women in the Greek world, especially when compared to Athens that treated its women with Persian-style misogynic disregard. Athenian women were there to cook and to bring forth boys. They were in the custody of their husbands, legally minors. An Athenian man caught having sex with them or any other woman in the household could be killed on the spot with total immunity. As men married in their late thirties and women married virgin when they were around 15, boys looked for sex among themselves.

If Spartan women couldn't produce offspring with their husbands, they bred for their country by being serviced by studs known for the fecundity of their seed. Husbands fully accepted this because they understood that they had to produce boys who would someday stand for them when they entered a room, as they now stood for their leaders.

Most of what we know about Sparta (and it's incredibly confused and limited) comes through Xenophon who sent his sons there to be educated much as, today, a father sends his boys to a military academy in the hopes that it will straighten them out. A Spartan boy had his admirers, who were many, and his lover, who was unique and with whom he exchanged emotive pledges. Nature being what it is, a boy may have wound up having many lovers, one at a time, and a lover many boys--*perhaps* one at a time. The boy then grew to become a man and took a boy, and the eternal cycle was repeated. It was good for a boy to have as many admirers as possible, good for his ego and for his future place in society, as each admirer would place a stone in the construction of the boy's ascendancy (it was good for his father's status too). The criteria were a beautiful face and a beautifully made body, but these were often ephemeral in comparison to a boy's courage, intelligence, personality, charisma and general lovability--not to mention his or his family's wealth and social status.

The boys crept out of their barracks to have intercourse with their wives, the stealthy stealing into the night firing the lust of their young, healthy loins, insuring the powerful inseminations that would bring forth sons of their own (and who would one day, it has to be repeated, rise to their feet for them, as they now rose to their feet for their current commanders). The girls were said to have had shaved heads and to have worn cloaks like the boys. Their husbands slipped into their cots at night and left nearly immediately to return to the barracks and their companions. Plutarch says that in many cases the men even had children before seeing what their wives looked like in daylight (which is hard to believe, I grant). Again, it's highly possible that this exceptional way of lovemaking--charging around in the dead of night like thieves--had been decided on in order to charge a boy's sexual libido to the maximum. Once they had children, Spartans could continue in this way or set up housekeeping in homes of their own. Sparta was a wild country, full of trees, bushes, ferns, boulders, brooks, meadows and mountains, all of which provided veils in acts of love and passion, although the usual sites for trysts between men and boys were just outside the barracks, gymnasia, training fields and campsites. As noted, a man too old to reproduce was obliged by law to get a young man whom he admired to do for his wife what he couldn't.

Men could impregnate boys but one had to be discreet about it. The tyrant Periander was murdered because during a drinking bout he asked his belovèd, in front of numerous friends, whether by this time in their friendship the boy was not yet with child. The boy leaned over as if fiddling with his sandals, and when his lover bent to see what he was doing, he thrust his knife into his lover's chest. When word spread as to the reason he had acted as he did, he got off with the approbation of his peers, the other boys.

Xenophon goes on to describe a tender battle scene in which a certain Episthenes, seeing that a handsome enemy boy was about to be executed, ran to Xenophon and begged for the boy's life. Xenophon approached his general, Seuthes, in charge of Episthenes, to ask if the lad's life could be spared, as Episthenes had shown himself a valiant warrior. Seuthes asked Episthenes if he would be willing to take the boy's place and be executed. Episthenes stretched out his neck and told Seuthes to strike off his head if the boy so ordered. The boy came forward to save Episthenes, but dropped to his knees and begged that both their lives be spared. Episthenes rose and enfolded the lad in his arms, telling Seuthes that he would have to kill them or let them both go free. Seuthes laughed and, says Xenophon, winked at him. The story is certainly true as someone of Xenophon's value would never have recounted it otherwise.

A Spartan had no life of his own; he had no existential problems to solve. Who knows? Perhaps there was something satisfying in the comradeship among men, knowing that when one awoke his day was planned, that he and his friends would eat, train and exercise together, march, sing and laugh in the fullness of men raised as brothers. Nothing to question; nothing to fear so long as they remained united. A visitor to their country must have been very surprised: an unwalled city of men and women who chose a healthy existence, one of bravery and simplicity, who followed the Apollonian ideal of moderation in all things.

Before leaving Sparta to fight Xerxes Leonidas sent to Delphi to learn what the Oracle had to say about the coming conflict. To say the least, the Oracle was, this time, precise:

> To you, courageous and brave men of beautiful Sparta,
> Either your glorious city will be wasted by Persians,
> Or you will mourn your greatest king, from Heracles' line.

At Thermopylae Xerxes' spies reported to him that the Spartans were exercising, bathing in the sea and caring for their hair. He asked the Spartan renegade Demaratus what was going on. Demaratus told the king that this was the Spartan way to prepare for death. When the king asked for more, Demaratus went on to tell the king that the Spartan army was the greatest the world had ever known, for they were free men fighting freely. Demaratus then said that the law was Sparta's only master, from which we have the incredibly moving Spartan epitaph known to every schoolboy, in honor of the 300: *Go tell the Spartans, stranger passing by, that here, obedient to Spartan law, we lie.*

Xerxes held back until Leonidas was betrayed by a local, Ephialtes, who led the Persians along a mountain track that outflanked the Spartans. The Persians, still afraid of the Spartans, shot thousands of arrows from a safe distance into the enemy ranks, killing them off one by one. When Leonidas, the descendant of Heracles, fell, his men covered his body with their cloaks. When they too died, Xerxes had Leonidas beheaded and his body hung from a stake. The Persians then sailed to Salamis and the final countdown for Xerxes who fled back to Persia like the dog he was.

The hallowed year of the Battle of Thermopylae was 480 B.C. (2)

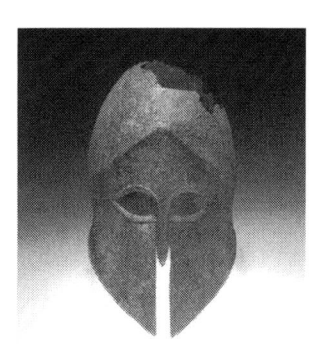

A Thermopylae helmet

SCHOOLING IN ROME

EDUCATION AND SEX IN ANCIENT ROME

Compared to Greek Love

Roman education was based on Greek education because the Greeks had founded schools based on Homer, Hesiod and their poets, while during the foundation of Rome Romans needed knowledge only in military arts, as their time was spent in war or in the fields producing food. Livius Andronicus was a captured Greek slave who gave private lessons to the sons of his wealthy captor, and for hundreds of years, before Augustus and Empire, education developed in this way, in private homes with private teachers, Greeks and freedmen. The instruction was in Greek and eventually in Latin as Greek texts were translated into Latin by Greek scholars. Later still the Romans developed their own poets, among the world's finest, but should a Roman wish still more knowledge he went to Athens or Alexandria.

In times before the engaging of private tutors, the father of the household, who held life and death sway over his sons, taught them what they needed to know to be a good Roman citizens, as well as the merest basis in reading, writing and arithmetic, enough to enable them to carry on a minimum of daily functions. But bit-by-bit it was noticed with what alacrity children could retain information, so they were offered more enlightenment, although the Romans would have a pragmatic approach to education throughout their entire history. A case in point was the importance of studying music for the Greeks, but not for the Romans, and athletics for Greeks who wanted their lads to be beautiful, while the Romans wanted theirs stout enough to kill Rome's enemies.

Education was never obligatory in Rome and most wealthy families employed tutors for children's elementary levels, while public schools were open for less rich Roman families. Early education was given in sites rented by teachers or, if they didn't have enough money, were taught in the open. They instructed the fundamental 3Rs, after which the students returned to the fields or became apprentices, and girls, rich or poor, contented themselves with household duties or, for the rich, preparation for a good marriage, while boys of the rich, 9 to 12 years of age, went on to grammar schools.

As in later boarding schools, grammar school teachers could whip the boys into obedience. The poorer teachers taught outside, others rented space, as said, and the best entered the service of the rich, one of whom, Verrius Flaccus, pitted boys against each other in learning competitions, which gained him such a reputation that Augustus himself hired him for his grandsons, making the man rich and in huge demand. A grammar school education continued until the boys were 14 or 15, after which only boys of the very affluent went to schools of rhetoric, the teacher called a rhetor.

These were highly qualified teachers who taught geometry, literature, geography, mythology and public speaking--declamation, oratory and other fine points in the art of delivery. The boys went on to become advisors to senators or specialized in criminal law and became lawyers, thanks to which they earned great sums of money and prestige, as did Cicero. They could also earn enemies: Marc Antony saw to it that Cicero's head was separated from his body when he continued to insult the oaf that was Anthony.

The pinnacle of education was in philosophy, which meant boys were sent to Athens. But learning for the sake of learning would always be a Greek imperative, rarely a Roman one, except for the most advanced men in the Empire, Virgil, Ovid, Horace and Cicero.

All historical sources conclude that the Romans couldn't care less if a man stuck his dick in a girl or a boy: it just didn't matter. Caesar himself was known to be a man to every woman, a woman to every man. His soldiers sang ditties to that effect as they marched along, perhaps not always to Caesar's amusement; in fact, Caesar was far more sensitive about losing his hair than having lost his cherry, when young, to King Nicomedes who happened to have been a Bithynian like Antinous, and like Antinous Nicomedes was noted for the dimensions of his member. The words hetero and homo didn't exist yet because the distinction between them was immaterial, and would remain immaterial until after the Renaissance.

Whereas Greek boys were encouraged to have older lovers and to learn from them, the Romans had sex for pleasure as long as the participants respected two iron-clad principles (although, as we all well know, all iron-clad principles, especially in sex, are made to be disregarded): A Roman male could not have sex with another Roman male. If he was horny and a slave (or a foreigner or anyone else, as long as he wasn't a Roman) passed by, he was fair game. The second principle was that a Roman male had to do the penetrating. It was he who was *vir*ile (*vir* meaning man in Latin). A corollary to the two principles was the very strong preference for young smooth hairless bodies, often between the ages of 14 and 20, marked by the onset of down on the boy's cheeks (permissible too on his butt cheeks). Greek boys had Greek lovers, often many, from whom the boys gained the key to life: *knowledge.* The boys were normally passive, the men active, and when the boys became men, the roles were inversed: they took on a boy of their own, their belovèd, and they became the boy's lover and teacher. There was also a practical side to Greek love. A lover would never ever show weakness before his belovèd and vice versa, which made them the fiercest fighting force the world has ever known.

The Romans and Greeks practiced vaginal and anal penetration, intercrural insertion and, rarely, fellatio. Mutual masturbation and circle-jerks were rarely mentioned because they were so common between schoolboys, a little like boys pissing together, and perhaps also because this took place between Roman boys. Parents despaired of keeping their sons, if they were beautiful, chaste. Roman boys did have access to slaves, just like their elders did, on whom they could practice intercourse, intercrural or anal. As today, the Romans associated male/male relations with Greece (in France one says, for the English Go Fuck Yourself: *Va te faire voir chez les Grecs).* In the same way that one drinks anything when thirsty or eats the food offered when hungry, a man will go with any male slave or foreigner when he has a hard-on. Diogenes the Cynic says that of the three appetites, food, drink and sex, sex is the easiest to fulfill as one need only rub oneself to obtain instant satisfaction.

Sex was found in brothels and latrines and taverns, parks and gardens and any other place sheltered from public view. Hadrian's successor, Lucius Verus, opened a tavern in his own home in order to create a climate for debauch. Male prostitutes showed their wares in parks and gardens as they do today, and many turned to acting to supplement their incomes, as did Hadrian's favorite Pylades and, later, Shakespeare's comedians.

Lucius Verus

As just being a wife was enough status for most women, men were free to look elsewhere for pleasure. In Rome love was always in the air (just like today). The Romans had adopted many of the Greek gods and their myths, especially those which dealt with Apollo and Hyacinth, Hercules and Hylas, Achilles and Patroclus, Zeus and his cupbearer and bedmate Ganymede. Antinous' role was strikingly similar to that played by Ganymede, and as he was Greek he was a safe foreigner, although it's doubtful that Hadrian would have turned him away should he have been a Roman citizen. The Greeks were not obliged to look for sex in gardens or taverns or back alleys. They had academies and gymnasiums where they could openly entice boys, although not those under age 18. Rich parents sent slaves to accompany their sons to and from the gym. Sex between boys was so current that we have the story of the Greek boy who didn't share his schoolmates' interest in men. He prayed to Zeus so that he too could be moved by the love of boys, but when this failed to happen, he committed suicide.

A huge difference between the Greeks and the Romans was that the Greeks preferred their boys with modest members, the perfect size to fit the anus and the mouth, whereas the Romans followed the cult of Priapus, and, as today, thought that bigger was always better. Clapping could be heard in the Roman baths when a man of healthy dimensions paraded through the corridors. One Roman, Cotta, was known to invite only guests to his lavish dinners whom he had first seen at the baths--a word often on his lips was donkey. Presumably, even heteros today show deferential admiration for those who show more manliness than they do themselves, which does not necessarily have anything to do with the desire to be penetrated. Roman boys often wore phallic amulets to protect them from the evil eye, and even today Roman men and boys quickly touch their balls to ward off evil, as when, for example, they see a passing priest.

Some hoopla developed concerning the roles of the Greek lover and his belovèd. Lovers didn't just fall in love with any boy, but only those who showed intelligence and maturity. The sexual link was ephemeral and came to an end with the growing of a first beard. From then on the boy and lover became loyal friends and remained so throughout their lives. Love was to be simple and undebauched, built on education and physical maintenance. But if intelligence was the primary criteria, wondered Cicero, why did lovers only fall in love with handsome youths and never ugly ones?

Boys, then as now, were mantraps: The poet Tibullus tells us that we have no chance against tender youths, who give us ample reason to love them. This boy is pleasing due to the masterly control he has over his horse; this other one causes our hearts to flutter when he breaks the surface of the water, showing his snow-white chest and nipples; so and so captures us by his daring; such and such by his peaches-and-cream complexion. At times youths objected for the form when men made advances, even menacing to tell their fathers if the men didn't cease. But once bridled, and the man could find rest after expulsing his lust, it was the boy who sought more, awaking the man from sleep by the gentle entreating of his buttocks. Again satisfied, man and boy plunged back into the arms of Morpheus for an hour before the boy asked if the man would like to do it again. The man did, but when the boy stirred still again, an hour later, it was the man who threatened the boy, "If you don't stop I'll tell your daddy!"

Fellatio and cunnilingus were both looked down upon as being unclean. The former, fellatio, was often associated with grown men with beards. Women were there for fucking, boys for sodomy and bearded men for cock sucking. Another degrading aspect was the use of sex to further one's advancement. From multiple sources we learn that this was Hadrian's way with Trajan's entourage: he advanced through fucking the emperor's influential friends, and by being fucked by them. But given the known promiscuous nature of Trajan's court, and the incredible sexual arousal in a climate of lustful males, most of whom were not simply Trajan's buddies but youths recruited to fulfill the needs of the emperor and his associates, Hadrian's task had certainly not been arduous.

In the ancient world, as today, boys and men knew pining, tears, longing, despair, self-sacrifice--the entire panoply of sentiments. In Thebes the Sacred Band was formed, 300 lovers and their belovèds, fed at public expense and housed on the acropolis, they formed a group of warriors who would sacrifice themselves at the snap of a finger for their companions. Love between men was so special in Thebes that it was, says Plato, illegal for anyone to maintain that it was *not* beautiful. Thanks to the Sacred Band Thebes freed itself from Spartan domination, until it was totally destroyed by Alexander the Great, he who was said, as related, to have known defeat only once in his life, when confronting the thighs of his lover Hephaestion.

Naturally, had there been only homosexuals in Thebes, Thebans would have died out. Plutarch relates the story of a rich Theban woman who arranged the kidnapping of a handsome ephebe that she then kept at her side until he understood that she was as interested in his welfare as she was her sexual satisfaction. She married the lad, to the fury of his male suitors. (This brings to mind the wonderful scene in *Some Like It Hot* in which Jack Lemmon returns from his date with Osgood and declares to Tony Curtis that they're going to get married. "But why would a guy marry another guy?" asked Curtis. "For *security*!" exclaims Lemmon.)

Pederasty referred to, in ancient Greece, young men, not young boys. There was, naturally, no *legal* age in Greece. The boys involved were military age, which infers that they had left boyhood. In Greece pederasty was simply the socially accepted erotic friendship between a man and a boy, a boy being between the ages of 15 to 17 (many Greek poets refer to 16 as the perfect age for the belovèd). In Crete it seems to have been a vital ingredient in military life, sanctioned by Zeus himself, an active pederast. In all other aspects of Greek life pederasty was clearly apparent: nude athletics, nude sculptures of ephebes (kouroi), historically famous cohorts of men and boys such as the Sacred Band of Thebes.

From this distance in time it's hard to pin down the behavior of the belovèd. Some poets claim that his role was passive in the sense that he contented himself with being beautiful, looking meekly at the ground as his lover greats him, allowing the man to stroke his cheek and gently nudge his genitals through the boy's chiton, as Phitotime did in *Alcibiades the Schoolboy*. Today this would seem erotic and daring, but also how arousing! Perhaps the lad did feel he had to play a submissive role, but I'm sure all masks fell away while he was being, later and in private, tenderly caressed by his lover.

Boys in Greece were free to choose their suitors, while the boys' sisters had to comply with theirs father's wishes, wishes based on political and economic advantages. The boys received continual gifts and tender attention from their lovers, the girls were paid for and sent to the kitchen or the bed according to their husband's needs. Girls remained virgin until marriage and remained loyal to their husbands. Boys could have as many relationships with other boys and men as they wished, each serving as a step upwards in the boys' advancement through society. As related, the same was true for Hadrian who sought influence with Trajan by plowing the buttocks of the emperor's consorts or allowing access to his own. In Athens as well as in Rome boys and their multiple lovers remained friends, often throughout their entire lives, a phenomenon that we find later between Cambridge and Oxford boys when they became men.

Prostitutes served as an alternate form of sexual outlet. Romans and Greeks had the choice of women, girls, wives, men, boys and pleasuring themselves. The only difference, as said, was that Roman men could not have sex with other Roman men or women (other than one's own wife or husband), but only with foreigners, slaves and prostitutes--a rule certainly broken on occasion. And they had to be the top, in today's parlance, never the bottom. In Greece anything went down as normal and good, although throughout all time the penetrator has always been more respected than the penetrated. Prostitutes were looked down upon and Roman or Greek nobles thought to have sold their wares were tainted through the rest of their lives.

Virtus, manliness, was the quality that drove the Roman state and gave the Romans *imperium*, power, over their women, over foreigners and foreign countries. This manliness was tied to sexual dominance. A Roman man was expected to penetrate the rest of the world as he did mistresses and his boys, and it was he who would decide who would be allowed to penetrate the females in his household.

In Plato's *Symposium* we learn that man-and-boy love was advantageous because no army could overcome the bond between lovers, and it worked in the favor of democracy because no despotic ruler was more powerful than the loyalty between men and their boys. We have the case of Harmodius and Aristogeiton: Hippias and Hipparchus were joint dictators in Athens. Hipparchus fancied Harmodius who refused his advances. To gain revenge, Hipparchus refused to let Harmodius' sister take part in the Panathenaea Games, accusing her of not being a virgin, a requirement for the games. Harmodius and his lover Aristogeiton decided to rid Athens of the dictatorship and thusly redeem the honor of Harmodius' sister. With daggers hidden in their chitons, the boys fell on

Hipparchus at the foot of the Acropolis, stabbing him to death. Hipparchus' guards immediately killed Harmodius and Aristogeiton was captured. While being tortured to reveal any coconspirators, Aristogeiton swore to tell the truth if Hippias would promise him clemency, sealed with a handshake. When Hippias complied, Aristogeiton laughed at his having shaken the hand of his own brother's murderer. Hippias, mad with fury, thrust his dagger into Aristogeiton's throat (2).

Plato claimed that the ideal nation would be based on lovers, because no lover would ever dishonor his belovèd. To the contrary, he would do everything in his power to build him up, to educate him, to do for him all that was virtuous and good and honorable. All the great gods, all of them with the one exception of Ares, god of war, were lovers to their belovèds. (Ares was too unfeeling to appreciate tender friendships: he killed and maimed, maddening men so they would take nursing babies from their mothers and dash their brains against walls or tree trunks.) The poet Theognis justified his own love of boys by relating, to friends, the story of how Zeus had abducted Ganymede. As in Rome, the Greeks too were unaware of the concept of sexual orientation. Men quite simply did what they wanted to do (as the enlightened ones do to this day). Only the role in the act was of importance. In Rome and in Athens the penetrator was masculine, adult and of high social status; the penetrated was a youth or, if not, he was categorized as being effeminate or socially inferior. Not only did men share a sexual relationship with boys, they saw to it that boys were educated in the Greek way, meaning in the responsibilities that would be theirs in manhood. The period between the moment the man took a liking to a boy and the moment he quenched his desire, could be several weeks or months, giving the youth time to assure himself that the man had a genuine attachment for him, one that surpassed sexual lust. Normally the youth had body hair, but cases of boys being appropriated at age 12 were not unknown. Such was Patroclus' role with his beloved Achilles: friend, teacher and protector.

In Rome men may have preferred the passive role, desiring to be penetrated by their slaves, but such men were not considered as being *vir*, real-men: only the penetration of a handsome youth, by a man, was judged conventional. The use of perfume and cosmetics and others forms of effeminacy were tolerated by some men when they concerned youths, but not adult men. Roman boys and men were allowed male-slave-sexual-partners as a way of discharging one's lust, an alternative form to pleasuring oneself. The male-slave-sexual-partner was generally replaced, sooner or later, by a wife. The slave would then cut his hair short and join the domain of the other slaves. A slave boy could be castrated to preserve a youthful aspect, as Nero had castrated Sporus before marrying him. Naturally, slaves could service their mistresses as well as their masters. As with Caesar (and King Nicomedes), Roman males often went through stages during which they evolved from being sexually passive to sexually active. In one well-known case, involving a youth who did not manage the transition from passive to active, his father, Quintus Fabius Maximus Eburnus, had his son killed for being "unchaste." The hypocrisy of the matter was that as a youth Fabius himself was called a "chick", signifying a boy-love-object. He was known for his good looks and availability. His reaction towards his son was perhaps a counter-reaction against his own juvenile misdeeds. The satirist Juvenal states that male prostitutes were found in streets known to all, as well as the baths, especially valued as one could check out the potential of what one was buying. As previously mentioned, the key word for most same-sex-enthusiasts was "hung". Apuleius, the irreverent writer of *The Golden Ass*, mentions a banquet in the midst of which a "*well-endowed*" young man was fellated by all the participants.

Same-sex marriages were not legally recognized in Rome. The aforementioned Juvenal criticized them because he felt that one day they would be legalized. Nero purportedly married several men, Pythagoras and Sporus among them. Nero was the bride and wore a bridal veil, the men received a substantial dowry. Cicero accused Mark Antony of being a slut in his youth and married to one Curio. This is one of many reasons Antony insisted on Cicero's death the moment Antony gained power. The exquisite Emperor Elagabalus is reported to have married his charioteer, Hierocles, and the athlete Zoticus. He was assassinated at age 18.

Rapists were subject to death if they raped a woman, boy or man. Slaves, prostitutes and entertainers were public property, and as such couldn't be raped (even up to Shakespeare's time actors often rounded off their monthly earnings through prostitution). A man who was raped (anally or orally) was legally exempt from public stigma. It goes without saying that rape was the perfect vengeance, and according to some sources it occurred as often between men as it did between men and women among the Romans. When it happened to a Roman citizen it was thought to equal, in horror, parricide, the rape of a virgin or the robbing of a temple.

Augustus banned soldiers from marrying, a ban that held good for 200 years. Soldiers could not have sex among themselves in the same way that no Roman citizen could have sex with another Roman citizen outside of marriage. Many took mistresses and had children that they recognized after leaving the service. All turned to prostitutes of both sexes and gang rapes following military conquests. As with all other Roman citizens, a man was forbidden to lose his masculinity by allowing his body to be violated. The historian Polybius wrote that a soldier found guilty of being penetrated was clubbed to death. Plutarch recounts the story of the handsome recruit who was pursued by his commanding officer. He shunned the unwanted advances until the officer ordered him to, in effect, bend over. The recruit drew his sword and plunged it into the chest of the commander. Not only wasn't the recruit sentenced to death, the mandatory sentence, he was awarded the Crown for Bravery, the equivalent of today's Medal of Honor.

It seems evident that due to the multiple ways of appeasing one's lust, Roman males put off marriage. Naturally, if a woman was of the high nobility and wealthy, she didn't remain without a husband for long, but with husbands seeking release with young girls and boys who were foreigners, slaves and/or prostitutes, and with one entering into adultery as freely and guiltlessly as did the Romans, the birth rate diminished to such an extent that the great Augustus never stopped chewing out the men who frequented his court. Finally, laws were drawn up, forcing men to marry at the very latest between the ages of 25 and 30, and to produce a child before age 26 if they wished to escape penalties. Women were to marry between ages 20 and 30, giving birth during her twentieth year. Men who fathered three children or more received rewards and rapid career advancement (as they did, years before, in Sparta). As boys sought fortune by giving themselves to older men (an example being Marc Antony and the wealthy Curio whose relationship lasted so long that it was considered an unofficial marriage by some) in hopes of a rapid and rich inheritance, a law was passed allowing such legacies only from close relatives. Widows were obliged to marry within two years of their husbands' deaths and divorcees within 18 months. Also, Augustus, knowing that theaters were the preferred sites for men who hoped to waylay boys, set aside special sections where the boys could be accompanied by chaperons, an extremely difficult task as handsome boys always found a way to men who knew the art of flattery and knew of boys' ever present need for the sound of sweet jangling pocket change. Of course, Augustus too had been a beautiful boy and had certainly had his share of suitors (in truth, his beauty could only be described as have been exquisite). Where before one had looked the other way concerning adultery, now adulterers were punished with banishment or flogging. Augustus had his daughter Julia sent to rot on an island, as she was found to have spread her thighs for literally any virile male. Male/male relations were never punished, but the loss of one's seed between a boy's buttocks or through autoeroticism were considered a waste in times when the state needed kids, and plenty of them. (5)

SCHOOLING DURING THE RENAISSANCE

COSIMO DE' MEDICI
1389 - 1464

In Florence Cosimo de' Medici helped found humanism with his friend Niccolò Niccoli. Cosimo offered Niccoli the funds necessary to send him far and wide, even to the Holy Land, in search of the ancient manuscripts that would bring the words of the likes of Plato into the very living rooms and libraries of the Medici, hundreds and hundreds of volumes. Each discovery that Cosimo made, each old text he unearthed, was like Howard Carter peering into the tomb of Tutankhamen. Cosimo employed forty-five copyists to spread the liberating concepts of the ancients, assisted by Niccoli who wore a Roman toga to the embarrassment of his entourage. Greek studies became a part of Florentine university instruction and artists like Donatello and Brunelleschi built their art along classical lines.

One of the first great schools was established in Mantua by Vittorino da Feltre, around 1410, where Latin, Greek, Cicero, Caesar, Plutarch, Virgil, Homer and Cicero were taught, along with mathematics, philosophy, history, rhetoric, poetry, music, mythology, and astronomy, accompanied by dancing, fencing, hunting, swimming, all under the Greek ideal of a sound mind in a sound body. The education was for the upper classes, the lower ones at times attended elementary schools where they acquired a smidgen of reading, writing and how to do basic sums. Erasmus and the invention of the printing press helped things along, and immense strides took place in painting, sculpture, architecture and literature.

Renaissance School Boys.

DA VINCI
1452-1519

Leonardo was gorgeous and so were his boys, beginning with Salaì, magnificent in da Vinci's two paintings, *St. John the Baptist* and *Bacchus*, the absolute ultimate in homoerotic art. The beauty of Leonardo can be admired in Francesco Botticini's *Tobias and the Three Archangels*, Leonardo shown as the first angel; and Verrocchio's *Archangel Michael*.

Salaì was Leonardo's nickname for his boy lover, meaning Little Devil, bestowed when Salaì, unmanageable and stubborn, hotheaded and careless, proved to be a liar and a not-so-accomplished--although highly assiduous--thief. This at the prepubescent age of ten. A very close friend of Leonardo's, Giacomo Andrea, was present during one of the first meals shared with Salaì. It is suspected that Leonardo's idea for the *Vitruvian Man*, the male body made up of two superimposed figures showing four arms and four legs, was originally Andrea's invention, and bares an amazing resemblance to Leonardo himself. Of Salaì Andrea said he was a glutton who ate as much as four monks, spilled the wine and broke whatever his fingers came upon. Another friend, the painter, architect, writer and historian Giorgio Vasari wrote that Salaì was "a graceful and beautiful boy with curly hair and a delight to Leonardo." There is no doubt that he was Leonardo's bedmate, the only question being from what age? Along the line Leonardo drew him with a huge erection, a drawing called *The Incarnate Angel*. But Salaì was such a prankster that he may have drawn in the phallus himself on one of his master's many drawings of him. (Another drawing is entitled *Salaì's Ass*, the boy's buttocks shown surrounded by penises.)

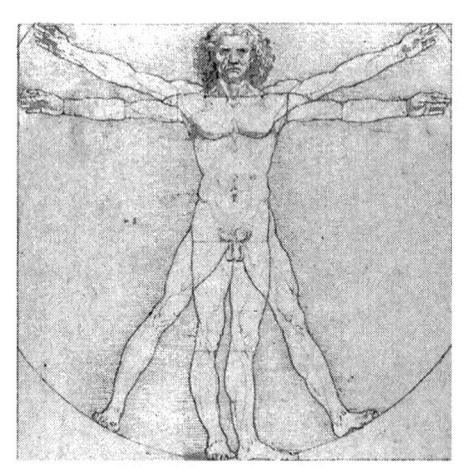

The Vitruvian Man

Numerous times Salaì made off with Leonardo's money, but as the painter had endless commissions, he was rich and, at the end of his life, even wealthy. Salaì is said to have bought clothes with most of the lucre he swiped, at one point possessing thirty pairs of shoes. Throughout his entire life he remained by Leonardo's side, at times replaced, as with the handsome Melzi. Melzi to whom Leonardo left half of his fortune, the other half going to Salaì. But most importantly, both boys remained loyal to the master, both present at his side to witness his last breath.

Some find it incomprehensible that Leonardo, known for his exactitude (most sources say it took him 4 years to paint the *Mona Lisa*, others as long as 14), painted *John the Baptist* as an erotic young man and not the usual old prophet in most paintings. The surprise is greater still when we learn that in Leonardo's painting the Baptist was at first totally nude, and that only later were animal skins added (which reminds me of the "artist" Daniele who covered up the genitals of Michelangelo's Sistine Chapel men, earning the sobriquet "the painter of breeches"). At any rate, Leonardo kept the painting with him to the very end, understandable as *John the Baptist* is the most beautiful portrait of a young man that has ever been put on canvas. He kept the *Mona Lisa* until the very end too, at the Chateau of Clos Lucé, a chateau given to him by François I, who is believed to have held his head as he expired, perhaps his last gaze on Salaì at his bedside or Salaì, much younger, the model for *John the Baptist*.

John the Baptist

Leonardo's exposure to boys was literally limitless. In the workshop artists and their models came and went as they discussed artistic issues and gossiped, most of whom were sexually available. And as Leonardo gained in reputation, he was surrounded by a constantly renewed court of extremely beautiful boys and young men, friends and models, many of which adorned his paintings and notebooks: thighs, buttocks and penises from repose to full erection, or, in his words, "long, thick and heavy" to "short, slim and soft," writes Leonardo, and he continues: The male member "has a mind of its own. When we desire to stimulate it, it obstinately refuses, or the opposite. When a man is asleep it is awake, and when he's awake it's asleep. It remains inactive when we want action, and wants action when we forbid it." He maintains that "it" can at times be dangerous, inundating the world with human beings the world in no way needs, as well as being the entry point for diseases (syphilis having reached Italy in 1495). On one page of his notebook he noted: "A woman's desire is opposite to that of a man's. She wants the size of his member to be as large as possible, while he wants the opposite (in the woman's sex), so that neither gets what he's/she's after." Leonardo, both gorgeous and good natured, must have made a lot of boys extremely happy.

Vasari wrote that "there is something supernatural in the accumulation in one person of so much beauty, grace, strength and intelligence as in da Vinci." Da Vinci was also said to be preternaturally gentle for the period, kind to rich and poor alike, generous, always in good humor and possessing a sense of humor. Vasari goes on to say, "Leonardo had such a great presence that one only had to see him for all sadness to vanish." As a person he personified what Plato would call the perfect alloy of *virtu*, intelligence and knowledge. Leonardo was born, out-of-wedlock, in 1473 in the Tuscan hill town of Vinci, near the Arno River that flows through Florence. His father was a wealthy legal notary and his mother a peasant. His full name was Lionardo di ser Piero da Vince, meaning Leonardo son of Messer Piero from Vinci. He lived his first five years with his mother, then with his father who married four times, but never Leonardo's mother.

At age fourteen he was apprenticed to the painter Andrea di Cione, known to the world as Verrocchio, in whose *Archangel Michel* we see the incredibly beautiful Leonardo. The choice of Verrocchio was fortuitous as his paintings are exquisite, the demonstration that Fortune never ever stopped looking over Leonardo's shoulder. Verrocchio's shop was in Florence, another lucky break as it was then, as today, arguably the most beautiful city in the world. Verrocchio never married, but this was true of half of the male population of Florence for whom freedom to live their lives as they wished was of prime importance. Verrocchio's apprentices included Ghirlandaio, Botticelli and Botticini, whose *Tobias and the Three Archangels* features da Vinci. At age twenty Leonardo's father set him up with his own workshop, but his love for Verrocchio was such that they worked together until Verrocchio's death. Verrocchio was a father figure, perhaps the most important man in the artist's life.

Verrocchio was described by Serge Bramly in his marvelous *Leonardo* as "a sort of one-man university of the arts." He knew and taught literally everything with the exception of huge wall murals, the reason for the disastrous destruction of the *Last Supper*. When Verrocchio was only 17 he had struck a boy, age 14, with a stone, killing him. He was jailed but released when it was proven that the incident had been an accident. Verrocchio was nonetheless haunted by what he had done to the very end, especially as he was a good man, sensitive in the extreme. Verrocchio's father died the year of the accident and Verrocchio found himself at the head of a family consisting of his mother and six brothers and sisters. Years later, now well-off, he was still providing for them as well as his nephews and nieces. Verrocchio was apprenticed to a goldsmith and began learning the skills of drawing, engraving, carving and metallurgy, followed by other jobs in which he would master sculpturing, painting, the basics of architecture and his favorite subject, mathematics. He was commissioned to make the tombstone for the person who started the Italian Renaissance, Cosimo de' Medici. Verrocchio established his own workshop, a large room with all the instruments an artist uses on the surrounding walls, plus sculptors' turntables, workbenches, easels and kiln, as well as shelves bent by the weight of busts and plaster body parts. Around the workshop and upstairs were the living quarters for the boys and the kitchen. An apprenticeship lasted around thirteen years, which started with sweeping the workshop and cleaning the materials, moved to the rudiments of drawing, making paintbrushes, preparing canvases and pigments freshly ground every day; sculpting, painting, drawing, decorating; even learning how to make salts out of human excrement--from dawn to dusk, seven days a week.

At age twenty-four Leonardo was arrested for sodomy. Four years later he moved in with the Medici, with Lorenzo *Il Magnifico*, thanks to whom commissions began to rain down on the lad. From there he went on to the career for which he is known the world over. Salaì followed in his footsteps, helping with his paintings, constructing the machines inspired by the master, keeping shop for the man who would reward him with a golden retirement, providing Salaì with a piece of land and the money on which to build a home. Salaì would later die in a duel, some say by sword, others by firearms, still others by a crossbow.

Salaì was the gift of God that those of my sexual persuasion could rightly give thanks for each and every day left to us on earth. A saner man than Leonardo would have thrown him out when the boy stole his first lire, or when caught in bed with another of the master's apprentices. But the genius whom we are all acquainted with, the master of every domain that took his interest, revered the boy as his source of inspiration, as the cherished love of his life. Leonardo could see beyond the daily tribulations and petty treasons. Instead, he held firm to the companion with whom he would walk the rocky path of life, right up to the end. That Salaì was beautiful and beautifully built was important, without doubt, but in a land like Italy, with apprentices he had to turn away in droves, he could have found a dozen replacements. But Leonardo knew that in the end one goes ahead alone or one grants the concessions necessary to share the route with another. The alternative is sterile old age.

The second love of Leonardo's life was Giovanni Francesco Melzi who became his apprentice around 1508. The boy's father was a senator and a captain in Louis XII's army. Unlike Salaì who only partially succeeded as a painter, Giovanni Melzi did some remarkable works. As handsome as Leonardo had been in his youth, Giovanni followed his master to the end, inheriting half of his oeuvre.

Vasari tells us that it was around this time that a boy, 20, living in Urbino, decided to forget everything he had ever learned about art and dedicate himself to copying Leonardo's paintings, paintings that had just come to his attention. The boy had a magnificent name, Raphael.

Finally came his encounter with the man with whom he would end his life, François I, age 19, a giant at more than 6 feet, who loved war, placing himself in the front lines, and was an insatiable womanizer. The year was 1516; da Vinci had 3 years left to him. He became François' tutor, and their days and nights were filled with discussion, often in the presence of Salaì and Melzi, all three immeasurable comforts to the old man, old beyond his years as seen in his self-portrait. Personally, I have never, ever come across a life as perfect as de Vinci's; never has there been a man as deserving of the name Man.

Giovanni Francesco Melzi

The last words will be Melzi's, in a letter he sent to Leonardo's surviving brothers: ''He was the best of fathers to me and the grief I feel at his death is impossible to express. As long as I have breath I shall feel an eternal sadness, for every day he gave me proof of a passionate and ardent affection. Each of us will mourn the loss of a man such that nature is powerless to create another." (7)

MICHELANGELO
1475 - 1564

Few men had lived a longer, fuller life than Michelangelo, perhaps none has bequeathed as much artistic wealth to humanity as this tortured genius, dead at age 89, with a chisel still in his hand, at work right up to the end. The body was destined for burial in the Basilica of St. Peter's still under construction, but was stolen by Florentines in the midst of the night, destination a city Michelangelo had not visited for 30 years, his nonetheless beloved Florence. Paraded through the streets to his last resting place, word of mouth spread as to who it was, and soon the streets were jammed with crowds. At the Basilica of Santa Croce the coffin was opened for the benefit of the crowd. The body within was intact, clean and totally lifelike a month after his passing, proof to the assembled masses of the artist's sanctity. But he had not had the luck of going to his tomb in company of his lover, as da Vinci did with Salaì and Melzi. The love of Michelangelo's dreams, Tommasso, was absent, and the love of his life, Urbino, had preceded him in death.

Michelangelo was born a Florentine and he died a Florentine, even if his birth had taken place outside of Florence in Caprese, and he had been destined for burial in Rome. The Florence of that epoch was the most beautiful city in the world, 30,000 Florentines massed together between walls that surrounded the town, a space so narrow it could be walked across in less than an hour. Divided in half by the Arno where ruddy-cheeked boys swam naked in its refreshing waters, Florence was the birthplace of the Renaissance and home to the hallowed sextet, da Vinci, Michelangelo, Raphael, Botticelli, Cosimo de' Medici and his grandson Lorenzo *Il Magnifico*.

His full name was Michelangelo di Lodovico Buonarroti Simoni, his father was Lodovico who was forced to place him in the bustling workshop of the immense painter Ghirlandaio, at age 10. Forced because the lad was headstrong despite, says Ascanio Condivi, a painter and Michelangelo's biographer, Lodovico's "outrageously beating him." Lodovico had destined the boy for more literary quests, beginning with the obligatory study of Latin, a language Michelangelo would always regret not having learned as it separated him from the ranks of the nobility he admired, a regret that burned like a coal until the day he died. But he did make it to Ghirlandaio's, as if directed by the hand of God, in the same way that Leonardo had been fortunate in finding Verrocchio. Michelangelo's older brother, Lionardo, didn't fare as well. Destined for commerce, his father placed him in a school where an abacus teacher, Raffaello Canacci, sodomized the boy, age 10, "often and often from behind," he admitted to the court. He was fined 20 florins and a year in prison which was dropped because he confessed his sin. Lionardo entered the orders, became a Dominican friar, and disappeared from history. Lodovico had five sons about whom he said, "None of them would give me the slightest help or even a glass of water."

In the workshop apprentices learned to look after the tools and keep them clean and in working condition, as well as keeping the shop clean and doing the shopping. They became familiar with the materials used in fresco and tempera, and in the preparation of paints, and how to prepare the surfaces over which the assistants and the master would paint. In exchange for their labor they discovered the secrets of their trade. Michelangelo soon became better than Ghirlandaio, which was bad enough, but he bragged about his superiority in frescoes and tempera to the other boys, earning Ghirlandaio's disdain for the boy's arrogance.

Michelangelo learned about Ghirlandaio's workshop thanks to a boy two years older, Francesco Granacci, who would remain his friend until his death. Together they were sent to work for Lorenzo *Il Magnifico* de' Medici who owed a part of his prestige to his position as patron of the arts. At the moment Lorenzo lacked sculptors and Ghirlandaio sent him the two promising boys. Here Condivi recounts the charming story of Lorenzo coming on Michelangelo as he was sculpting a faun. He pointed out to the boy, then 15, that a faun as old as the one he was creating wouldn't have had a mouth of such perfect teeth. Michelangelo is said to have not been able to hold still until Lorenzo had left so he could knock out a tooth, and then he couldn't wait until Lorenzo returned and admired what he had done. Alas for boy and man, Lorenzo, although still young, had but four years left to live. About Lorenzo the great historian Guicciardini wrote, "No one, not even his enemies, denies that he was a very great and extraordinary genius." Lorenzo provided him and Granacci a room and a place at his excellent and refined table, the table conversation itself an exceptional education. Yet despite the refinement, Lorenzo's household was run on an extremely informal basis. One was free to come and go as one wished, and to say what one wished, and Lorenzo himself was always available to boys like Michelangelo, whereas visitors of high rank often had to cool their heels for days before being admitted into his presence. A grown man was present, Poliziano, a professor and Latin poet, a founder of humanism. He translated works from the Greek, especially Plutarch and Plato. He was also a rampant lover of boys, and one can only wonder what effect his intelligence and enticing talk had on seducing the young artist. He took an interest in Michelangelo and was said "to have loved him greatly." Another boy was also present, Pietro Torrigiano. He too was a sculptor under Lorenzo's patronage, and later he brought the artistic segment of the Renaissance to England where he finished his life. He was also Michelangelo's boyfriend, a lad of startling beauty. When Michelangelo made some disparaging remark concerning his work, he broke the artist's nose, an infliction that greatly diminished Michelangelo's faith in himself, as he felt he was no longer handsome.

Thanks to his sculptures Michelangelo became rich, but the money was put away in banks or under his mattress. His brother Buonarroto found him living in dingy, humid lodgings, dressed like a beggar. But Michelangelo would always live in avarice, collecting and hiding money, and at his death a whole chest of gold was said to have been found under his bed, a fraction of what he had horded away. He never slept enough, ate enough, or dressed warmly enough. He made it known to those around him that he was penniless, perhaps to keep them from asking for alms.

Julius II became pope, taking Julius Caesar's first name as his own. Julius asked Michelangelo to build his tomb and asked where it should be placed. Michelangelo answered "in St. Peter's that I will build." "At what cost," asked the pope. "100,000 ducats" was the artist's answer. "Make it 200,000" was Julius' rejoinder. Julius advanced 1,600 ducats, money that Michelangelo immediately invested in land around Rome and property in Florence, especially houses in the Via Ghibellina, as well as depositing a part in the bank. He then started work on the Sistine Chapel, painted daily on fresh plaster, a technique of such huge difficulty that even da Vinci is suspected of having given up work on his *Battle of Anghiari* because of his failure in mixing the right components, and then, later, making mistakes when doing *The Last Supper* which, consequently, is lost to us forever. That Michelangelo succeeded on just the mechanics, mechanics on such an incredible scale, is in itself a miracle, not counting, afterwards, the choice of the right oils and right pigments. A patch of plaster to be covered during a day's work was called a *giornata*, the seams of which cannot be seen from afar. Errors could be made up for by painting over the dried plaster, *a secco*. Differences in temperature and humidity complicated the making of the plaster, and the mixing of the colors was a daily challenge, especially as the final result could only be verified once the plaster had dried. Mistakes, when not corrected by painting *a secco*, led to the destruction of the day's work, starting again from scratch. The Sistine paintings are a homage to the male body. In the part dedicated to the story of Noah, called *The Drunkenness of Noah*, Noah is painted in the nude, his sons, shown covering the body while averting their eyes, were also painted--for absolutely no biblical reason--stark naked too. Four years later, at the end of his labors, Michelangelo wrote in a letter to his father, ''I work harder than anyone who has ever lived!'' And it was so. But at age 37 the King of Florence, thanks to *David*, became the King of the World. (For much more, see my book *Homoerotic Art*.)

On the sexual front Michelangelo could solicit whom he wished, although longer, more intense relations were known to have existed with Piero d'Argenta, an assistant, and an assistant known as Silvio, whose bedside he refused to leave when the boy became ill. Antonio Mini, 17, replaced Gherardo Perini, 19, who wrote that he was ready to offer Michelangelo any service. Niccolò da Pescia, "who lives with me," wrote the master, followed. There was Febo di Poggio and then Federico Ginori that Cellini describes as a young man with a fine spirit, noble, with handsome looks, whom a princess later took for lover.

He had his models and assistants, all of whom happened to be among the most beautiful and desirable boys found wherever he decided to set down roots. Michael Rocke, in his *Forbidden Friendships*, tells us of a letter Machiavelli wrote to a friend, describing, in couched terms, what men did at night in Florence, what Michelangelo certainly did: "A man of my acquaintance went from one site to another that lads are known to frequent, and then wound up finding 'a little thrush' agreeable to being kissed and having 'his tail-feathers ruffled.' After this successful find, the man sealed his conquest," as Machiavelli put it, "by thrusting his *uccello* (dick) into the *carnaiulo* (ass)." Benvenuto Cellini writes, in his autobiography, about a youth called Luigi Pulci "whose singing was so lovely that Michelangelo, that superb sculptor and painter, used to rush along for the pleasure of hearing him whenever he knew where he was performing." The boy became Michelangelo's lover. Cellini goes on to say that Pulci's father had been beheaded for incest and that the boy had "just left some bishop or other, and was riddled with the French pox (syphilis)." Cellini nursed him back to health, after which the boy had an affair with the nephew of a cardinal and with Cellini's own mistress, in revenge for which Cellini wounded him with a sword. Pulci was later killed falling from a horse while showing off in front of Cellini's mistress whom the lad was still seducing. All this is proof again that, in Florence, as in ancient Rome, a boy took advantage of literally any orifice that presented itself. Another source tells us that Michelangelo "spent time without end helping boys, like Andrea Quaratesi, to learn how to draw, as tutors "helped" boys in schools since *Alcibiades the Schoolboy*."

Michelangelo met Tommaso de' Cavalieri and sent him a letter in which he said, "I promise that the love I bear you is equal or perhaps greater to that I ever bore any man, nor have I ever valued a friendship more than I do yours." Thanks to Tommaso Michelangelo would know his own Renaissance, a new life at age 60, and he still had 30 years left to share it with this young gentleman. Michelangelo immediately set himself to drawing, the most rapid way to offer presents. One was *Tityus*. Tityus was

Zeus' son who tried to rape Leto, in punishment for which he was eternally attacked by a vulture. Next came the drawing of *Ganymede*, being carried off to Olympus where he would serve as Zeus' servant and bedmate. Then came *The Risen Christ*, a full-frontal nude, followed by *Phaeton*, the son of Apollo who nagged his father until allowed to drive the chariot of the sun. He lost control and Zeus had to kill him before he hit the earth, destroying it. Another highly unique drawing was *The Dream*, showing a naked young man surrounded by a ring of vices, a woman (a man with breasts) awaiting copulation, the exquisite buttocks of another young man, and a fully engorged dick. They were gifts to Tommaso, all accompanied by what would turn out to be dozens of sonnets.

The Dream

Paul III became pope. He had been named a cardinal by Alexander VI because he was the brother of Alexander's mistress. The Romans changed his name from Cardinal Farnese to Cardinal Fregnese, "Cardinal Cunt." Paul III had been waiting years to get his hands of Michelangelo and did so now by ordering him to paint *The Last Judgment* in the Sistine Chapel, an immense work that would require scaffolding seven stories high and take five years to finish, longer than he had taken on the entire ceiling. In other Last Judgments only the damned were featured naked. Here nearly everyone was, the saved and canonized alike.

Then absolute disaster struck. Francesco d'Amadore, whom he called Urbino, died. He had come into Michelangelo's service as a young man when the master was himself but 30. Michelangelo grew to love Urbino, but in a decidedly different way from Tommaso. Urbino was well cared for, fed and clothed, and he did whatever was needed, from the marketing to the grounding and mixing the paints. But he never received a drawing as did Tommaso. Nor did he merit a sonnet. Yet he was always there. Michelangelo would never put on a clean shirt to greet him, nor, when the sap rose while painting his nudes and he wanted relief, would he need more than pull the ribbons that released the cloth covering his engorged manhood, waiting for Urbino to do the rest. Urbino was always there. Just there. Until he was there no longer. It was then that Michelangelo died, not the biological end that came later. God may not exist but we need Him to exist, He must exist in something, and that something, for Michelangelo, was Tommaso de' Cavalieri. He was the love of Michelangelo's life but not *the* love. That was Urbino, the only person permitted to accompany him during the painting of *The Last Judgment*. Just before the end Cellini had pleaded with Michelangelo to return to Florence, leaving Urbino behind to take care of his master's workshop and belongings. As Cellini related in his autobiography, "Hearing this, Urbino, in an uncouth way, shouted out 'I will never leave Michelangelo, not until either he or I is under the ground'."

Surrounded by what the world has to offer in supreme beauty, Michelangelo died alone, having pushed away even Tommaso at the end, thusly sparing himself the cruelest of all destinies, seeing his own ugliness reflected in the eyes of those he had cherished most, the eyes of his lovers, models, assistants, apprentices, boys he met and offered to draw or to teach how to draw, boys in taverns and in alleys after dark in a city, Florence, reputed for its warm nights of sublime encounters--with the imperishable boys of imperishable Italy. There would be no Salaì or Melzi at his side. Like Hadrian who lost Antinous, he too would meet his maker alone--the world's supreme artist, not just in his time, but of all time. (7)

CELLINI
1500 - 1571

Persius detail

Giovanni, Cellini's father, was Cellini's first great love, and no son was more adored by his dad than was Benvenuto. He loved the man and the man loved his boy with every fiber of their souls. This was Cellini's first great luck in life. When Cellini went off, they both had tears in their eyes. When he returned, they both wept with joy. In (nearly) the same way, Cellini loved his lovers, boys and men to whom he was fiercely loyal. When Cellini returned to Florence from his first adventures, he came across a former friend who greeted him with kisses and an open bed, and when Cellini went off again, the boy plucked a few nascent whiskers from Cellini's chin to keep in memory. Such was Cellini.

The second lucky break was being born in Florence. Nothing surpassed the beauty of the Piazza della Signoria with its statue of *David*, nor the splendor of the immensely imposing and beautiful Palazzo Vecchio, as well as the Duomo with Brunelleschi's dome, the Baptistery with its Gates of Paradise and the Pontevecchio Bridge, spanned by jewelry shops that would one day sell, at prices only the wealthiest could afford, Cellini creations.

At around age two--younger even than a later prodigy, Mozart--Giovanni put his boy to practicing the flute, the rigor of which Cellini hated, but nonetheless became highly proficient at playing, a proficiency that would serve him well when at the end of a long workday of sculpting or jewelry making he would take out his flute, to the wonder of the workshop boys around him, many who knew nothing of his hidden talents, and enrapture them like the Pied Piper, leading any who might have been hesitant into his welcoming arms.

Cellini's father wanted him to become a musician because all of the great courts of Italy employed them all year round, from festivals to nightly entertainment during dinners. To become a musician was to have assured employment. But when it became clear to Giovanni that his son would never give in, he allowed the boy to join the workshop of Michelangelo Brandini, but took him away after a few months. Cellini may have been removed due to the reputation of artists' workshops, where sex between the master, the apprentices and the models was daily routine. These kinds of relationships were totally par for the course, totally accepted by parents and society as being the only way boys could learn about life, as girls were shut away. Some workshops, however, gained reputations as nothing more than whorehouses where one could go for sex as one could at any tavern that had rooms.

Florentine sexuality seemed ideal. Men like Cellini passed from boys to girls and back with disconcerting regularity. The reasons are unclear as to why this should have been. Today we're used to a world divided sexually, where there are straights, gays and those who are bi. In Greece women served to keep the home and to produce, basically, sons. In Rome women were far better educated but were still homebodies, and homosexual encounters were frequent if somewhat smirked at. A Roman woman, unlike Greek women, could really be a helpmate and sincerely loved. In Florence, as we'll see again and again, men--all men--were intimate with boys and other men, despite laws to the contrary, but, again, what is puzzling was the ability to go from one sex to the other with abandon and frequency. Cellini usually took his girls from behind, certainly to avoid pregnancies, perhaps for the increased pleasure of a tighter sheath. Cellini ranted about his boys, covering them with every kind of complement and the most sublime of adjectives: beautiful. He never complimented girls, although about a certain Angelica he did say, in his autobiography, "I enjoyed such pleasure as I never had before or since."

At age 15 Cellini gained the right to enter the workshop of Antonio di Sandro di Paolo Giamberti, (luckily) known simply as Marcone. He learned to draw, to work gold, silver and jewelry. As his father paid for his instruction, he was not obliged to perform menial tasks like sweeping the workshop, marketing, preparing food, cleaning the latrines and the hundred other chores involved in the daily care of boys. Cellini tells us he liked the trade so much that soon he had caught up with even the very best of Marcone's craftsmen. But his father was not forgotten. Cellini would return home to play the flute, rejoicing in his father's tears, fulfilling his filial duty "to give my father contentment."

By the age of 16 Cellini knew how to protect himself with sword and dagger, as did his younger brother Giovanfrancesco, called Cecchino. "At that time I had a brother, younger by two years, a youth of extreme boldness and temper." In Florence a fight could begin if a boy looked at another a nanosecond too long. For some unknown reason, Cecchino got into a brawl at age 14 and Cellini came to his aid. Several boys were hurt and because boys 13 and over were considered adults, they could have been severely punished. Due to the daily violence in Florence, punishment was harsh in an attempt to stem it, but in the Cellini boys' case they got off easy, with an order to banish them for a period of six months. They went to Siena where the goldsmith Castoro, with Giovanni's permission, took them in. Cellini worked on jewelry while Cecchino wandered around the town whiling away time, hooking up with boys and bothering the girls.

Boys then prided themselves far more on how they dressed than they do today. Some belt buckles were very large, and Cellini made his with sculpted masks and incredibly intricate foliage. Nowhere did boys like to dress up more than in the Florence under the Medici, where costumes for festivals and carnivals were magnificent: Boys' trousers so tight they looked painted on, ample shirts that fell from the collarbones to the upper thighs, taken in by a thin belt at the waist. A headband with perhaps a feather adorned the forehead. Niccolò Machiavelli wrote, "The city's youth, being independent, spent excessive sums on clothing, feasting and debauchery. Living in idleness, it consumed its time and money on gaming and women."

It was now 1517 and the seventeen-year-old Cellini had his first real love affair. The boy was Giovanni Francesco Lippi, grandson of the painter Filippo Lippi, and the same age as Cellini. About Giovanni Cellini wrote: "So much love grew up between us that we were never apart, day or night. For two years or thereabouts we lived in intimacy."

A new boy and a new workshop. He entered that of Francesco Salimbene. Here he created a silver belt buckle of supreme beauty, about three inches in diameter, showing leaves, vines and masks. Two years passed and he decided to change workshops again ... and boyfriends. The new lover was Giambattista Tasso, a woodcarver, and one day during a stroll ... but let Cellini take over: "By this time we had reached the San Piero Gattolini gate--the gate by which one leaves Florence to travel towards the Holy City. We looked at each other, tied our aprons around our waists, and set off along the road. It had been God's will that we came to the gates without noticing that we were that far. On the way I asked him, 'Oh, I wonder what our old folks will say this evening?'" Words that ring as true then as today. "I had just reached nineteen, and so had the century."

It could have been the Yellow Brick Road, for it led to a long life of astonishing adventure.

In Rome Cellini and Tasso found work in a shop of Firenzuola. He was well received, especially as he was wearing some of the silver pieces, clasps and a belt buckle that he had himself made. He carved a saltcellar that he sold for enough money to wander around the Eternal City and copy the works of art by other artists. He joined a new workshop when his funds were low, that of Paolo Arsago. Firenzuola didn't see things that way and went after Cellini, as he had spent time and money teaching Cellini his trade, but Cellini brushed him off with "As a free man I'll go when and where I please." When Firenzuola lost his temper, Cellini put his hand on the hilt of his sword. "The dispute waxed warm as Firenzuola was a far better swordsman than he was a goldsmith." Luckily a passerby who had been Firenzuola's old master stopped to find out what was going on. He got both talking, and in the end Cellini became godfather to one of Firenzuola's children.

Cellini passed much time wandering around Rome, discovering its hidden corners, adding, always adding new knowledge and new experience to his art, drawing, learning perspective, and the incredible difficulties in making moulds and mixing and pouring molten metals. He says he also made a great deal of money that he gave his father.

Cellini landed a commission, the crafting of a silver vase, for the Bishop of Salamanca. He spent months on the oeuvre in company of a new lover, this one 14, Paulino, about whom, he writes, "I had a passionate love. He was honest and had the most beautiful face I'd ever seen. The love he had for me and mine for him bordered on the unbearable. His splendor was such that he would have driven the Greek gods themselves mad!" Paulino's father met Cellini, and although adventures between men and boys were known and practiced by one and all, there's no indication that he suspected Cellini's attachment to his son. On the other hand, Paulino had a sister that his dad hoped would interest Cellini. "He wanted me as a son-in-law," resumes Cellini in his autobiography. As Paulino loved music, Cellini spent many a languorous night playing his flute for the fourteen-year-old who was entranced by his lover's talents, artistry and expertise in the art of virile domination--acquired since Cellini himself was but 13--all of which took Paulino's breath away.

Cellini opened his own workshop at age 23. One of his first wealthy clients was Giacomo Bergenario da Carpi, a doctor who made his fortune treating syphilis, called the French disease because it entered Italy at the same time as Charles VIII. The good doctor ordered several silver cups. Thanks to the Bishop of Salamanca's vase and the doctor's cups, commissions flowed in. Cellini nonetheless studied on the side, especially with Cristoforo Foppa, an expert in enamelling, thanks to whom Cellini would later make a *chef-d'oeuvre* for François I of France. From here on in Cellini began to make immense amounts of money, much of which, he says, he sent home to his father.

Cellini attended a party given by Giulio Romano, a painter notorious for his *I Modi* sexual-intercourse drawings. Romano thought it would be amusing to have a dinner in which the men invited their mistresses (whom Cellini reveals later as being, for the most part, whores). Cellini had none, but he did have a boy of wondrous beauty, 16, whom he dressed as a girl. "Diego had a handsome figure, and a complexion of marvelous brilliancy. The outlines of his head and face were far more beautiful than those of the antique Antinous. When I begged him to let me array him in women's clothes he readily complied." Diego is recorded to have made such a splash that one of the men present fell to his knees before him and said, "Behold ye of what sort are the angels of paradise!" One of the mistresses left in a huff, followed by another when one of the men put his hand in the little lady's panties and discovered the truth. The men broke up in laughter and Diego, the "girl" of wondrous beauty, was said to have passed an equally wondrous night.

In Florence Alessandro de' Medici, age 19, whose specialty was robbing girls of their virginity, was named ruler of the city by his purported father, none other than Pope Clement VII. To thank the pope and to gain his blessing, Alessandro went to Rome accompanied by a group of boys, louts like him, who came up against even trashier men, the pope's own guard. Among Alessandro's boys was none other than Cecchino, Cellini's brother. The pope's guard arrested one of Alessandro's men--we don't know under what pretense, but Alessandro and his ruffians were known for everything vile, including the mass rape of nuns. The arrested boy, Bertino Aldobrandi, was a friend of Cecchino's--who, like his brother, nurtured extremely intimate friendships with his pals. Cecchino learned, falsely as it turned out, that his friend had been killed by one of the guards. Mad with fury, Cecchino got a description of the man he thought to be the murderer, found him, and "ran him right through the guts," says Cellini. Another guard then shot Cecchino in the leg with a harquebus. The wound festered and Cecchino died. Clement wanted Cellini to return to work despite his mourning, saying that Ceccino was now gone and nothing more could be done. But Italians are extremely bound to their families, and Cellini no less so. He found out who had shot the boy and, as he wrote, "followed him as closely as though he were a girl I was in love with." He attacked him with a dagger, a first blow that grazed the neck as the man, aware of an approaching figure, was able to move slightly out of the way. He tried to run but Cellini was on him like a lion on a fleeing antelope, downing him with another blow, to the back, and as he lay on the ground another and still another to the neck and upper back. He then ran to Alessandro's palace near the Piazza Navona where guards caught up with him. Alessandro explained the motive for the killing and the guards left. Later, the pope simply asked him if he "had gotten over it now", and gave him a commission. Cellini had murdered and gotten off scot-free.

A newly elected pope, Paul III, gave Cellini a commission saying, "Men like Cellini, unique to art, are above the law." But a problem arose: the pope's son, Pier Luigi Farnese, a homosexual who had raped the bishop of Fano, was a friend of the man Cellini had murdered, a man who had a daughter that Farnese wanted to marry to his lover, a young peasant boy, in order to confiscate the girl's dowry (!). Despite what the pope felt for Cellini, Farnese had the power to order Cellini's arrest, which he did. He also hired an assassin to kill Cellini. The assassin met him in a tavern and, seduced by his charm, told Cellini of the plot. Cellini then immediately fled to Florence and the open arms of Alessandro de' Medici.

Alessandro took advice from no one, living for his own pleasure, his motto being "They made me duke, so I'll enjoy it!" By enjoying it he meant wandering the streets at night fully armed, pushing aside anyone in his way, looking for a fight he was destined to win for the simple reason that he had barred the carrying of a sword or a firearm, both of which never left him, nor did his dagger. And he had reason to fear, as the nobility of Florence wanted him replaced by legitimate blood, noble blood. He had gained power at age 19 and had by now fully tasted every perversion, so that what was left was taking the hymen of those who still had one, notably nuns, and that of those who kept guard over theirs, virtuous women. He liked his boys too, for quick, easy couplings, as heated and virile as possible. His favorite companion was his cousin Lorenzino with whom he shared his bed and more when not exhausted from a night of whoring. And when he awoke with a lustful urge, Lorenzino was always conveniently spread out, naked, at his side. This is how Cellini had caught them many times, as the artist was permitted to come and go as he wished, and as Alessandro had no modesty and no need to hide his vices, Cellini was aware of everything that went on. "Meanwhile I went on making the Duke's portrait and oftentimes I found him napping after dinner with that Lorenzino of his."

No one knows why Lorenzino turned against Duke Alessandro, aided by a professional assassin, Scoronconcolo. In his play, *Lorenzaccio*, Musset writes that Lorenzo wanted the duke dead so that Florence could become a Republic again. Others suggest that he was just jealous of the duke's powers and privileges. As Duke Alessandro was so unpopular, he was never without his body armor, weapons and guards. But Lorenzino told him that he had found a Florentine lady of exceptional beauty and, especially, ironclad virtue, who had been abandoned by her husband. Lorenzino would bring her to the duke, and from then on it was up to the duke to prove that he could triumph over virtue. Lorenzino convinced the duke to dismiss the guards for the night, to take off his armor and to slip naked into bed. From then on it was easy for Lorenzino to strike him with a dagger. Afterwards he rode off to Venice, a glove covering a finger Alessandro had nearly bitten off. There, he published his version of what had taken place in his *Apologia*, claiming to be a second Brutus. Lorenzino himself was later stabbed to death by a poisoned dagger on a bridge in Venice.

Due to the events described above and his problems with the pope and the pope's son Pier Luigi, Cellini had had enough of both Rome and Florence. So with two new boys, Ascanio, "the most handsome boy in Rome," and another handsome lad, Girolamo Pascucci, he and they headed for France and the wondrous court of the courtly François I (he who had held da Vinci's dying head).

François, who had already lost his virginity to his sister at age 10, was a lad 6 ½ feet tall and so big some girls couldn't accommodate him although most tried, and, it was said, virgins literally lined up around his bed awaiting their chance to be deflowered--his specialty. His bed accompanied him while he was out hunting, using it between kills, to the utter amazement of Henry VIII who had accompanied the king during his visit to France (Henry went far in such things, very far even, but not *that* far). François took whomever he wanted from the nobility, whether the ladies liked it or not, and apparently not all did as one woman had her husband infect himself with syphilis before infecting her so that she could infect the king. Another woman had her face slashed, which didn't dissuade François as it wasn't her face that interested him.

François offered Cellini a commission: six colossal gods and six goddesses, all in silver, more than life-size as François wanted them his height, the purpose of which would be to hold candlesticks. That he asked Cellini to create these giant candelabras was a surprise, given the expense of the project, as Cellini was only noted for his belt buckles, silver plates and vases.

Cellini set to work making a clay model of one of the statues, a male figure, that was cast in bronze over which he hammered sheets of silver with a wooden hammer. During this time Cellini had problems with accountants, with jealous artists who badmouthed him and, far more deadly, with Madame d'Étampe, François' mistress, whose ass (to be honestly frank) he just hadn't sufficiently kissed.

The day came for Cellini to present the finished statue to the king and his mistress. "The Jupiter was raising his thunderbolt with the right hand in the act of hurling it; his left hand held the globe of the world. Among the flames of the thunderbolt I had very cleverly introduced a torch of white wax." Cellini had the king observe the statue from several angles, informing him that a sculpture should always be viewed from at least eight different standpoints. Cellini had draped some tissue around the statue's private parts, knowing a woman would be present, but when d'Étampes saw the statue she suggested to the king that the tissue was there to hid some imperfection. Cellini had Ascanio take it away. Madame d'Étampes stared at the incredible detail of the pubic bush, balls, penis and ample foreskin, and Cellini asked, "Do you find it all as it should be?" Madame d'Étampes left the room in a huff. As soon as she was gone the king "exploded with laughter," says Cellini. The statue had taken 4 years to make, at the cost of 40,000 francs. There would not be a second, and the first has not survived.

Back in Florence Cosimo I de' Medici promised that if Cellini produced a great work of art, he would not be disappointed in his reward. Cellini suggested doing the statue of Perseus, Cosimo agreed, and thus began the countdown to Cellini's Immortality. The year was 1545.

A new boy, handsome, naturally, was found, a very young lad, Cencio, the son of a prostitute. He took on Bernardino Mannellini, the exquisite head and body of whom would be the model for the future *Perseus*. "He was 18 and I asked him if he would enter my service. He agreed on the spot. He groomed my horse, gardened, and soon essayed to help me in the workshop, with such success that by degrees he learned the art quite nicely. I never had a better assistant than he proved." Cellini decided to enlarge the horizons of Bernardino and his assistants by taking them to the Old

Market, the Chiasso de' Buoi, the Tavern Buca and the baths, all pleasure zones where the lads could enjoy both sexes, singly or in bacchanals. In fact, he was, in a sense, making up for lost time. He had kept boy-love to a minimum in France because there the penalty was death, one that seems to have been enforced by François who much preferred female plumbing to that of males. Back home in Florence, he seems to have let out all stops. Be that as it may, Bernardino turned out to be intelligent, loyal and hard working, and was Cellini's first assistant from then on.

In 1548 Cellini cast the figure of Medusa and in 1549 work on the rest of the statue began. Just before the actual casting he fell sick with fever, brought on, certainly, by the incredible stress related to his work. Luckily Bernardino Mannellini was there to see that things went along correctly. *Perseus* comes through as a real living youth, his brow knitted as is Michelangelo's *David*, his look grave. The body of the Medusa is just as living, just as wondrously human. A marble block had been brought to the workshop in 1549 to serve as a base for *Perseus* and in 1552 Cellini cast two figures which would go into the block, Mercury modeled after Cencio and Danaë modeled by a new girl Dorotea. Cencio, as *Mercury*, is totally naked and eminently desirable. He had shared Cellini's bed since the age of 12. Dorotea also shared his bed and gave him a son he legitimized. She also accommodated Cencio. All told, Cellini was living and creating, creating and living, in the most beautiful city in the world, under skies warmed by the unstinting generosity of Helios, his *Perseus* complete, his Immortality guaranteed.

Cencio as *Mercury*

He went to work on his book which, next to *Perseus*, was his greatest triumph. He was aided by a boy, age 14, and seemed to have liked the experience of talking about himself while the lad noted all. Part of his memoirs had been a tell-all outing of the true nature of Cosimo, but he burned the papers, following the French adage: *Toutes les véritées ne sont pas à dire*. In that respect his relationship with the truth was always hesitant, as was his love for women. He never admitted anally contenting himself with boys, yet when he loved a boy he was as frank--or even franker--than the times permitted:

"We are never apart, day or night."

"We loved each other more than if we had been brothers."

"My passionate love for the boy."

"'The prettiest face of anyone I have ever met in my whole life."

"He's amazingly beautiful, and the great love he's shown me made me love him in return--almost more than I could bear."

"His beautiful smile would have driven the gods themselves mad."

"Extreme personal beauty."

"The most handsome young fellow in Rome."

He weakened. He died, accompanied to his resting place by hords of admirers--I can't say *last* resting place because, for this man who had never stopped moving, it was, in reality, his first. When I entered the Peace Corps, a very young boy, I received a huge box of books, as do all volunteers. One was *The Autobiography of Benvenuto Cellini*. I read it with great pleasure, totally unaware of the volcano who had produced it, only vaguely aware of my own sexuality, never dreaming that I would eventually, like countless other boys, fall in love with this incredible creature, proof that God truly does work in entirely mysterious ways. (3)

PERSIUS

RAPHAEL
1483 - 1520

The first thing to known about Raphael comes from the art historian Vasari: "So gentle and charitable was Raphael that even the animals loved him."

Self-portrait

The second key is found in those around him, beginning with his student and lover Giulio Romano who became known for 32 drawings called the *I Modi*. Sixteen represented scenes of heterosexual intercourse, 16 others of homosexual couplings. The first 16 were reproduced by the engraver Marcantonio Raimondi and gained such notoriety that they were banned and destroyed under the order of the pope. But they had been more or less well copied by others. The 16 homosexual drawings were considered too outrageous to be copied, and so have been entirely lost (if they ever existed). The first 16 came to Shakespeare's notice: In *The Winter's Tale* Queen Hermione mentions, "that rare Italian master, Julio Romano." Besides these, he did some beautiful paintings, for example his *St. John the Baptist in the Wilderness*, a beautiful young boy *à la da Vinci*. His *Jupiter Seducing Olympias* is an oddity, Jupiter's fully engorged penis just inches away from insertion.

66

Romano's *Jupiter*

The second personage associated with Raphael is Pietro Aretino who wrote dirty sonnets to go alone with the *I Modi*, but is especially known for his satirical writings, so sharp, witty and revealing that Charles V and François I (whom we've already met, twice) paid him blackmail under the guise of patronage so he wouldn't include them in his satires. He was, if you will, the talented Renaissance Walter Winchell (known by millions but himself so unpopular that only three people attended his funeral). Aretino too was unpopular with hordes of Italians, barely escaping assassination on several occasions.

The third man is Federico II Gonzaga of Mantua. Mantua, beautiful but dull until the arrival of the Duke, became a center of art, as had Milan under Ludovico Sforza, a vulgar condottiere until he visited Lorenzo *Il Magnifico* in Florence. Seeing the splendor of Lorenzo's court and the magnificence of the city--where, after all, the Renaissance began--Ludovico had an epiphany. Back home, he changed the face of Milan, architecturally first, then artistically, bringing aboard da Vinci himself. Federico was so afraid of Pietro Aretino that he literally became his pimp in procuring boys, as witnessed in this highly-abbreviated exchange of letters that Federico wrote to Aretino, in answer to a request: "I would willingly satisfy your wishes regarding this kept boy who you write could remedy your trouble, if I knew who it was, but I do not know this boy Bianchino." The Duke finds out who the boy is and writes back: "I truly love you more than any other and the fruits of your splendid intellect have so impressed me that I will never forget them. If I could possibly satisfy your desire for Bianchino I would do so gladly. But having understood his reluctance when I spoke to him on your behalf, I did not think it fitting to plead with him or otherwise to exhort him, and I surely can't order him, it not being either just or honest to command him in this case. So pardon me if I have not pleased you. If I can in any other way, you know very well I am only too glad to do it and you will always find me ready...." It was true that boys who sold their favors could gain not only money but a position in the upper hierarchy of government and/or church.

Raphael Sanzio (or Sanzi or Santi) was born in Urbino in 1483, the fief of Federico da Montefeltro. His father was a court artist and it was at court that Raphael, young, learned proper manners and social skills. He was helping his father at age 4, thanks to which he progressed in talent (as did the equally young Mozart, years later). His self-portrait at age 16 shows a boy of unsurpassed beauty. He was apprenticed very early, some say around age 8, to Pietro Perugino, "despite the tears of his mother," states Vasari. Around age 11 he went to Florence for 4 years and then around age 15 he went to Rome where he lived until his death, 22 years later. It was there that Pope Julius II put him to work on several Vatican rooms, in one of which he painted his most famous work, the huge mural *The School of Athens* showing da Vinci, Raphael himself, Sodoma and Michelangelo sitting in front. Here we have the trinity of the times: the Everest of men, da Vinci, followed by the world's Annapurna, Michelangelo, and Raphael.

Raphael opened his own workshop with, says Vasari, fifty apprentices and assistants, among whom were his lovers, Giulio Romano and Gianfrancesco Penni. Thanks to these boys and men, Raphael was able to produce an amazing number of paintings, all of which looked as though they had come from the hand of the master. Raphael was especially noted as someone who would take over the techniques of others, incorporating any and all external influences. He was also a perfect collaborator, establishing peaceful relations between men of extremely varied characters.

After Raphael's death Giulio Romano and Gionfrancesco Penni continued his workshop, their inheritance from Raphael. One of their assistants was Caravaggio. Unfortunately, they separated and died apart. Raphael died of fever, at age 37.

CARAVAGGIO
1571 – 1610

Caravaggio – self-portrait

Michelangelo Caravaggio was noted for his use of chiaroscuro to such a point as to be thought, by some, to be its inventor. Chiaroscuro is the contrast, often very strong, between light and dark, enforcing the three-dimensionality of objects. Around 90% of Caravaggio's life resided in the *oscuro*, the bleakness of which made his biography far more difficult than the chapter on Cellini. Despite the dark side of Cellini, the fact that he had murdered several men (stalking and knifing them from behind) and the even more disconcerting fact that he was a confirmed sadist towards women (confirmed by his own autobiography!), the *chiaro* portions of Cellini's life were by far the more important. Like Caravaggio, Cellini was an artist of genius, but one--and this was the winning point, for me, concerning Cellini--who worshipped the boys he loved.

What was engaging concerning Caravaggio was the *chiaro* of his first paintings, the eroticism found in the close-ups of certain works--here I'm thinking of his *The Musicians*--which show the boys' faces in the very throes of immanent orgasm, the eyes glazed over, the lips sensually parted, the tongue just visible and lascivious. Or the boys' shirts, in this and in other paintings--always boys, as his first painting of a woman came only much later with his *Repentant Magdalene*--shirts at times undone to the waste, open on skin glistening through effort, perhaps sexual, the nipples erect, the underarms reeking of pheromones, the odor of sex so invasive that one can guess at the traces of sperm smeared somewhere over the lower belly.

The Musicians

But I was enthralled too by the *obscuro*, the blood gushing from the jugular of the virile male in his *Judith and Holofernes,* as the knife is halted forever in mid-distance, as it cuts through the throat. Or the nearly naked soldier in *The Martyrdom of Saint Matthew,* sent to murder the saint so that the king of Ethiopia could have access to Matthew's niece: the horror being that one so young and virile would dare destroy one so old and helpless. Then there's the *Sacrifice of Isaac* in which the withered mind of Abraham pushes him to slit the throat of his screaming son, his hand stayed at the last moment by an angel. And *David and the Head of Goliath*, David holding up Goliath's severed head, the self-portrait of Caravaggio himself, one eye clearly dead, the other harboring a lingering thread of life. *The Beheading of John the Baptist* is of disgusting reality: his executioner, muscular and shiny with sweat, the ultimate in homoeroticism, leans over the saint whose head he holds firmly against the floor, while blood spurts from the severed throat. But the worst is *The Martyrdom of Saint Ursula*: A withered old man, unable to achieve his ends with a young woman, shoots her in the breast with an arrow at pointblank range. Ursula looks down at the wound, as if in wonder that she has been pierced and that blood is flowing.

The Beheading of Holofernes

Caravaggio worked alone, had no assistants, no workshop. He strode through the streets of Rome in the company of a wild bunch such as he, looking for action in the form of fights, his sword by his side and his dagger reassuringly in his belt. His eyes were wide-open and seeing, mean and blasé, his lips ridged. His motto was said to have been *nec spe nec metu*, without hope or fear.

He lost nearly every male member of his family to the plague while still very young--his father at age 5, the rest at age 6--the plague that had killed over half of the population of Italy one or two generations earlier, around the 1350s, but reappeared from time to time to claim the survivors. This might have instilled a sentiment of abandonment, a child's first and greatest fear, a scar on the mind that pushes one incessantly from place to place, person to person, never at ease, never satisfied, always angry, violent, physically and sexually aggressive. Perhaps only a man of such unhinged and brutal appetites could create the works of this totally unique individual, stark, aggressive and sexually explosive segments of human life. This may partially explain the brutality of his nature, as well as the fact that the times in which he lived were in themselves ultraviolent.

Caravaggio was a man of great strength and a first-class swordsman. That he was also an artist whose delicate strokes created works of genius must not mask the fact of his indomitable virility, capable of downing a man with a blow--temporarily if done with the fist, life-threatening at the end of his sword. The proof of this was his slaying of the handsome Ranuccio Tomassoni in a sword duel. Caravaggio ran with a pack of toughs, armed to the hilt in a city where arms were forbidden. He and his goons drank and whored, pushed fellow revelers aside as they made their way through the alleys from tavern to tavern. They were constantly picked up by the Roman police, held the night and then freed as they had powerful friends, friends like Cardinal del Monte who was smitten by boys and who appreciated homoerotic art, bringing much of it into the Vatican. Del Monte provided lodging for Caravaggio and his lover Cecco, a boy of only ten when he appeared as a prepubescent *St. John the Baptist*, a beautiful, brooding lad when painted a handful of years later in another *St. John*. Caravaggio and his ruffians broke windows, sang bawdy songs, hurled animal bladders filled with blood or ink at buildings, smeared excrement on door handles and, naturally, drew erect, usually discharging phalluses on walls. An unknown source had this to say at the time: ''After a fortnight's painting he swaggers about for a month or two with a sword and like-minded friends at this side--Prospero Orsi, Orazio Gentileschi, Mario Minniti and Onorio Longhi--ever ready to engage in a fight or an argument, so that it is awkward to get along with him.'' To say the least. Another of his acquaintances, Agostino Tassi, was accused by a father of ''repeatedly deflowering'' his daughter! (Perhaps, like Aphrodite, her virginity continually rejuvenated by bathing off the shores of Cyprian Paphos.) For every outrage that I'll recount, there may have been a hundred others unknown to us or too little known to relate or were covered up by the people looking out for Caravaggio, the most important of which was del Monte. We known that Caravaggio lived for his art, but it can be said that he lived too to impose himself, violently, on others.

He whored, but his preference was men, a choice far from unknown in the Florence of his epoch where men chose freedom over marital bondage, where one could take one's pleasure when and where one desired, with a boy or a man, free of nagging and the expense of a meal. This is what Andrew Graham-Dixon says in his wonderful *Caravaggio*: ''Caravaggio was capable of being aroused by the physical presence of other men. He could not have painted such figures in the way that he did if that were not so. Caravaggio's painting suggests an ambiguous sexual personality. On the evidence of his paintings he was neither heterosexual nor homosexual, terms that are in any case anachronistic when applied to his world. He was omnisexual.''

Boys at that time loved to dress to kill. Churches abounded in Renaissance Italy, and especially in Florence and Milan, perfect stages for a young sire to show off his splendid forms, silk-adorned chest, form-fitting trousers, elegance out to swoon the fair sex, a dagger at the belt and a sword ever handy, a youth's tools. For the daily, reliable and rapid purging of one's lust, there were bordellos, taverns with frisky and economically cheap servers, as well as back alleys where, indeed, all cats were grey in the absence of light, and a lad had but to pull the strings attached to the cloth that covered his private parts to take his pleasure with whomever engorged his manhood, or when he simply wished to relieve himself against a wall.

Michelangelo Merisi da Caravaggio was born around 1571. Famous while he lived, he was immediately forgotten after his death, to be rediscovered in the twentieth century. He was blessed with two beautiful names, *Michelangelo* which evoked the famous Florentine genius, although

Caravaggio's first name had been chosen after the feast day on which he had been born, Archangel Michael, and *Caravaggio*, the site of his birth. His father, Fermo Merisi, was the chief architect of the Colonna family household, a family known for its military glory, and he directed its staff.

A two-hour ride from the stiflingly dead town of Caravaggio brought one to the big city, Milan, under Spanish rule at the time, the bustling center of commerce and manufacturing, 100,000 souls--as many as London and Paris--and the epicenter of the silk industry as well as the finest workmanship in swords and daggers in Italy. Gold from the New World caused a rise in prices in Milan that impoverished the majority of the Milanese, and what had been considered a miracle of riches would soon lead to the bankruptcy of Spain. Milan was inhabited by the young Caravaggio until he went to Florence, later in our story, at the age of 21. Florence was the capital of art, and da Vinci and Michelangelo, soon followed by Raphael, were its kings. What a change Caravaggio would bring to all this. Michelangelo Buonarotti's muscular lads looked as fresh and scrubbed as if they'd just stepped out of an hour-long shower. Caravaggio's boys were so realistic that one could nearly whiff the pheromones from the lads' beautiful but slightly rank bodies, and in his *Jupiter, Neptune and Pluto* we have a full under view of Neptune's pubic bush, scrotum and penis with its full prepuce. I insist on this point: the boys in Caravaggio's pictures are totally alive, and even when just sitting, surrounded by fruit or flowers, their shirts open over their naked chests, one has the impression that they've just left a bed after making sweet love, and, as I've said, that unwashed sperm still coats their bellies. And their eyes; look into their eyes--the ultimate erogenous zone. The realism in his paintings was such that he even showed the dirt under the toenails! But all this is in the future. For the moment he's 13 and apprenticed to Simone Peterzano, a painter of mediocre repute who taught the boy little except for a smidgen of drawing, stretching canvases and the art of grounding colors. Caravaggio is thought to have been rowdy even at that age, controlled with difficulty. He ran around with gangs as he did later in life, and he certainly had his first sexual experiences with boys in his workshop. And as Milan was noted for its violence he may have done more, he may have killed someone, as is suggested in several texts, but at any rate he left the city, never to return, and headed south to his destiny in Rome.

Rome, where he spent 14 years, had once been like Caravaggio in a new array of the best clothes, it had been the center of the ancient world and had reigned supreme for half a millennium, but now it was decrepit, the buildings crumpling among fields of mud, rats and stench, with only a few favored islets inhabited by the rich and powerful. During the Cesares there had been 2,000,000 souls, now there were 100,000. Then as today the Romans rose early, slept the sweltering afternoons away and spent the nights in earthly amusement. The city was violent, the streets unsafe, men carried stilettos and swords, and the most vile could poison an enemy through the prick of a death ring.

Caravaggio spent much time with his friends roaming the vicinity of the Piazza Navona and, if they wanted sex, the Piazza del Popolo where women and boys plied their trade in ill-lit alleys or behind the parted curtains from their lodgings where they appeared naked, enticing men who often found that what they were buying was far more sordid than what they could get for free among their own sex. Caravaggio was an earthy realist. His paintings show dirty feet, soiled hands and fingernails rigorous right down to their grooves. Caravaggio makes one think of an animal, with an animal's spontaneity and boldness; there was nothing shy or hesitant about him. If he had to kiss his masters' feet and hands it was with the awareness that he could just as easily bite and, if need be, go for the jugular with the dagger he was never without. Reality in painting, reality in life: this was Caravaggio's creed.

He was given employment in the atelier of Lorenzo Siciliano, specialized in the heads of the ancients that he sold cheaply to those who wanted to decorate their homes with the portraits of the Caesars. It was here he met another painter, Mario Minniti, first his lover, then a friend, and finally a benefactor at the end of Caravaggio's life. With Mario he moved on to the workshop of Cavaliere d'Arpino. D'Arpino was an arrogant tyrant who mistreated him, and if this were not enough, he was kicked by a horse and forced to spend several weeks in a free hospital, Santa Maria della Consolazione. He had placed some paintings with an art dealer, Costantino Spata, who sold one, the wonderful *Cardsharps*, to Cardinal del Monte who took him in. The palace housed as many as fifty boys, artists like Caravaggio, actors who took part in plays dressed as women when the role demanded it, rent-boys when out of work, and castrati. Caravaggio came with his baggage: a tormented mind, a character as unruly as his hair, violent fists and a sword and dagger at his side, despite their interdiction in the holy city famed for its bordellos. Rome's clergy lived in palaces and needed architects, sculptors and playwrights to fill their theaters, painters like Caravaggio, and warm bodies to span their nights. One Englishman described Italians as being addicted to ''the art of Epicureanism, the art of whoring, of poisoning and of sodomy.''

One of his early biographers, Giovanni Bellori, describes Caravaggio as being dark, dark in his looks, in his temperament and in his art, an extremely apt insight. Another description of Caravaggio's place in Rome and Roman violence comes from Tommaso Garzoni, relayed to us by Graham-Dixon: ''Every day, every hour, every moment, they talk of nothing but killing, cutting off legs, breaking arms, smashing somebody's spine ... For study, they have nothing other than the thought of killing this or that person; for purpose, nothing more than to avenge the wrongs that they have taken to heart; for favor, nothing more than serving their friends by butchering enemies..." With Caravaggio we will continually go from summit to summit, one in blazing light--that of his art, the other in princely dark--his intimate nature. Caravaggio was Alex in *Clockwork Orange*.

Ranuccio Tomassoni is a case in point. Ranuccio had a stable of women he put on the streets. Known for his extreme good looks and for being well-endowed, his women were jealous of whom he chose to bestow his favors, to the extent of attacking one another with daggers, hoping to scar a pretty face, or splash it with acid. The Roman police were called in numerous times to bring calm to the domestic situation. Ranuccio was always armed despite its unlawfulness, but invariably defended himself by stating that in his business being armed was necessary due to the girls' rowdy clients. At the same time, it appears that Caravaggio might also have had girls who disputed their places on the streets with those of Ranuccio, the basis of an explosive situation that would lead to Caravaggio's attempt to knife the boy, perhaps aiming at his genitals but striking instead the femoral artery, a place certain to cause nearly instant death. Both Caravaggio and Ranuccio had been accompanied by three men each. Onorio Longhi was there on Caravaggio's side and a captain of the guards was with Ranuccio. The captain too was run through but whether he died or not is uncertain. Caravaggio was put out of action with a blow to the head. The surviving six men stated that the incident had been over an unpaid wager on a tennis match although, most probably, it was a duel over prostitution, but as dueling in Rome carried the death sentence.... Caravaggio fled before his trial and was therefore sentenced to death, duel or no duel. A bounty was put on his head, a head that could literally be presented, severed from the body, in order to claim it.

He fled to Malta where thanks to the paintings he did for several Knights of Malta he gained near godlike admiration and was even knighted. Most sources believe that becoming a Knight had been a wish Caravaggio had often expressed, and it played in well with the extremes of his character, from a painter nearly as acclaimed as Michelangelo, to a killer on the run, to a monk in the service of Malta. He would renounce the princely life he had led with del Monte, eating and drinking and fucking the best that life had to offer, pushing his way through the alleys of Rome, dagger at easy reach, spending the wild sums his paintings now procured. He would exchange instant justice at the end of his sword in favor of vows of poverty, obedience and chastity. He, Michelangelo da Caravaggio, would trade the good life for the life of a saint. He had convinced himself that this was the right path, just as he and the people about him had convinced themselves throughout all their lives of the existence of good and bad, that a soul left purgatory the instant a coin hit a priest's alms bowl, and that absolution came through confession. Like sex, after the first act of faith one was no longer virgin.

The promise of a painting or two had opened all the doors to knighthood for Caravaggio. But the Grand Master, Wignacourt, needed the consent of the pope himself, a pope who, for the moment, hesitated to absolve Caravaggio of the killing of Tomassoni, but who planned, too, to squeeze, like a lemon, the last *chef d'oeuvre* from the rustic artist. Wignacourt was intelligent, modest, always ready to accept advice, generous and, when he had the information he needed, decisive. He had rule over 1,800 monks (Knights), half on Malta itself, and was ever ready to protect his subjects from the Moors who would capture and sell them as slaves. He even set up a fund to ransom those captured before he took power. To say the least, he was lionized.

In Wignacourt's request to Pope Paul he didn't mention Caravaggio's name as the recipient of the knighthood, but he did mention that the man in question had been accused of murder, and as all of Italy had had little to gossip about other than Ranuccio's killing, there was no doubt in the pope's mind as to the recipient's identity.

While waiting for word from Paul, Caravaggio did several portraits of Wignacourt, one of which showed him in the presence of one of his many pages. Every historian since that time has added two and two, making Wignacourt the king of pederasts, but no one will ever know. The pages were lads chosen from the ranks of poor nobles, and it is said that Wignacourt paid for their education from is own pocket.

Wignacourt loved Malta and had been literally there to see the spectacular capital, Valletta, an immensely fortified town, rise from the island's cliffs and throne over the deep harbor. Although he died at age 71, before the cities' completion, he wished to beautify it with churches and Caravaggio's art. Caravaggio came through with his most outstanding creation, the *Beheading of St. John the Baptist*, the only painting he signed with his name, *F Michelangelo*, the F for Fra' as he had succeeded in being made a monk. His signature was in blood--how seemingly typical of this man who had personally known and personally been responsible for so much suffering--blood from the throat of the saint, his head pressed solidly against the ground by his assassin, while the assassin's other hand hides the offending knife behind his back. He stares down at his victim, set on the sight of the gushing blood, hypnotized even, as if thinking, *''I, the living, have ended this life. I am God. I am misery. And the sight of your suffering has engorged my penis with the blood of the living, and I shall insert it into the living, and my orgasm will confirm my being alive!''* John the Baptist was the Knights' protector, then as he is today.

Beheading of St. John

And then, when things were going perfectly, Caravaggio, in Malta, threw a wrench in the works. Everything had been going so well! He was adored by the Grand Master, adulated by the Knights, even worshipped by the Maltese. True, he couldn't stride the streets armed to the teeth, accompanied by his faithful dogs, like Onorio Langhi, when he had lived in Rome, pushing citizens out of the way, eating and drinking without paying, and fucking alongside his buddies, when not fucking his buddies. He just had to wait it out, a few weeks longer, perhaps even just a few days, until a red-and-gold Maltese boat brought word from Paul that his hand was needed in Rome to paint pictures, and that all was pardoned and forgiven. After all, who was Ranuccio Tomassoni, other than a boy who had wished to live out his life?

But he screwed up--the least that can be said. Again, not only are details lacking, but we don't even see the big picture. Some said he buttfucked one of Wignacourt's pages--the Grand Master's own personal reserve (this according to some sources certain of Wignacourt preference for boys--but far from all sources). Others say he killed someone in a duel, this on an island where there were hundreds of testosterone-engorged men and boys, and where men may have had the title of monk but were first and foremost warriors. Any pretext for a duel is conceivable, from making a pass at a man's whore to looking at a man, as I've written, a nanosecond too long. One major source believes that what he did so deeply offended Wignacourt that he set out to destroy the artist. Another major source believes he offended an important personage (through an insult? by physically injuring him?) who got him locked in jail and, when he escaped, set the wheels in motion that finally led to his death at age 38. In this version not only was Wignacourt not against him, Wignacourt did everything necessary to ensure his escape.

He stowed away on a ship to Messina where, besides visiting the taverns and back streets known for their vice, he was denounced for his too assiduous interest in the lads bathing nude in the port, and indeed had hired several to pose and otherwise entertain him. He was forced to leave quickly when right-thinking citizens rose up in force against him.

He went to Palermo where he embarked for Naples by way of glorious Capri and Ischia. Back on familiar ground, he went to the Osteria del

Ciriglio, a tavern in a back alley of Naples frequented by both the dregs of society and the upper-class slumming for sex, a place known for its orgies, possessing a secret door for men who preferred boys, a door Caravaggio took as he certainly took the lad or lads within. But after one of these visits, on his way out, he was waylaid by a group of men who beat him up and then badly scarred his face, a fate reserved for whores. No one knows who these men were. Had Wignacourt been responsible he would have been punished in exactly this way as Wignacourt would have wanted revenge, not his death. Some put blame on the family and friends of Ranuccio Tomassoni, but the Tomassoni family was stationed in Rome and logistically it would have been difficult for them to organize an attack in Naples.

It was perhaps in Naples that Caravaggio did his darkest painting, *David with the Head of Goliath*. Painted in the year of his death, 1610, *David with the Head of Goliath* is Caravaggio's most stunning painting: David a small lithe boy, deadly solemn, showing neither fear nor awe at having decapitated the giant, thanks to which David would become king of Israel. The painting is moving in many senses. Did Caravaggio have a premonition of his coming end, and wish to join both extremities of his time on earth, he as a boy in the form of David, he as an older man, dead in one dull, sightless eye, a glint of still-existent life in the other, his mouth ajar in an eternally silenced scream, his face still lacerated from the beating in front of the Osteria del Ciriglio? Or was David his lover Cecco, his shirt open and in disarray as in life, a child he had ''known'' at age 10, had painted again and again as he grew into manhood, finally portrayed here from memory, the inextinguishable memory of a lover, Caravaggio, for his belovèd, Cecco. Caravaggio had called David *il suo caravaggino*, his little Caravaggio, which could have meant Cecco, who later adopted Caravaggio's name, or it could have meant Caravaggio as he was as a little boy.

Caravaggio offered the painting to Scipione Borghese, a friend, a patron, and the official power who held Caravaggio's blood-dripping head in his hands, as did David, in that Scipione had the power to have Caravaggio cleared of killing Tommasoni ... or have him decapitated.

Besides being disfigured during the attack in front of the Osteria del Ciriglio, Caravaggio was perhaps even partially blinded. His convalescence near Naples took six months. It was then that he painted what was one of the darkest paintings of a lifetime of dark masterpieces, his *Martyrdom of St. Ursula*, that I described at the beginning of this chapter.

Word came from Rome for him to return. Glory would once more be his. Scipione had commissions by the bucketful. He would be pardoned. He would be acknowledged and rewarded as the greatest living painter. He would be enriched as only Michelangelo Buonarotti had before him. His knighthood would be reestablished. The young twerps on Malta would be obliged to kowtow despite their nobility--the gift of accidental birth, not merit. And, of course, there would be boys without end, the husky lads of the country, the slim boys of the towns, the red-blooded glory of glorious Italy.

He sailed from Naples to Rome. Why he landed farther north to Rome, at perhaps Palo, is unknown. An ill wind in the form of a gale perhaps blew him there. He landed and was arrested for being a bandit, perhaps due to his clothes, always thread bare, and the cuts that disfigured his face, following the attack at the Osteria del Ciriglio. When he was released he learned his boat had gone to Porto Ercole. He went after it, perhaps on foot, perhaps he had enough money on him after his arrest to hire a mule, although the arresting guards had most probably appropriated his valuables. Some sources believe he made it that far. Others that, ill, feverish and in deep sufferance from his Ciriglio wounds, he was taken in at a hut along the way. At any rate, at age 38 the life of the choleric genius that has so enriched humanity, affixing his seal until the end of time, came to an end. He was a man who certainly abused life, but one that allowed life, in its turn, to use him--for me the paramount accolade.

It is improbable that Cecco Boneri accompanied Caravaggio to Malta. We last view him in Caravaggio's *St. John the Baptist*, a brooding lad of exquisite beauty, but so different from the laughing carefree boy in *Love Conquers All* that the contrast is heart wrenching. Cecco took the name Cecco del Michelangelo and one of his paintings, *St. Sebastian*, is exquisite. He vanished from history, having lived a life of infinite rebounds, sharing the air and more with the fabulous, enigmatic artist known as Caravaggio. (4)

CAPTAIN ROBERT JONES'S TRIAL, 1772, THE RESULT OF BOARDING SCHOOL NOSTALGIA

I'm not going to belabor the contacts between ship officers, cabin boys and young crewmembers because much of what took place was certainly abuse of power on the part of the captains, repugnant in every aspect. Which doesn't mean that youths didn't have sincerely affectionate relations with men, captains included, or use them for their own personal advancement. The captains were warriors and thusly have their place in this book. The cases I've included in this chapter clearly show what comprised a crime during this period.

Robert Jones was such a captain and was responsible for popularizing skating in England, in part thanks to his published book on the subject. Written for men as women didn't skate at the time, Jones's book described figure skating and figure eights, literally inventing a field that until then had been known only for speed skating. He was also known as an expert in fireworks, popularizing their usage throughout the kingdom. He was a gay blade, openly frequenting known homosexuals, although his reputation as a womanizer put him above all suspicion of harboring homosexual tendencies. In fact, he was on the verge of marrying a woman of wealth. Jones had been signaled out at the time for his disguise as Punch during one of Teresa Cornelys' famous masquerades, the entry to which, at her Carlisle House mansion, was prized by the nobility.

The story of Teresa Cornelys began when her actress mother put her on the road to seduction, teaching her how to hold off the rich and powerful until she could extract maximum value in exchange for her charms. At times she did so for pleasure, as with Casanova, to whom she bore a child, and gave up another of her children in his care, a boy Giuseppe, when she was imprisoned for debt. She adopted the name of one of her lovers, Cornelys, and took on a pimp, a cellist who worked at the theater where she made her début as an actress, a man who later claimed to be a preacher and took her to London where they opened a whorehouse under the guise of a chic salon, at a rented manor, Carlisle House, assiduously frequented by Robert Jones. Besides herself and her girls, she offered card games, dancing and masquerades--Thackeray's book *Barry Lyndon* took place there. Casanova returned later, writing that she had 32 servants and three secretaries. The rooms of her manor were so crowded that she had to outlaw hooped skirts, which took up space, and so numerous were the carriages that dropped off clients that she initiated the world's first one-way traffic system. But the wealth of the furnishings and the cost of publicity were such that she spent more money than she brought in, and eventually had to close down and auction off her belongings. She was jailed for dept, escaped, tried her hand at other sources of income, like breakfasts destined for the nobility. Her children, boys and girls, raised as aristocrats, had at least been well educated, allowing them to fend for themselves. She died in prison at age 74.

Because a man's life was at stake sodomy had to be proved beyond doubt, making two concordant conditions imperative: The anus had to be proved to have been penetrated and sperm deposited therein, a seemingly impossible task until one reads the transcript of the trial of Robert Jones, in which one admires the prosecutor's thorough attempts to arrive at the truth; his in-depth questioning; and his success in bringing facts to light. The handling of the boy witness was exemplary, for the avuncular nature of the questioner visibly put the lad at ease, enough to detail acts made sordid due to the lad's extreme youth.

Punch

The boy had been 12 at the time, but because he was but a month from his 13th birthday, it is that age which is most often referred to. Had the acts taken place but a year later the consequences would have been greatly different, as the boy would have been 14, the age of consent in England (the act of *sodomy* remaining, nonetheless, punishable by hanging). Because a man's life was in play the interrogation had to be extremely precise and the boy's character beyond reproach. And indeed, the boy rose well above his contemporaries in that he was deemed by all who knew him as serious, trustworthy, scrupulously honest in speech, acts and testimony, and such was the lad's impact on the jury.

Puberty came later at that time than today, and the boy seemed to have been sexually indifferent to what he went through, himself incapable of being aroused or achieving orgasm. Had there been masturbation alone, Jones would have faced a simple misdemeanor.

The bare facts of the matter are these: The boy's uncle had a shop that did, among other things, shoe repairs. Captain Jones was a valued customer and had had ample opportunity of observing the lad. During one visit he suggested that the boy come to his residence in search of a pair of shoes in need of a new buckle. Because Jones's manner--open, warm and amusing-- was appreciated by all, because he was important to his father's affair, and due to the possibility that he could earn a coin or two, the boy was happy to consent.

Immediately on entering Jones's apartments Jones locked the door and proceeded to fondle the boy through his trousers, before lowering the boys pants and his own, prepatory to penetrating, after which he apparently had a second orgasm by masturbating on the floor. The boy was requested to return the next morning where the man masturbated himself while fondling the boy, the whole scandal ending in a third visit where the same masturbatory act was repeated. The boy was paid all three times, trifling amounts in today's terms but back then a house could be rented for a shilling.

At home the lad fell ill and was bedded with pain between his thighs. Humiliated for what he had done for a few coppers, he kept the provenance of his suffering--the exact area and what had taken place--to himself.

Jones returned to the shop and requested that the boy deliver a pair of shoes he had ordered. When he left, the boy admitted to a friend of his uncle's that he didn't wish to go. The friend pursued the matter when the boy's uncle had left the shop on an errand, and the boy, yearning to get it off his chest, admitted all, the genesis of the trial and the following transcript. The boy's name is Hay:

Q. How old are you?

Hay. I shall be thirteen next January.

Q. Are you to tell the truth?

Hay. Yes.

Q. What do you know against the prisoner?

Hay. I was walking up St. Martin's Lane, I believe on Tuesday.

Q. Did you go to school?

Hay. Yes, I did. I live with my uncle a jeweler in Parliament Street. I met Captain Jones the prisoner, in St. Martin's Lane. He told me he had a buckle to mend.

Q. How long is that ago?

Hay. I believe about a month ago. He took me up stairs into his lodgings, in St. Martin's Court. He took me into his dining room, and he locked the door.

Q. Had you ever been in company with him before?

Hay. No. He always used to look at me, and give me halfpence when he met me. He pulled down my breeches and then his own.

Q. Were not you frightened at this?

Hay. Yes, I was a little. He set me in an elbow chair; he set me down and kissed me a little; then he made me lay down with my face on the chair, and so he came behind me; he put his cock into my hole.

Q. Did you submit to it quietly, or make any resistance?

Hay. I submitted to it quietly.

Q. How long might he keep it in your hole?

Hay. About five minutes I believe.

Q. Was he quite in?

Hay. A little.

Q. Was he in at all?

Hay. Yes.

Q. Did you find anything come from him?

Hay. Some wet stuff that was white; I wiped it off.

Q. Can you describe to the jury how far it was in your body?

Hay. No.

Q. What did you wipe the wet off with?

Hay. My shirt.

Q. You are sure it was in you?

Hay. Yes.

Q. What did he do after this?

Hay. He spouted some on the ground.

Q. Did he spout some into your hole?

Hay. Yes.

Q. What did he do after this?

Hay. He set me down in the elbow chair, kissed me a little, and gave me some halfpence and told me not to tell anybody.

Q. How long did you stay?

Hay. About half an hour.

Q. Did he attempt to do anything more to you?

Hay. No, not then.

Q. How came you not to cry out?

Hay. I was ashamed.

Q. Had ever anybody served you in this manner before?

Hay. No.

Q. Did you tell your uncle, or anybody, when you came home?

Hay. No.

Q. How soon did you go again?

Hay. He desired me to come next day; I went; he unbuttoned my breeches again, and then his own.

Q. What time did you go next day?

Hay. About eleven o'clock. He made me rub his cock up and down till some white stuff came again.

Q. At the time he put his cock into your hole, it was stiff and hard, was it?

Hay. Yes.

Q. Did he attempt anything behind then?

Hay. No.

Q. How long did you stay with him then?

Hay. About ten minutes.

Q. You quietly submitted to all that?

Hay. Yes. He gave me the buckle and some halfpence then, and desired me to come again next day; I went next day about eleven o'clock. He unbuttoned his breeches again, and mine too. He did the same again that time as he did the last day.

Q. What happened next?

Hay. I was taken very ill after this. I was ill a week. I had a pain in my thighs and legs that I could not stand. About a fortnight ago, after I was well, he came to the shop one day, and looked on the show glasses. He bespoke a shirt buckle of my uncle. It was to be sent home to him. My uncle ordered me to go with the buckle. I told him he had better go, and perhaps he might get the captain's business.

Q. When you went so willingly two days together after the first offence was committed, how came you to make the objection to go now?

Hay. I was afraid he would serve me the same thing again.

Q. How came you to object to go now and not before?

Hay. He told me not to tell of it, and I was ashamed. The reason was because I was so ill.

Q. Did you think you had been doing a wrong thing?

Hay. Yes. As soon as he left the shop I told Mr. Rapley of it. He is a jeweler.

Q. What time was it the captain came to look at the show glass?

Hay. About twelve o'clock.

Q. How came you to tell Mr. Rapley, and not tell your uncle?

Hay. I was ashamed to tell my uncle.

Q. Did you go there before dinner?

Hay. Yes.

Q. Did you tell your uncle the whole story, how he had served you these three times?

Hay. I told him what he had done to me the first time, but not the last times.

Q. How came you to tell it now, when you kept it a secret so long.

Hay. I thought I would tell of it all the while, but I was ashamed.

Q. Did you think you had been doing a wrong thing with him.

Hay. Yes.

Q. Then how came you to go of your own accord the second and third times?

Hay. I thought my uncle might get business by it.

Q. Did anything more happen than what you have told us now?

Hay. No.

The newspapers related that it took the jury 5 minutes to reach a decision, death by hanging, a verdict later rescinded in exchange for Jones's exile from England, for which he was allowed two weeks. The clemency granted by the king was due to a petition by a large number of notables who vouched for Jones's character, with the exception of this brief error in judgment. In reality, Jones--like a huge percentage of the English who had undergone boyhood boarding-school adventures--was bisexual, and it was most probable that usually Jones found contentment with adolescents, not pre-pubic children like Hay.

One paper claimed he went to Florence for a time, not the worst of exiles, and then to Lyons where, said another paper, he lived with his footboy (male domestic worker). He was reported as going to Turkey where he served assorted Beys, but during a conflict that arose between several pretenders to the throne, he championed the wrong side and had his head separated from his body.

ENGLISH BOARDING SCHOOLS (and one French example)

OXFORD - CAMBRIDGE
HARROW – ETON – AND OTHERS

Oxford and Cambridge are referred to together as Oxbridge, schools for the rich and aristocratic where the dons, following a Middle-Ages custom, were not married, but where an inexhaustible supply of highborn boys were at their disposal. Lads were trained academically and homosexually on courses of Greek and Latin classics, the first step of which were the prep schools of Repton, Harrow, Winchester and others. Of disputed educational value in the past, today Oxbridge rank in the top 5 of the world's universities, and many of the schools that prepare students for entrance into Oxbridge are often, intellectually, *today*, the *crème de la crème*.

Oxbridge were ruled by dons, professors who lived in the upper-class world they created in their image, exclusive, privileged to an unbelievable extend because they could do as they pleased with university monies, live in lavish surroundings, kowtowed to like emperors by teachers and staff. One was Benjamin Jowett who ruled Balliol College, Oxford, from 1870 to 1893, about whom one wrote:

> First am I; my name is Jowett.
> There's no knowledge but I know it.
> I am Master of this college:
> What I don't know isn't knowledge.

John Sparrow held sway over All Souls College, Oxford, in the 1950s and was a homosexual who cruised London. He was against the decriminalization of homosexuality because, as another don, Noel Annan wrote in his book *The Dons: Mentors, Eccentrics, and Geniuses*, Sparrow felt two things were necessary for homosexual pleasure, a sense of both guilt and danger.

Margaret Thatcher ended their paradise in the 1980s by asking the question What-the-hell-are-they-doing with Britain's money?, and, when she found out, she put a stop to it.

Cambridge was founded in 1209 by scholars fleeing Oxford because of disputes between the great Henry II's far-less-great son King John and Pope Innocent III, as to who should appoint the Archbishop of Canterbury. In 1231 both Oxford and Cambridge received charters from Henry III which freed them from paying taxes, as well as the right, accorded by Pope Gregory IX, for graduates to teach wherever they wished.

During the Middle Ages grammar, rhetoric, logic, mathematics, geometry and astrology were taught, augmented with mind-liberating Humanities during the Renaissance. Six new colleges were added to Cambridge between 1430 and 1496, for a total of 31 today. With the Reformation Henry VIII named Cambridge don Thomas Cranmar as the first Protestant Archbishop of Canterbury, who was soon afterwards beheaded by the Catholic Queen Mary. The Cambridge teacher William Tyndale translated the Bible into English, and because the Bible was exclusively the church's domain, he was burned at the stake.

Oxford, the world's 3rd greatest university.

Cambridge men were among the Pilgrims that founded America and Cambridge graduate John Harvard endowed the university that adopted his name. Cambridge Oliver Cromwell saw to the beheading of Charles I.

Isaac Newton was a Fellow of Trinity College who didn't believe in the religious Trinity but was personally supported by Charles II who left him free to discover his laws of motion and gravity, in addition to calculus, and tell men that although God set all in motion, He had other things to do than the day-to-day running of the universe, thereby freeing men's minds to look into the subject themselves.

Cambridge man Francis Bacon was making progress in science while giving his lover Buckingham advice as to how to manipulate *his* lover James I/VI. The Cambridge atheist Halley was discovering his comet, while people began to talk about the Cambridge student Charles Darwin--and have never stopped.

The Enlightenment at an end, women were allowed into Oxford in 1869 and into Cambridge in 1920, although without full rights until 1947. The likes of the Bloomsbury Set set the pace afterwards, the subject of a following chapter.

The Society of Apostles was formed at Cambridge in 1820 where homosexually physical friendships were formed, called Lower Sodomy, or what was called Higher Sodomy, non-sexual male bonding. Society members created, later, the Bloomsbury Set.

Schools were homosexual settings in the 1800s where the highborn went to do boys, where learning was far less important than playing both musical beds and sports, the athletic heroes of which were chosen to be Fag Masters and had their pick of the prettiest lads, employing them to bring them off manually or lying on their stomachs, and whose influence was reinforced by handing the lads, post-orgasm, to their friends for their personal gratification. Among themselves, in their own dormitories, the young boys continued their inexhaustible sexual hijinks which John Symonds called ruthless orgies. Symonds wailed against the abuse of boys by headmasters, yet purportedly had sex with a choirboy, William Fear Dyer, and in addition was forced to flee to Switzerland when accused by his private student Shorting of aiding Shorting in Shorting's pursuit of the choirboy Walter Thomas Goolden. Symonds always claimed to have practiced High Sodomy, for example having loved his pupil Norman Moor but without having sex with him, although Symonds wrote in his diary, "I stripped him naked and fed sight, touch and mouth on these things," which means what it means, and is the reason why when boys became men they formed packs with their friends to burn their papers, diaries and other proofs of pederasty that could tarnish their earthly reputations. Symonds was an example of repressed, sexually unsatisfied poofs, in stark contrast to those like Byron who exulted in their physical possession of an unlimited number of young asses, Bryon claiming to have had full intercourse with 200 in Greece during just one trip, coming down and nearly dying of fever, probably *not* the result of homosexual exhaustion, although Byron did write that he was so sated he envisioned an extended halt to any form of lovemaking.

Getting back to the sexually unsatisfied Symonds: like so many Brits who drooled over Italian boys--similar to Ashenbach in Thomas Mann's *Death in Venice*--Symonds too breathed his last in the city of the Doges (his papers later burned by Edmund Gosse), although Symonds did write this, that has come down to us, concerning Jonathan and David:

> In his arms of strength
> And in that kiss
> Soul into soul was knit
> And bliss to bliss.

In tandem with the mediocrity of an education in both Oxford and Cambridge, was the poor physical condition of the writers, poets and other aesthetes, of the 1800s and early 1900s, that frequented both schools. Yet they were convinced of their excellence, even if many were nothing but arrogant wimps, often moneyed, who paid for rent-boys in pre-W.W. I Germany and Italy, an easy task in those years where a lad would sell himself for the proverbial Hersey Bar (after the war most boys sold themselves for even less because they were *starving*). Many Exbridge boys didn't see war because physically unfit to be induced, poor eyesight, bird-breasted chests, precocious varicose-veins, girlish biceps. The exceptions were spectacular: Rupert Brooke, Byron and several others, yet even Byron was only attractive when illness brought his weight down to human levels. Few of the men from Oxford and Cambridge resembled the boys seen in gymnasiums or on the wrestling mats, although the boys they paid for were often physically splendid. Proud of the clothes they donned for extravagant meals and the robes they wore in the inner chambers of their rooms, coquettish and swishy, they wouldn't have turned on even a girl, let alone far more demanding males--effeminate twits that make England, today, the last place virile males seek out their own, although there are, and have always been, remarkable exceptions. The writer Wyndham Lewis called Duncan Grant ''a little fairy-like individual who would have received no attention in any country except England.'' In a nutshell, that's exactly what I'm talking about. Which is why the English themselves look to other lands for good sex.

Tutors and students took sherry together and shared meals, after which what naturally happened when young men wished to please their masters did happen, consisting most probably of little more than mutual masturbation, but when it took place one time it was hard to see how the inexperienced student could (or would dare to) ward off a second and then a third occasion, and so on, which meant, in the end, that it was a disgraceful debasement of what should have been a striving towards academic excellence. It was putrid exploitation. In the Greek way the lover served as a tutor, whose quest was to instruct the boy as well as sexually share acts of love, but the difference was that the boy always chose the man, and that the man was but a few years older, handsome thanks to boys being physically trained, from childhood, to care for their bodies, whereas in Cambridge and Oxford the tutors were flabby, pale-skinned, often androgynous wrecks. We know nothing of Byron's sexual encounters with his tutors, although they most certainly took place, but we do known he had the consolation of lads younger than he, for whom his experience, eloquence, fine clothes, wealth, title and tastes made him a god, a god who willingly released them from their virginity if they had managed to keep it till then, which, knowing boarding schools that catered to lads 12 and over, was highly improbable.

About his own schooling, John Addington Symonds wrote: "The talk in the dormitories and studies was of the grossest character, with repulsive scenes of onanism, mutual masturbation and obscene orgies of naked boys in bed together. There was no refinement, just animal lust." The first order that Thackeray received on his first day at school from a schoolmate was "Come & frig me," he wrote later.

How much the men who left both universities, to become truly great warriors and administrators, owed to Oxford and Cambridge training cannot of course be known, but there were many who thought that bonding through the exchange of sexual favors was destined to ready the graduates for their role as builders and leaders of the British Empire, an inane belief but one supported, in a way, by Plato who had Aristophanes put this in one of his plays: "While they are boys they love men and like to lie with them and embrace them, and these are the best of the boys and youths. The evidence is that it's these boys, when they grow up, who become the best men in politics."

Many of these aristocratic pansies were in no way comparable to the admirable *men* who died at Thermopylae and in the ranks of the Sacred Band of Thebes, nor those who fought in the Crimea and Gallipoli, who ruled the seas for generations and made the second most populous country in the world, India, a democracy, who were decimated in the First World War and saved England from disaster in the Second, and most assuredly had nothing to do with the homosexual trio of fops, Blunt, Burgess and MacLean, who betrayed their country to the murderous Soviets. Other Oxbridge and Eton men:

William Johnson Cory was characterized as "the most brilliant Eton tutor of his day," loved by his students who called him Tute (for tutor), "the wisest master who has ever been to Eton." He wrote a justification for learning Latin, stating that it "enforced the habit of attention ... assuming at a moment's notice a new intellectual position ... entering quickly into another's intellectual thoughts ... [encouraging] minute points of accuracy ... and mental soberness."

He wrote a book of poems, *Ionica*, dedicated to pretty-faced Charles Wood, that laid "down the principle that affection between people of the same sex is no less natural and irrational than the ordinary passionate relations."

After 27 years at Eton he was forced to retire due to improper relations with boys, of whom Eton was a limitless source.

An ode of sorts to homosexuals can be found in Christ's Church, Cambridge, a white and black marble tomb shared by Sirs John Finch and Thomas Baines, both intellectuals and accomplished physicians. They founded the Royal Society in 1610 and perpetuated the fascination of the English for Italian boys by residing in the country for 20 years. As stated earlier, **Italian boys have been an Englishman's wet dream since the Renaissance, and deservedly so.** Charles II sent Finch on a diplomatic mission to Constantinople, and personally made sure that Baines was allowed to travel with him. When Baines died Finch wrote that Baines' death "cutt off the thread of all my worldly happiness."

The Baines and Finch memorial
in the chapel of Christ's Church,
Cambridge.

Robert Thistlethwayte, a Warden (head of an institution) of Wadham College, Oxford, was accused of sexually abusing a student, William French, as was John Swinton, Finch's tutor. Thistlethwayte fled England in 1737. About Thistlethwayte we have this limerick:

> There once was a Warden of Wadham
> Who approved of the folkways of Sodom,
> For a man might, he said,
> Have a very poor head
> But be a find Fellow, at bottom.

It was Godsworthy Lowed Dickinson who initiated the idea of the League of Nations. Called Goldie, he was in love with Roger Frey that we meet in the Bloomsbury Set, perhaps platonically as Fry was heterosexual and Dickinson's philosophy was based on Neo-Platonism.

Goldie entered the boarding school of Beomonds, then Charterhouse School, from ages 14 to 19, followed by King's College, Cambridge. In 1896 he wrote *The Greek View of Life*. Forster wrote the biography of Dickinson after Dickinson's death in 1932 but omitted all information concerning Dickinson's homosexuality and foot fetishism. Dickinson had been involved in both the Apostles and the Bloomsbury Set. He wrote dozens of books, one of which was *The Magic Flute: A Fantasia* to *Plato and his Dialogues*. His relationships with young men were both sexual and fatherly, certainly an ideal figure for a boy needing warm guidance from a man who would show him the way, instructing him intellectually while satisfying him tenderly and perhaps physically, yet without the virile dimension so vital in Ancient Greece.

Cambridge, the world's 5th greatest university.

Dickinson was reputed as having been remarkably candid in exposing Platonic homoerotism by stating, ''That there was another side to the matter goes without saying. This passion, like any other, has its depths, as well as its heights.'' Daring for the times, apparently. Paul Robinson summarized Dickinson's sexual life as ''an intensely romantic attachment, passionate kisses and warm embraces (with a hint of fetishism [feet]), followed by relief by masturbation.'' Dickinson himself confessed to masturbating, when young, over his father's boots.

Forster was handicapped in what he could write because homosexuality was illegal when the book came out in 1934, and any revelations could have seriously damaged the reputations of his friends. (The Buggery Act of 1533 punished homosexual acts with death; the death penalty was removed in 1861; a limited decriminalization was voted in 1967; the age of consent was lowered from age 21 to age 18 in 1994; and in the year 2000 it was lowered to age 16.)

Finally, Dickinson wrote that for those whose ideal was young men, King's College, Cambridge, was perfect.

Nicholas Udall was headmaster of Eton from 1534 to 1543. A graduate of Oxford, he was convicted under the Buggery Act of 1533 for sodomy with 14-year-olds, as well as being accused of merciless flogging with a birch switch with buds, capable of scarring a boy for life. Thanks to impassioned letters from friends in high places he got off with a year in prison, after which he went on to become headmaster of Westminster.

One man was accused of holding back women's rights to a full university education: Oscar Browning. In a feud with Virginia Woolf she accused him of not only thinking that "the best woman was intellectually inferior to the worst man," but she outed his preference for boys.

Browning was educated at Eton, a student of William Johnson Cory. He went on to King's College, Cambridge, where he became a fellow and a member of the Apostles.

He was dismissed from Eton as a result of a homosexual scandal there, in 1875. He went on to teach at Cambridge and founded a training college for teachers. He was also president of the Cambridge Footlights.

His nephew and biographer purportedly destroyed his diaries and letters as protection against further scandal concerning his involvement with young men. (Only thanks to diaries that have survived do we know a little about the sex lives of Roger Casement, Keynes and a few others.)

In love with Italy like so many before him, Browning died in Rome in 1923.

The first English school was thought to have been establish in 598 A.D., the purpose of which was to produce those who ran the church, and as the members were priests they were also celibate, a tradition that continued later on, encompassing the first university dons. The nobility was educated in Latin in which the Bible was written, although the curriculum was extended to rhetoric, mathematics, astronomy and music, exactly the same classes taught in ancient Rome, which were carbon copies of those in earlier Greece. As pure, unbroken voices were necessary for church services, boys from every horizon were recruited, especially among the poor, boys who were offered the rudiments of an education, free of charge, boys who filled the countless ranks of those sexually used by the celibates who ran the schools. Convinced in one way or another that they were accomplishing part of God's will, little convincing was necessary to have them bend over. Later thousands of men became priests thanks to the infinite pool of boys that made up the church, from the very first schools right up to today's, religious institutions where, for some recondite reason, the church can keep clericals out of prison simply by paying damages. For the boys, historically, this was nonetheless their ticket out of poverty, many becoming church clericals and boy abusers in their own time.

While nobles were taught at home by private tutors, the poor were welcomed into schools like Eton that Henry VIII set up in 1442 to provide pubescent lads for his choirs. Dozens of schools were founded by Henry and

Elizabeth on the ashes of those destroyed in order for the Anglican church to reign supreme.

Because schools were far between, boys eventually became boarders in towns around the schools. This was easily accepted because the nobles had farmed out their boys to be educated in the houses of other nobles for years, at around age 7. Eventually it was realized that these fee-paying lads could become a huge source of profit if they were housed in schools. This helped too for disciplinary reasons as the closer the boys were physically to their tutors, the easier it was to control them. Thus the advent of boarding schools. Soon an incredible *esprit de corps* formed between the boys, meaning that a boy interviewed for a job by someone who had been to his college was nearly certain to be hired. And it was not uncommon that boys dying in war had a last thought for their college house before that of their God. When the tenderness of first love is mingled with all the other first experiences of life, an inherent part of youth, no armed concrete is more solid.

The early schools were based on Latin and scriptures, Greek and the classics came later, during the Renaissance. And although England was making incredible strides in exploration, discovery, rule over other lands, advances in medicine under Harvey and science under Newton, public schools continued on as arrogant social functions aimed at showing off one's eccentricities in fine clothing, to honor the best in food and wines, and to have free, unsuppressed and unlimited sexual access to new boys entering each year. Nothing the world has known could compete with the wild orgiastic no-holds-barred sex in the entirely unsupervised dormitories. Moreover, boys slept two to a bed in the first boarding schools, until 1805 at Harrow. No wonder men would later die with the burning memory of youthful lust alive in their breasts like incandescent coals, and why men, become fathers, tolerated nearly every excess in their sons, an exclusively British phenomenon, and the reason that once a Brit ended his school years he exiled himself for extended and numerous visits to more liberal skies, especially those of Italy and pre-W.W. I Germany, while in Britain homosexuality was punished by death until 1835, when the last man was beheaded.

As there were few masters in the early schools to control hundreds of lads, beatings were among the most appalling to have existed, and they and other forms of abuse have continued right up to the present as the reader will soon see. Floggings by headmasters inspired cruelty among the boys, and even Bertrand Russell wrote that the big boys hit him so he hit the little boys, "that's fair", he concluded.

Dormitories were no more than male brothels. To make sex easy and accessible, (a healthy boy being able to ejaculate six times daily), the linings of their pockets were cut away so they could play with themselves, even in class, but two boys could especially practice mutual masturbation, withdrawing their hands from the other's pocket in a second if interrupted. For unknown reasons homosexuality was more fashionable in some schools than others, and even in schools where it was fashionable it suddenly ceased being so, whereas where it was little practiced it might come back with a bang. In one school a headmaster who succeeded in rounding up a huge number of boys, said to have been around 100, and having them all beaten for some forgotten rascality, was applauded by the boys afterwards for having been clever enough to catch them all.

It would seem that the earlier boys start having sex among themselves, the easier sex is throughout their lives. On the other hand, boys who enter into sexual relations with girls later on are more stressful and fearful, and the sexual satisfaction is far less to what they had known with other boys at puberty. The result is unhappy marriages and divorce. Sex is easy between boys because they are simply clones of each other; there is little that is unfamiliar for them to discover; they've known from puberty what turns them on. (Young heterosexual Italian boys were recently interviewed concerning their preference for transvestites, answering that first sex was easier with them because physically the heterosexuals knew what to expect.)

The holidays in those early schools were short, 20 to 30 days a year from 1500 to 1700, while the academic part of the day was short, 4 hours at Eton in the 1750s, half-days on Thursdays and on Saturdays, and no schooling at all Tuesdays and Sundays.

But the age was brutal--the 1600s and 1700s--when sailors were lashed to death, parents were cruel to their children, children could be imprisoned for stealing a handkerchief, poor houses where children were beaten and exposed to every form of sexual vice, several children to a bed, and where headmasters were told explicably by parents to birch them at their first obstinacy. It was a time when children were farmed out to wet nurses until around age 7 when, if they hadn't died of a childhood disease as at least half did, they were packed off to boarding schools. An example: like Byron, Talleyrand had had a clubfoot and had been sent to poor provincials to be brought up without the slightest education. Miraculously, a relative discovered him and took him to Paris to the rich residence of his parents where he and the boy walked in on a party of wigged noblemen, Talleyrand in filthy rags, bringing an immediate end to the chamber music and festivities. "This is your son!" the relative bellowed to the amazed parents.

Abuse in schools could go on unhampered because the headmasters washed their hands at what went on between the lads, especially as they knew they couldn't control it, and because they had their own lives to lead. The fact that boys were in class for so few hours gave them acres of free time, and nowhere was the saying idle hands are the devil's workshop more true. Their parents bought their own freedom by dispatching the boys to schools, giving them enough money to buy the drink and food and whores they coveted, rampaging through the streets, free to wreak havoc because the towns people could not complain to headmasters who would do nothing, nor the boys' parents who were most often their betters and who resided far away. *And* the money jingling in the lads' pockets would eventually find its way into town shops.

Because so much research has been done on Byron and Shelly, both Etonians, we know that Byron was often the leader of some revolts, Shelley the victim of boy abuse, boys who tore his clothes and knocked his books out of his hands, although nothing else more violent is indicated, yet even Shelley is reported to have electrified the knob of his door to literally shock visitors (unless this was his way of getting even with his tormentors).

Education in these schools was wholly secondary to the comfort and prestige of the place parents parked their children, and such academic dinosaurs should have disappeared eons ago had it not been for the fact that they evolved, and thanks to their wealth are now able to hire the best teachers who give the best education, and today rank among the world's top institutions. In public schools the sanction is immediate: when a school drops in rank its rich subscribers turn elsewhere, while *state* schools go on and on, no matter how mediocre the instruction. Luckily for America its universities are so wealthy the students are admitted through exams, meaning that the poorest church mouse can become a veritable pillar of society, even if the vast majority of the students are prepared by the best American prep schools, something out of the reach of all but the most dedicated, hard-working poor. Yet the tradition of starting off cleaning school toilets and ending up the school dean (in America, of course) still (I hope) prevails.

The attitude today, sexually, is that boys can do what they want as long as they are discreet and there is no sexual exploitation, a form of don't ask/don't tell. And that's the way it should be. Boys should be left alone, in the sense that adults must be excluded because they can force boys by their positions (priests and headmasters), their sweet talk (as men are infinitely more experienced and knowledgeable than boys), money and other forms of pressure and coercion. The rule of older boys poses a conundrum because young lads can be drawn to their prowess, especially when they're successful athletes. Older boys can show responsibility in the Greek way, become a teacher and protector, encouraging the boy to greater heights. In that case, who can rightfully cast the first stone?

The question of the age of consent comes in. The age of consent is when one is permitted to have sexual relations, and has nothing to do with one's majority, which envelops the age of criminal responsibility, voting, driving and drinking.

In Ancient Greece a boy married around age 30, leaving him lots of time to play the field (although marriage in no way curtailed the fulfilling of his lust for boys afterwards), whereas in Rome Augustus wanted his citizens to have children before age 30, and heavily fined them if they didn't, because the state was in dire need of men for wars, the running of government, for agriculture, construction, etc. Girls married around puberty or a little later.

In Medieval Europe one could marry between ages 12 to 14, and in the 1500s and 1600s girls could have intercourse around age 12. After the French revolution, which abolished laws against homosexuality, intercourse was allowed at age 11, and Spain, Portugal and Denmark followed with the age of consent between ages 10 and 12.

In the 1800s the age increased to around age 13, while in the 1900s it was raised to 16 as one became aware of sexual abuse concerning girls. It went to between ages 16 and 18 in the U.S. in 1920 thanks to female reformers. Only Spain held out, allowing intercourse at age 12, and that to 1999 (!), when it increased to age 13 (!), and only in 2015 did it go to age 16, but as we all know, everything ripens faster in sunny Spain.

To my way of thinking, 16 would be perfect (although kids in the Internet Age frequently replace masturbation by intercourse around age 15).

Canada, where the age of consent is 16, allows sex between ages 14 and 15 if the partner is not more than 5 years older, and between ages 12 to 13 if the partner is less than 2 years older. The age of consent in Finland is 16, but anyone can have sex at any age if they're the same age. Both countries are stunning models.

Today boys educated in British public schools leave with diplomas in engineering, science, economics, law, medicine, accountancy, the Classics and in the service industries. The wealthier schools are Eton, Winchester, Rugby, Dulwich and Whitgift; nearly all public schools charge enormous fees. Twelve years of education, starting from prep schools, is a *minimum* £420,000.

Winchester

Eton

Robin Maugham was a handsome Eton boy not unlike the lad on the cover of this book, black hair and eyes and a perfect boy's body. In later life he discovered that he was ''omnisexual'' as he put it, for me a far better and more accurate word than bisexual. At 18 he went to Vienna where whorehouse girls were paraded in front of him naked, one of whom gave him great sexual pleasure. He fell in love with a boy that his host in Vienna was paying £3 each time Robin fucked him, unknown to Robin of course.

What interests us here were his Eton years when, at age 14, a boy he later fell in love with stretched out on his bed beside him, both in pajamas, and asked him how green he was. When Robin assured him he knew the facts of life, the boy reached into his pajama bottoms and jerked him off.

Later, when a teacher was dismissed form school, Robin's friend admitted that he had spied on him in the company of two naked boys and turned him in because he didn't like that particular prof.

Although Robin apparently was faithful to his friend, the friend had other boys, some of whom would tell Robin they knew what was going on, and so Robin could share himself with them too, which he said he didn't do. Maugham cuts off the action every time he and a boy are together naked, but is seems apparent that what's going on is fucking, Robin the top.

During his last year at Eton a student told him what had happened when the headmaster himself caught him having sex with a boy and then, back in his chambers, had both strip naked and, making the boys stand face-to-face, encouraged them to frot together (see chapter: More about the Princeton Rub) until both came. You must keep this a secret, the headmaster told them, because people are so stupid they think it's a crime.

The student then asked Robin if they could make love, dropping his dressing gown and standing naked before him. Robin admitted ''that his genitals seemed almost obscenely large'', and that he broke out in laughter ''because I was happy'' And ''presently our bodies were joined together.''

I've never read a better book on prep-school first love--honest and as erotic as was good form at that time--than Robin Maugham's *Escape from the Shadows*.

Dulwich

HOMOEROTIC GREEK AND ROMAN TEXTS

The goal of headmasters and teachers was to create a justification, based on the solid reputations of poets, playwrights and philosophers whose ancient Greek and Roman texts would put the lads at ease with their masters' wish to slip a hand into their briefs, doing for them what the boys did for themselves or among themselves from, literally, the moment they awoke in the morning to their bedtimes, when they slipped into other hands, those of Morpheus, their briefs pleasantly warmed by the ejaculation they or they and their friends had induced.

XENOPHON

Xenophon was not only a general of genius, a valiant hero among men who fought for Cyrus the Younger during his youth, the stirring adventure that is the heart of his *Anabasis*, he was in addition a philosopher, historian, the author of *Hellenica*, the story of the Peloponnesian War. Born in Athens but an admirer of Sparta where he sent his sons to be educated, this man among men was a lover of boys whom he galvanized thanks to his courage, protection, guidance and education, the ultimate for those who seek a model for the belief that true good, profound inspiration, the very finest in what mankind can offer, comes through a lover's will to better the boy who-- tenderly, gratefully, willingly--fills his bed with his perishable warmth. His works are studied by first-year students of Greek.

Xenophon describes a tender battle scene in which a certain Episthenes, seeing that a handsome enemy boy was about to be executed, ran to Xenophon and begged for the boy's life. Xenophon approached his general, Seuthes, in charge of Episthenes, to ask if the lad's life could be spared, as Episthenes had shown himself a valiant warrior. Seuthes asked Episthenes if he would be willing to take the boy's place and be executed. Episthenes stretched out his neck and told Seuthes to strike off his head if the boy so ordered. The boy came forward to save Episthenes, but dropped to his knees and begged that both their lives be spared. Episthenes rose and enfolded the lad in his arms, telling Seuthes that he would have to kill them or let them both go free. Seuthes laughed and, says Xenophon, winked at him.

Greek love.

PINDAR

Pindar's great love was Theoxenus of Tenodos about whom he wrote:

> One must pluck love, my dear heart,
> In due season, in life's prime.
> But whosoever catches with a glance
> The rays flashing from Theoxenus' eyes,
> And is not tossed on the waves of desire,
> Had a black heart forged in cold flame!
> But I, like the wax of the sacred bees
> When smitten by the sun, melt
> When I look at the young limbs of boys.

He lived around 500 B.C. and celebrated the Greek victories against the Persians at Salamis and Plataea. His home in Thebes became a must for his devotees.

SOPHOCLES

Sophocles was the author of 123 plays of which 7 remain, notably *Oedipus* and *Antigone*. An Athenian born to a rich family just before the Battle of Marathon, he was a firm supporter of Pericles. He fought alongside Pericles against Samos when the island attempted to become autonomous from Athens. He was elected as a magistrate during the Sicilian Expedition led by Alcibiades, and given for function the goal of finding out why the expedition had ended disastrously. Sophocles was always ready and willing to succumb to the charms of boys. Plutarch tells us that even at age 65 "he led a handsome boy outside the city walls to have his way with him. He spread the boy's poor himation upon the ground. To cover them both he spread his rich cloak. After Sophocles took his pleasure the boy took the cloak and left the himation for Sophocles. This misadventure was eventually known to all."

A himation.

THEOCRITUS
FATHER OF HOMOEROTIC POETRY

Theocritus, a bucolic poet, was a Sicilian who lived around 270 B.C. In his 7th Idyll (a poem describing a pastoral scene) Aratus is passionately in love with a lad. His 12th Idyll refers to Diocles who died saving the life of Philolaus, the boy he loved, and in whose honor kissing contests were held every spring at his tomb. In his 29th Idyll a lover warns his belovèd that he too will age and his beauty will lose its freshness. He is therefore advised to show more kindness as "you will one day be desperate for a beautiful young man's attentions." Although lads are often disappointing, says Theocritus, it is impossible not to fall madly in love with them. In the 30th Idyll the poet states that when a man grows old he should keep a distance from boys, but in his heart he knows that the only alternative to loving a boy is simply to cease to exist.

A Theocritus boy.

Idyll V is a back-and-forth verbal wrangling between a man, a goatherd named Comatas, and a boy shepherd over whom Comatas had once had guardianship and had on occasion poked (variously translated as screwed or fucked). The setting is a grassy woods-encircled glen in the south of Italy. They enter into a singing contest judged by a mutual friend passing by, Maroson, the prize for which will be either a sheep or a goat.

The boy Lacon talks about his maiden and how he'll catch a bird for her and make a fine cloak for his darling from the black ewe he'll shear. Comatoas, with a sly smirk, asks him if he remembers ''when I fucked you, and you, grinning, held out your ass while you held on to that stout oak?'' ''Indeed I do, and I remember when Eurmaras tied you to that same oak and screwed *your* ass!''

Idyll XII (greatly condensed): Just as spring is sweeter than winter, so am I gladdened to see you my belovèd, and together we can admire those of old, whose love is our inspiration, like Diocles who gave his life for Philolaus. Let their love be on every lip, young men's most of all! Let the gods honor them for a hundred hundred years, in spring, when boys come together in a kissing contest over their graves, and the winners are those who most sweetly press lip upon lip.

Idyll XIII: The brazen-hearted master of the Nemean lion once loved a boy, the beautiful Hylus of the curly locks, and as a father his son, so too did Heracles teach him the story of past good men and how they gained fame, fashioning the boy to his mind, making him a true man.

Hylus and his lover Iolcus boarded the *Argo*, as did Heracles and his belovèd Telamon. One day the gold-haired Hylus went off to fill a pitcher with spring water from a nearby source watched over by Nymphs, Eunica,

Malis and Nycheia, who, seeing the boy, fell in love with him. As he bent to fill the pitcher they grasped and pulled him into the dark depths where they comforted him with sweet speech.

Hylus and the nymphs.

Heracles, alarmed at his absence, went bellowing after him. Hylus heard his cries and answered, but weekly from the depths. Like a lion who hears the reedy cry of a fawn and leaves his den mad with hunger, so Heracles, like a madman for his boy, goes in search of Hylus, not from hunger but from longing. Hylus joined the Land of the Blest and the *Argo* set sail without Heracles.

Idyll XXIII: There was once a beautiful belovèd who lacked kind ways as he spurned the man who loved him, offering no understanding and showing immunity to Eros' arrows, which earned him the god's enmity. Never a pursing of the lips, a smile, flashing eyes, nor even a stealthy movement of the hips. Like a hunted beast, he looked at the man threw wary dread-filled eyes. The boy's wrath colored his cheeks, making the man desire him even more.

Finally the man, unable to accept more of the lad's cruelty, went to his home, kissed the door cornice, cried out against he with a heart of stone, offering him a last gift, a noose he placed over his head, freeing the boy from the sight of the man he couldn't stand, certain that what awaited him was oblivion, oblivion that in no way would quench his desire.

The man knew the fragility of life. The rose that faded, the snow that melted with spring, a boy's beauty destined to fade. He knew that for the lad he so desired the day would come when he too would love another, his heart on fire and his eyes brimming with tears. "So I beg you, lad," the man cried, "when you find me, lower me gently and offer me a parting kiss that will be welcomed even in the land of the dead. And fear me not! I will never harm you from the grave, and with your kiss, I will have a happy end." [The end of this Idyll I'll put in verse:]

Following a prayer for almighty Zeus,
Around his bared neck he tightened the noose.
He climbed on a stone that he kicked away,
And there, no more than a corpse, did he sway.
The boy skirted the corpse, off for the gym.
Where revengeful Eros awaited him.
He entered the waters, naked and slim,
While the statue of Eros looked on grim.
To kill him it fell over with a thud,
Filling the pool with the lad's wondrous blood.

A teacher's desire.

SOLON

Blessed is the man sweaty from the gym,
Having muscles, supple, strong and slim,
Goes home where he may drink wine and play,
With a fair boy on his chest all day.

Statesman, lawmaker, poet in his spare time, he is credited with founding Athenian democracy, and as such is the most important person in the history of that great city, and keystone of our very own culture. What we possess of him we possess in fragments, but his life was related through oral history up to the time of Herodotus and Plutarch, thanks to whom we have a portrayal of this wondrous man.

Solon lived to see the tyrant Pisistratus take power in Athens but did little to combat him as Pisistratus, according to Plutarch, had been Solon's belovèd when he was a boy, and ''the embers of the former love still burned strong." Aelian later confirmed this. Pisistratus was also the father of two other tyrants, Hippias and Hipparchus, murdered by Harmodius and Aristogeiton (their story told elsewhere).

The above poem is said to be Solon's.

Greek affection.

THEOGNIS

After Homer it is the oeuvre of Theognis that has come down to us most intact, a near miracle given his birth around 500 B.C. in Megara. What we know about the man and the boy that inspired his poetry, Kyrnus, as well as what we learn about archaic Greece, is in his poetry. In the finest tradition of male relations, he educated his boy-lover in the ways of the world. What he teaches is often self-contradictory, but no more so than one expects from men then, as today, who learn as they go along, who change their minds and opinions according to what they see, hear and read. Theognis stresses morality, the reason perhaps why monks copied his works over the generations and why we have so much today. Unlike Straton, there is no talk of cocks and asses to titillate young friars. Boy-love nonetheless exists in his texts, and it is herein that I'll dip for examples of his teaching, although, in my mind, of far greater importance are the truths in his wisdom, the reason for which I've peppered this entire book with his poetry.

Here are several poems that aren't part of the book:

Happy the man who's got boys for loving, and horses,
Hunting dogs and foreign friends.
The heart of he who doesn't love boys and horses
And dogs will never know pleasure.

Boys and horses have the same brain.
A horse doesn't cry when the rider bites the dust.

He goes off with another who will sate him with seed.
The same with a boy eating from the hand of a new friend.

Happy the lover whose boy gives him a workout at home,
And the whole day to sleep alongside his beautiful body.

Boy love is a wonder ever since Zeus,
King of the gods, found Ganymede,
And brought him to the garden of Olympus,
Making his boyhood-flowering eternal.

ARISTOPHANES

Although he wrote, "A boy's beauty relied on a powerful chest, a tanned body, broad shoulders, a muscular ass and a small cock", we know nothing about his sexuality. In *The Women at the Thesmophoria* we have this dialogue between Euripedes and a citizen:

Euripides: There's that guy Agathon.
Citizen: The tanned, strong guy?
Euripides: No, a another one. You've never seen him?
Citizen: The one with the beard?
Euripides: You don't know him?
Citizen: Not as far as I know.
Euripides: Well, you may have fucked him, without knowing it.

Men who prefer men, continued Aristophanes, are more manly, courageous and masculine than other men, and their love is more profound than that between men and women, and they "tend to cherish what is like themselves."

In Plato's *Symposium* Aristophanes said that originally Zeus had created three types of person, a man, a woman and one that had both sexes. When they became too powerful he split them in half. Each half wanted desperately to rejoin the other half. The cock half of a man rejoined the missing ass half. Women did the same and the person who had both sexes was able to have male-female intercourse and children. In this way the wound of the original separation was healed and one was again complete. "Love," concluded Aristophanes, "is the pursuit of *wholeness*."

EPHORUS

Ephorus of Cyme, ca. 380 B.C. was the author of the 29 books in his *Historiai*, a thirtieth added by his son Demophilus, organized along themes rather than chronologically. The first universal history, it was greatly praised during antiquity.

The paragraph to follow concerns the Cretan custom of ritualized abductions, the Cretans being perhaps the first of the Greeks to practice boy-love:

> The Cretans win their lovers through planned abduction before which the abducted boy's friends and family have been notified. If the abductor is unworthy, his friends do not allow the abduction. If his friends believe he is everything the boy could wish for, the abduction is permitted after a staged show of force to prevent it. Supposedly the bravest, most valorous, best-behaved boys--not the most beautiful--are the abductor's priority. He is taken to his lovers hunting lodge where they hunt between sessions of enjoying each other. The boy can be kept for no more than two months. He is then offered gifts, depending on the wealth of the boy's lover, but usually consisting of a drinking cup, military equipment, an ox, and so on. The boy's friends sometimes contribute to the price of the presents--the more he is deemed worthy, the more his lover and friends spend. A huge banquet is held between the youths, lover, belovèd and friends, during which the ox is sacrificed to Zeus and the belovèd describes his capture, publicly admitting his pleasure or publicly avenging himself for having been ill-treated. In this case he is free to return with his friends and not see the lover again. Being chosen by a good lover has a tremendous impact on the boy's future place in society.

ASCLEPIADES OF ADRAMYTTIUM

> You open your legs, but there's that hair!
> On your ass, it's more than I can bare!
> "Oh I like that ! Please do it once more!"
> But all that bristly down--What a bore!

So little is known about Asclepiades that I can't even give a vague date of when he lived and worked.

SCYTHINUS

> Aged 16 Elissus is made for love,
> A wonderful ass as tight as a glove.
> Parted lips, sweeter than honey to kiss,
> A wondrous voice, the sound of bliss.
> "Don't touch!" he says, and I'm left to my fate,
> I think of him all night and masturbate.

> Erect you are my tall flaming cock,
> Valiant, ready, as hard as a rock.
> When Nemensinos came to my bed,
> You deflated and my face went bright red.
> Now he's gone and you're swollen to the gland,
> You won't get any relief from *my* hand!

As with Asclepiades, nothing is known about Scythinus.

ATHENAEUS

Athenaeus of Naucratis is thought to have lived during the times of Emperors Marcus Auelius and Commodus. His book, *The Deipnosophistae, Banquet of Scholars*, is unique in that it's an enormous source of 800 writers and other participants spoken about or speaking during the banquet, thanks to which otherwise unknown authors have come down to us. Book XIII relates sexuality in Hellenistic Greece. The banquet was held in the home of Larensius by Athenaeus in honor of his lover Timocrates.

Some excerpts from Book XIII:

Chariton and Melanippus plotted the death of the tyrant Phalaris who found out and had them both tortured. When the boys refused to give each other up in exchange for freedom, Phalaris had them released, apologized and declared his admiration for the depth of their love. Apollo, aware of Phalaris' decision, postponed his death as a reward, saying:

> Blessed are Chariton and Melanippus
> Who show mortals the divinity of friendship.

Ion of Chios relates this story about Sophocles: At a dinner Sophocles saw a beautiful boy who had a bit of straw in his cup of wine. The boy made to remove it with his finger, but Sophocles told him to blow it away. As the boy bent over to do so, Sophocles approached the cup so that soon both his and the boy's foreheads touched. Sophocles then put his arm around the boy's shoulders and they kissed.

A story was told about Alexander the Great who saw a beautiful boy at a drinking bout organized by Craterus. The boy was Craterus' belovèd and adored him. Craterus, seeing Alexander's interest in the lad, told the boy to kiss Alexander. Alexander refused: ''A kiss from a boy who doesn't love me would pain him more than it would please me.''

About a boy blushing from desire for his friend, Sophocles said: "There shines on his crimson cheeks the light of love."

About Alexander's father, Philip of Macedon, Theopompus said: Philip was not interested in well-behaved men and boys but only those who drank and gambled with dice. Some of these men would shave the hair from their bodies but continue to be men, mounting boys, others would have full beards and mount each other. They caroused together in twos and threes, no better than courtesans, sluts and beasts.

ALCAEUS

Alcaeus, born at Mitylene on the island of Lesbos, was considered at the time equal to Pindar. Of his works, originally 10 books, only fragments remain. They are divided into categories, the first of which are political songs aimed at inspiring compatriots to valiant action and heroic defiance. Drinking songs celebrated victories and the death of tyrants, and exhorted his companions to drink ever more as life was short and *in vino* came *viritas*. His hymns glorified the gods and his poems ... well, here are two examples, proof of the dislike of body hair, giving credence to the point made by women that men only liked boys so long as they resembled girls.

>Your hairy legs were once smooth as glass,
>Keep the hair, boy, from covering your ass.
>If not you'll lose your lovers I fear,
>For one day your youth will disappear.
>
>The hair on your legs is spreading, alas!
>Soon, Nicander, it will coat your ass.
>Then you'll lose your lovers very fast
>Oh why god, can't youth and beauty last?

Alcaeus is thought to have been the sole survivor of a battle between Athens and Mytilene, and fragments of his poetry are vigorous denials that he had survived because he had fled the battlefield.

He actively took part in the governing of Lesbos, joining this or that revolt, at times for, at times against tyrants. His brothers went off to war, too, and one tender poem recites the return home of one of them.

He seems to have died embittered by the outcome of life-long friendships, but at any rate he had known love and glory on the battlefield during his many years of soldering. Tents, comradeship, banquets, wine, buddies and the nostalgia of campfire smoke are the basis of the few existent fragments of his oeuvre. With the loss of such stirring events--living and fighting among those one loved and, especially, the one boy one adored--and the coming of despicable age--who wouldn't feel embittered?

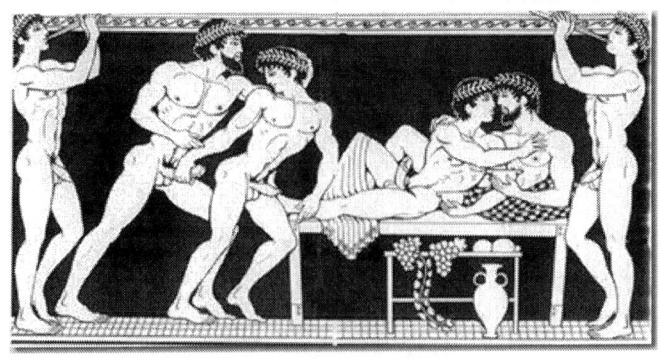

Banquet memories.

MELEAGER

Born in today's Jordan, educated in Tyre, he spent most of his life--and died--on the island of Cos. He spoke and wrote in Greek and his fame resides in his 134 existent epigrams that he collected, along with the poems of other poets, each poet represented by a flower, the whole forming an anthology known as the *Garland of Meleager*.

Meleager was a philosopher who was a Cynic. In Cynicism one frees oneself from futile influences like the search for wealth, fame and power; one contents oneself with the bare necessities required for existence. A Cynic was supposed to be free from the hold of sex, too, which was not the case for Meleager. He lived and loved like every other male, although the eroticism is far less explicit than in the works of Straton.

> This summer I hungered for the kiss
> Of a handsome lad, life's foremost bliss.
> Such a kiss Zeus had drawn from the lips
> Of Ganymede in tender sips.

And this:

> I saw Alexis pass through the street,
> His eyes, bright like the sun's, mine did meet!
> That night the sun's rays had ceased to shine,
> While his image made my dreams divine.
> Joyfully, sleep I refused to find
> As his beauty was etched in my mind.

STRATON OF SARDIS

Let's begin with my favorite poem by Straton:

> A hairless boy of twelve is sublime,
> A youth thirteen is in his prime.
> Fourteen is a sweeter flower still,
> While fifteen a man's heart will fill.
> Sixteen is destined for the gods divine,
> Seventeen is for Zeus' bed, not mine.

A credible source has it that according to the Greek calendar all these boys would have been, in reality, a year younger, a penchant that concords with my research which places the sublime age of boy-love at 16 (and thusly reserved for Zeus only). Greek statues, too, most often showed kouroi around age 16, and it was the preferred year to be portrayed on death steles, no matter at what age a man really died. Eleven may seem young but in the Florence of the Renaissance a lad could begin making money with his body at age 10. Da Vinci's Salaì was perhaps that age when introduced to the master, Cellini's Cecco was 10 also. Much is unknown about sexuality then. Why was it so important for the Florentines and the Greeks to possess a hairless boy when a lad was deemed most desirable by the gods, at age 16, when attired in nothing more than a full public bush, which is far from hairless? The imperative of possessing a hairless boy for the Greeks is reinforced by nearly all of their poems, which stress the "ugliness" of facial and buttocks' hair when it mutes from down to bristle. Men shaved until the Roman Hadrian grew a beard, popularizing the style.

> Theudis excites me more than any boy,
> His radiance makes others just a toy.
> He's my sun but that too will soon be gone:
> He'll soon be too hairy to turn me on.

Straton attempts to seduce a lad before he becomes hirsute:

> Why must we steal kisses and only wink,
> And into sterile platitudes sink?
> Why must we continue to play hide-and-seek,
> Until hair ruins a body now so sleek?

Born in Sardis in Lydia (today's western Turkey), perhaps during the reign of Hadrian, Straton was known for his anthology of love poems generally translated as *The Boy Muse*. His works went through many hands before coming to us, those of Greeks and Romans, Arabs, Byzantines and monks throughout the following centuries, altering, censoring, condensing or expanding.

> I don't like boys who refuse my touch,
> Who play dumb or protest far too much.
> I don't like those easy to entreat,
> Who show their wares the moment we meet.
> I prefer those somewhere in between,
> Who oblige me to guess what they mean.

Straton related the ups-and-downs of boy love, boys frisky as a horse but who refused to be ridden, arrogant boys, those with rye smiles, those blond and blue-eyed who quicken the heart and those with black hair and eyes blacker still, who brought it to a stop. His poems were highly autobiographical. Loneliness, the inconstancy of lovers, relief through self-pleasuring, boys jerking each other off--perhaps an endearing memory from early youth. The key word for Straton is desire, desire spawned by the beauty of a boy; desire that culminates in sexual union. Straton covers all aspects of love, beginning with the eyes, progressing to foreplay, deep tongue kissing, appreciation of the buttocks, the entering of same. The aim of Straton, as with most Greeks, was a hairless boy:

> You lean your dear ass against a wall,
> But a wall can't honor it at all!

Boys eventually marry, which is meaningless to the men that court them:

> Wondrous Diodore so ready for bed,
> I'll still be here even after you've wed.

The baths are a place of predilection for the hunt, distinguishing Straton from other poets by his edging towards the pornographic:

> In the bathing pool Diocles' cock
> Rose from the waters hard as a rock.
> If the goddess had seen his size,
> It's Paris who would have won the prize.

And this:

> Why wear a long robe down to your feet?

110

> Back then you raised it when we would meet.
> Now you greet me with silent disdain,
> I know the cock your robe doth contain!

Men appreciate the lack of trickery in males:

> The duplicities in curling hair,
> Don't touch me as they're for girls to bear.
> I want a boy sweaty from the gym,
> With oil covering every limb.

LUCIAN

Lucian of Samosata was a satirist and rhetorician from Assyria who spoke and wrote in Greek, forsaking his mother tongue, a dialect of Aramaic, the language of Christ, that he considered barbaric. He traveled widely, from Ionia to Gaul, via Greece and Italy, becoming wealthy and famous thanks to his recitations and teaching.

In his *Erotes* we have two boys discussing the merits of girl and boy love, Charicles is described as mad about girls, Callicrates passionate for boys. Charicles claims that heterosexual love is best because homosexual love is so intense in pleasure that it can be considered over indulgence (!). Plutarch, who favored women, weighs in by stating that women can be just as desirable as are boys, which infers that boys are more so (or such is my interpretation). Callicrates maintains that love between men is equal, implying heated on both sides, and it is true that rarely will a boy just lie there like the proverbial ironing board, waiting for the male to finish up. In Plato's *Symposium* we learn from the Stoics that males continue on together from youth to old age with love and desire becoming love and friendship. Charicles says that the love of women endures throughout life, while that of a boy lasts until he is bearded. The love of women is physical, says Callicrates, while that of a man combines virtue--learning, education--with pleasure. The love of women is a physical necessity, that of boys cultural and philosophical. There's an observer to the debate, Theomnestus, who appreciates both sexes. He says that both girls and boys give pleasure, and any talk about turning the love of boys into something philosophical is just bunk.

PHILOSTRATUS

Lucius Flavius Philostratus was a Greek sophist who wrote exquisite love letters to an unknown handsome boy. The letters are in pairs, one emphasizing purity, the other praising its contrary.

Three examples:

These roses make haste to join you. Welcome them as gifts from Adonis. Just as a wreath of olive leaves becomes an athlete and a helmet a soldier, these roses, by their fragrance and color, become a beautiful boy. They will not adorn you; they will be adorned by you.

You have accepted the roses I sent, a sign that you have a certain affection for the sender. If you wish to favor he who loves you, send back a few, since they are now enhanced by your fragrance.

In the name of what obsession do you hang on to your chastity? Do you scorn pleasure? Do you refuse love's delights? Crown yourself with flowers before you wither and die, anoint your body with sweet oil before it decays, find lovers before you find yourself alone. Live all the night through, eat and drink. How much time do you imagine you have left? Yesterday? Yesterday is dead. Today? You are wasting it with your chastity. Tomorrow? How do you know you will live so long?

HORACE

Horace personified the Roman attitude towards sex. As he himself wrote:

> When your dick is stiff
> And a servant girl or youth
> Is at hand,
> You can either take your pleasure
> Or hold off and burst with tension.
> Not me! I take my sex then and there.

For a Roman, the only guilt in having sex, it bears repeating, is being accused of the passive role in a sexual encounter. Just as the emperors had *imperium* (power) over their subjects, so too did the average Roman wield *imperium* over his household. Manliness was a necessary part of *imperium* and someone who allowed himself to be penetrated was not manly, and therefore could not hold *imperium*. Penetration means subjugation, while masculinity, *virtus*, is domination. The Roman male was expected to penetrate girls, women and boys. Sex with young boys, slaves or foreigners, was so common and accepted that erotic statues of youths were the rage in Rome, and dancing nude boys could be used as entertainment at weddings, to raise the male participants spirits as well as their robes, and set the stage for the taking of the hymen that would follow the wedding banquet.

Horace's rooms were walled with mirrors to enable him to see lascivious scenes wherever he looked, says Suetonius. Such scenes were certainly lascivious as he organized orgies thanks to the participants of rich friends such as Maecenas who offered him the farm where he wrote, partied and died. Friendship was the leitmotif of his life and his goodwill to others, as well as poetry said to be exquisite, brought him companions like Virgil. He was so small that when he sent a volume of his work to Augustus, the emperor replied, thanking him, but wondered if his books were always so small so as not to exceed him in size. Maecenas took him on his diplomatic voyages and such was the love between them that Maecenas vowed he could not live without Horace and Horace said he did not wish to outlive Maecenas, which was exactly what took place, as Horace died one month after his friend.

Instinctively Horace felt that his life would end young. Perhaps he had this in mind when he wrote about Lycidas. In reading this we must also keep in mind that men liked their boys young and girls liked them during their manhood.

> Life's too short for long hopes, Lycidas:
> In Hades you will no longer role dice
> And be the King of the Party,
> You who put all boys on fire when young,
> And made girls glow when a man.

His love of boys was evident throughout his poetry:

> Lirius! At midnight I dream I'm holding you.
> I dream I'm flying after you across meadows,
> Out over the sea, flying after you and your hard heart.

MARTIAL (Marcus Valerius Martialis)

Martial was an epigrammatist (an epigram being a concise poem dealing pointedly and often satirically with a single thought or event and often ending with an ingenious turn of thought) who had the great fortune of a loving family and friends in his hometown of Bilbilis in Spain. He then moved on to the big city, Imperial Rome, to further his education, surrounded by luminaries who were also his friends, the likes of Seneca and Lucan, also Spanish born (and soon to be murdered by Nero), as well as Piso, Juvenal and Pliny the Younger. As his family wasn't rich he didn't have it easy, especially living on his poetry, and so was obliged to literally beg for food and a few coins, which he did by being a client to wealthy Romans. (Every powerful Roman had his clients and was known to them as their protector. The protector provided food, money and judicial help in exchange for the client's vote on issues important to the protector, as well as various small services. The clients met at the protector's home in the morning and accompanied him to the Forum.)

He stayed alive under Nero through supine capitulation, and under Domitian by total submission. Only under Nerva and Titus did he find his voice.

Like all (or nearly all) Romans, he had intercourse with both sexes, but it was said of him that he was especially moved by the beauty of young men. About one Dindymus he wrote of the perfume of the boy's kiss. But such beauty too often takes second place, in Martial's work, to language which is far more crude. In fact, he seldom speaks of boys in a tender sense, and given the lewdness of his work, it's amazing that so much survived the Middle Ages, and one can hardly imagine what the young monks' physical response was while translating Martial's Latin into the vernacular.

But he was a recognized poet, and received gifts from his benefactors, a farm outside Rome, and later a small house within the city. After what must have been a period of intense intellectuality and sensuality, he retired to his birthplace, after having spent thirty-four years in Rome, dying amidst relatives and friends, all of whom he was happy to be reunited with, all of which seemed to have been content with the return of the wayward son--what I would consider a highly satisfying existence.

To start off with, a flavor of what he had in store for women: "Bassa: I never saw you with a young guy, and nobody mentioned your having a beau. No, just girls around you, doing your shopping, in the absence of men. I assumed you were chaste but was I wrong! You were a slut humping all the time with other girls, rubbing your cunts together, your clits in place of the male member." And this: "Barbarian hordes en masse you fuck /Odd types into your bed you tuck / You take on blacks and Asian forces / And Jews, and soldiers, and their horses / Yet you, voracious Roman chick, Have you never known a Roman dick?" His misogyny was fierce, but no more so than many Romans, which didn't stop him from accepting a villa from an admiring woman when he returned to his hometown.

About prostitution: "The pimp made you pay 100,000 for the boy. I thought you were crazy but his dick has earned you 2,00,000!"

What takes place in the baths in our own time took place then: "We bathe together but he only stares with devouring eyes at athletes, at their cocks, his lips drooling."

This man saves his last kopek on what moves him most: "Hyllus, you only have one silver coin to your name and it's as worn as your ass. You won't spend it at the baker's or the restaurant, but you will spend it on who has the biggest cock. Your unfulfilled belly watches while your ass feasts."

On the penalty of getting caught: "You're fucking the wife of a tribune because you believe that if you're caught he'll just fuck you in the butt, but I'm telling you, you'll be castrated. You say that's not allowed, but is your fucking his wife allowed?"

The uncomely shaving of one's pubes has it's origins 2,500 years back: "Labienus, you pluck the hairs on your chest and legs and arms, and you shave your pubes, all for your girlfriend. But for whom do you shave the cheeks of your ass?"

"Your prick is sore, boy, and so is your ass. I'm not a soothsayer but I know what you've been doing."

Here Martial talks about himself: "If some benefactor could give me what I want, Flaccus, this is it: A boy born on the Nile, because no land produces hornier lads. Let his eyes be an inspiration to the stars and his hair fall to his shoulders. Let his forehead be low, his nose with a slight bend and his lips as red as roses. Let him force me against my will and back away when I want it. Let him be the penetrating male to others but a boy to me."

And this conundrum: "Artemidorus had a boy but he sold his farm; Callodorus has a farm in the place of a boy. Who is better off? Artemidorus who plows the boy or Callodorus who plows his field?"

And this: "If you hear applauding in the baths, Flaccus, you know big-dick Maro is there."

Pleasuring one's self is rarely mentioned in ancient texts, perhaps because it wasn't all that necessary, given the availability of slaves and foreign prostitutes: "Ponticus, you never fuck pussy but use your left hand as a mistress, a friend to your lust. But what if everyone did so? There would be no children if we all jacked off and sent our filthy cum into our hands! This is what Nature is telling you: 'What's flowing through your fingers is a human being!'"

This one is especially raunchy: "When you fuck pussy, Polycharmus, you take a dump afterwards. But what do you do when you're butt-fucked?"

An amusing turn: "You're an informer, Vacerra, a crook and a salesman. You suck cock and you train gladiators. So why are you always broke?"

And this all-to-frequent plaint: "Lygdus, when I ask to be with you you always say yes and tell me the hour and the place. I await you there, in bed, for hours, with my horny prick stretched taut, eventually letting my right hand ease me in your place."

As boys married late, often in their thirties, they knew little more than butt-fucking: "Your bride is being prepared for you, Victor, and on your wedding night she may allow you to butt-fuck her, but her mother tells her to permit this only once, saying, 'You're a girl, my daughter, not a boy!' So before the wedding night get yourself to a whorehouse to learn a male's role with a pussy.''

And incest? ''Fabullus, you ask me why Themison doesn't have a wife. It's because he has a sister.''

Same-sex marriages were performed in Rome. We have the examples of Nero and Elagabalus, among others. Here Martial presents Callistratus and Afer: ''Bearded Callistratus gave himself to Afer who sported a stiff prick, in the way that a virgin gives herself in marriage to a virile male. There were torches, a bridal veil covered the face, toasts were exchanged and a dowry paid. Next on the agenda is what, a birth?''

Throughout the ages men have married to acquire position and wealth: ''Although your wife is young, rich, noble, educated and virgin, yet you cum in long-haired boys, Bassus, using your wife's dowry to pay them. And so your cock, that she paid for, comes to her limp, and no amount of enticing with her soothing hand will make it work. Have you no shame? We'll go to the law for your dick no longer belongs to you. She bought it!''

Martial vaunted his virility and his lack of esteem for effeminacy: ''Since you're always bragging that you're a citizen of Corinth, Charmenion--and no one denies it--why are you always calling me brother? I hail from the land of Iberians and Celts and the River Tagus. Do you think that we even look alike? You wander around looking sleek with your curly hair, while mine is wildly unruly in the Spanish style. Every day an epilator makes your body smooth, while I sport hair on my thighs and cheeks. Your mouth is lisping and your tongue is faltering, but I speak deeply from my guts; we're more different than a dove from an eagle or a timid doe from a raging lion. And so, Charmenion, stop calling me 'brother' or else I'll start calling you 'sister'.'' At the time 'brother', *frater*, implied a sexual union. And this proof of his virility: ''For veritable man I cannot pass? Then what's that in your mouth and up your ass?''

FAGGING

Fagging was traditional in boarding schools until the 1970s and 1980s. It consisted simply of new, young boys acting as personal servants to senior boys, and was supposedly invented for the purpose of teaching the young lads how to be of service, while being disciplined and receiving instruction from the senior. The lads cleaned up after the older boys, did chores for them, prepared breakfast and teas, polished shoes and ran errands, and spared them the need of exertion by masturbating them to climax, if ordered. What happened sexually varied enormously from one prep school to another--running the spectrum of testosterone-fueled orgies to nothing-happened-at-all (according to some). Seniors didn't need to revert to actually raping the boys, but as they had supreme power over them in the form of social status, age and physical prowess (captains of various sports were most often chosen as Fag Masters, rarely boys of intellectual ability), the boys had little choice, meaning that even in cases where the youths did not want their anuses invaded they submitted anyway, which of course was a form of rape. This did not stop the same youths from offering themselves to those they liked or loved, in the sanctity of their own dormitories.

In boarding schools boys naturally found sexual discharge among themselves, but fagging was a perverse addition, allowed by school authorities who insisted it was the best way to prepare their boys for later service to their country, an idiotic and disgusting perversion, the reason why British fathers were forgiving or understanding of their own sons' excesses, when they themselves may have had a cock up their asses when young--a vulgar assumption that might nonetheless be all too true.

At the end of the year fags were given a fag-tip by the senior for services rendered. The colleges saved huge amounts of money (as it often did on the boys' food) on domestic servants it didn't have to employ.

The head of a house, also called Fag Master, had 3 or 4 House Prefects to help him, usually aged 17 or 18, while the boys were 11 or 12. When they called fag! all the fags came running, because it was the last one there who had to do the job. The fags warmed the toilet seats in winter with their bare buttocks and the beds with their naked bodies. They could physically harm the boys. Roald Dahl wrote of being submerged fully dressed in a tub of winter-cold water as punishment for something he had said. As he was 15 at the time, and the boys 18, there was little he could do.

Dahl, 6' 6'', a student of Repton and a flying ace in W.W. II.

Sir Laurence Olivier spoke numerous times of being gang raped in boarding school, and of one boy he adored who would always say thank you when withdrawing from Olivier's ass. The difference was that Olivier adored being fucked, and as a child he would run home in anticipation of the coming night when his older brother would plow him. Later his brother went on to girls but Olivier could never live without being penetrated, using his later position as a star to get what he wanted (see my book *RENT BOYS*).

The fags could be thrashed by the older boys who would inspect their rooms wearing white gloves. Afterwards the boys were obliged to thank the prefects for the beatings. Dahl relates being beaten on his naked buttocks by the Headmaster who later provided a basin, sponge and towel, and was told to wipe up the blood (just writing this sentence makes me want to volmit). Fists fights were thought to develop a robust character, as well as preparing boys for Empire, maintained a later House of Lords asshole.

Repton

A writer, Francis Wheen, wrote this: "At my prep school, Copthorne, there was a fair bit of leaping in and out of beds in dormitories, comparing notes, and general exploration. I was sexually molested by a gym master called Charles Napier, who was always putting his hand down boys' gym shorts."

George Melly, a singer, wrote: "It's not uncommon, I believe, to be chased at public school, especially if you're pretty. I was gay at school, so I had a lovely time. My school [Stowe] was tolerant, too--they didn't follow you about trying to catch you in flagrante. I rather enjoyed it all."

Oliver James, a psychologist, gives an excellent résumé of what sex and fagging most probably is today: "I just missed--thank God--the Tom Brown's Schooldays era. When I was first at Eton, in the summer of 1967, it was still pretty authoritarian between senior boys and juniors, but that dissolved rapidly--certainly by the end of 1968. They abolished fagging not long after I left. You can only really talk about your own house, and in my case the headmaster was a very nice man. Any behaviour like that would have been unacceptable to him. Some heads would allow a more brutal regime than others.

"When we got older, nearly all of us fancied boys who looked like girls, but I think it was pretty rare that anything actually happened--there was a curious platonic, romantic attitude. Having said that, I can think of at least three cases in which actual homosexual acts were performed. In one case it was a boy who liked doing mutual masturbation with other boys his own age. In another case it was an older boy and a younger boy, but there was no coercion. And there was one notorious case, again between an older boy and a younger boy, and I'm almost certain that too was non-coercive, and agreeable to the younger boy. Unfortunately they got found out, and the older boy got sacked. I think the house master got sacked pretty soon afterwards too.

"The food was memorably disgusting, and I seem to remember being served at table by a sequence of Spanish men. No one tried to have sex with me. It may be that I was protected from older boys by having an elder brother at the school. I also had a spectacular outbreak of acne, which ran from one side of my brow to the other like the Himalayas. Relationships were going on, but it was less the love that dare not speak its name than the fact that if you put 1,200 testosterone-fuelled boys in an enclosed space there is bound to be some cross-fertilisation.

"While the Fag was the general servant, gofer and dogsbody, the Fag-Master was responsible for protecting his Fag from harm or exploitation by other senior students as well as dealing with disciplining the Fag and taking that responsibility away from the House-Master (an adult who would run the dormitory).

"The duties undertaken by fags, the time taken, and their general treatment varied widely. Each school had its own tradition. Until circa 1900 a fag's duties included such humble tasks as blacking boots, brushing clothes and cooking breakfasts, and there was no limit as to hours. Later, fagging was restricted to such light tasks as running errands, bringing tea to the fag-masters' study and fagging at cricket or football. At many schools, fag-masters were expected to reward their fags for their efforts at the end of term by giving a monetary 'fag tip'."

And a final excerpt from an unknown source but one that appears reliable: "The English public (that is, private) school has been the exemplar boarding school in this aspect. The prefect-fagging system in particular, established to enhance character building, quite accidentally, facilitated this bond between older and younger students. Under the prefect-fagging system senior boys (prefects, ages 17-18) were given a major role in governing the school, wielding discipline, and carrying responsibility while new boys (fags, ages 12-13), were appointed as servants to the prefects. Their duties consisted of almost anything prefects cared to impose, from running errands, carrying messages, cooking, kindling fires, warming beds and toilet seats, to sexual favours. Fags were chosen among the cutest young boys and senior students often made top 10 lists of the best looking ones. Cute boys were given feminine nicknames and, in cases where they welcomed the attentions of older boys, they were called tarts. Prefects on the other hand, were chosen by teachers (masters) according to their performance in sports (games) which were highly idealized by younger boys while their leadership and academic skills were taken into account only secondarily. Relationships between older and younger boys (or between prefects and fags) were sometimes chaste, sometimes overtly sexual, but always sentimentalized."

D.J. Peel writes about his Fag Master: "If for some reason my tormentor didn't require a hand job, possibly because he had already compelled another small boy to give him one, he loaned me to one of his two friends and I was obliged to service them instead.

"This man--and although it is tempting to name him, I'm not going to-- was, I think, the only genuinely amoral person I've ever met. Towards the end of our time together, he compelled me to agree to meet him in a public toilet in the cemetery on the outskirts of Shrewsbury, where he raped me. Oddly enough, much as I hated the experience, I think I had become so accustomed to systematic sexual abuse that I wasn't especially traumatized by the experience."

"The night was loud with the boasts and groans that resulted from this endless, and fairly evenly matched, single combat between chaps and their cocks. To even the dullest lad it would sometimes occur to think that self-abuse was slightly wasted on the self and might be better relished in mixed company," Christopher Hitchens brings us in his book *Hitch-22*.

The brutality of boys being flogged mercilessly by headmasters during the 1800s and the first half of the 1900s led to violence between boys, the big ones dominating the small, in an era where boys fought 30 rounds with their bare fists and murders were committed, as when the Eton boy Thomas Dalton stabbed his schoolmate Archibald Cockburn to death. Gradually the young boys became slaves to the older ones, with hopes that the situation would be reversed when they too grew to the ages of 17 and 18.

Headmasters who had hundreds of boys under their direction needed strong lads to keep them in line. What atrocities took place surpassed William Golding's *Lord of the Flies* in absolute horror, minus the sexual filth impossible to relate in a film made in 1963. (Filthy it was, but very often the dirtier the sex the greater the orgasm and the more vivid the memory of it--although I'm referring to uncoerced sex.) The boy victims who suffered from the cruelty were in one instance beaten bloody, pissed upon, their anuses violated, and not only by penises, their bodies actually burned while they screamed. Boys had coals applied to their hands, giving them what their comrades designated as iron-fists (as recounted in Jonathan Gathorne-Hardy's superb *The Public School Phenomenon*).

Shelley loathed Eton, but then Shelley, unlike Byron with whom he was friends and whose dead body Byron brought ashore, in Venice, was a thoroughly good person (Byron's chapter follows).

Thomas Arnold, Headmaster of Westminster and Winchester--he who created the concept of houses--saw life as a constant battle against sinning boys who had to be beaten in order to be saved. C.J. Vaughan, Headmaster of Harrow at age 28, was forced to resign 15 years later or face charges of sexually abusing boys. J.A. Symonds, a student there, had to sit beside him in his chambers, on the couch where he knew Vaughan had had sex with boys, yet Vaughan, a priest, ruthlessly beat the boys for the vice in which he himself was indulging.

Evelyn Waugh wrote that most school masters were homosexual, "How else could they endure their work?"

Fagging and beatings have largely vanished. In all walks of life public school boys are preferred by job recruiters. A huge percentage of government ministers and parliamentarians are from public schools, the top being Eton. It's true that a boarding-school atmosphere helps greatly in evolving social skills, in communication and in general sociability. But state universities are gaining in powers, especially due to the expense of a public education.

Schools of little academic interest in Byron's time, like Oxford and Cambridge, are today excellent, able to count on the best teachers thanks, in part, to a pay scale far superior to state schools. They are known for their athletes and their moderation concerning sex and discipline. As said, Oxford is the world's 3rd greatest university, Cambridge its 5th. But they will always remain an upper-class phenomenon, a British particularity along with their drooling in the presence of royalty, which is in place exclusively through the hazard of birth, a sad inconsistency for such a truly great empire.

The history of boarding schools in general is one of screaming pain and suffering, vile abuse, brutal masochism, headmasters who coerced sexual favors, certain prefects of nearly sociopathic tendencies who got off physically thanks to the misery they inflicted. They were showrooms for aristocratic bullies who could sport their clothes and have unlimited sexual access to whichever boy buttocks took their fancy, while sponsoring all kinds of secret-society inanities. Heathens of the most disgusting stripe, there under the pretention of an education, a pretext to display themselves before their equals, happily wallowing in their own filth. Were the schools worth it? I think not.

BYRON
1788 – 1824

Forward

Byron lived in an age when men were hanged for their love of males and/or pilloried, caged in public and punched by sticks, eyes stove in and throats pierced, at times causing death. The high and mighty in England didn't necessarily escape (although most did), as shown by Oscar Wilde's trial for homosexuality, a man of genius whose plays were immensely popular then as they are today. There was also the threat of blackmail that led to many suicides. In order to be hanged for homosexuality, both penetration and ejaculation had to be proved in a court of law, no easy affair. In France laws against sodomy were dropped after the Revolution, in 1791, and many other countries like Italy and Spain followed. But not England. Yet school was a protected sanctum, where boys could enjoy their puberty more or less unhampered. Boys were locked in their dormitories at night, left to themselves, at times exhausting their young bodies in orgies that would have impressed the Romans. *All* boarding schools were rife with sex.

Harrow

The Byron family history is one of licentiousness and handsome men, both of which very often go in tandem. Byron's father, called Mad Jack, passed his time in Paris gambling and going through a limitless number of females. Only when in bottomless debt, at age 22--having been cut off for years from his family as its black sheep--did he meet and mate with the Marchioness of Carmarthen who craved him for his beauty and virility, and who left her husband, taking with her £4,000 of yearly income. They married and produced Augusta, Byron's half-sister, who would, in the tradition of Caligula, become one of Bryon's many mistresses. The Marchioness died, perhaps under the hands of her husband, although Byron declared his father innocent of any wrongdoing, and as for his licentiousness, was it his father's fault that women threw themselves at him? One of these women was Byron's mother, Catherine Gordon, plump but possessing £30,000 and her own castle. Her family was described as having been bloodthirsty killers, generation after generation, but this only concerned the men. As for the Byrons, his first important ancestor was John Byron who bought his manor from Henry VIII. Another Byron had been shipwrecked off Patagonia. Still another was known as the Wicked Lord who set up his own whorehouse where one night he plunged his sword into the stomach of Viscount Chaworth in an upper floor of the brothel. This Byron had nine children, one of which had been our Byron's dad, Mad Jack.

Mad Jack bled his wife, Byron's mother, white, forcing her to sell her castle, farm lands and woods to pay for his need to assuage, in luxury, his gambling and his balls--not put too fine a point on it. Catherine's pain did not end in the long and painful birth of Byron. The boy was born clubfooted, a handicap that would handicap his mind and personality from his first breath, an impediment that would cause him anguish until his death, at first physical pain during his infancy, mental hardship afterwards. He never forgave his mother whom he accused of injuring him for life due to her insistence on wearing the tightest corsets. Rich, she could have had whomever she wished; now she was weighed down by a husband who wouldn't touch her, a step-daughter, Augusta, she immediately farmed out to whichever of her relatives would take her in, turning the poor girl into a timid, emotional recluse. Catherine was weighed down too by a son who despised her with each painful step he took (later, when his own beauty was in decline, he would realize that she was the only person who was truly selfless and had truly loved him). He called himself the *diable boiteux,* the lame devil, and felt life owned him a debt, its permission for him to commit every excess.

Every excess was what his father was at that moment committing. He returned to London but lived down the street from his wife, requesting money before begging for it, before abandoning son and wife to return to France where he lived with his sister, Francis, as dissolute as he. She made love to whoever was available, as did her brother Mad Jack, both comparing the sexual endurance and the quirks of their respective lovers, until they themselves fell into Caligulan incest, which they eventually enlarged to all comers.

With the death of their mother, and the hope of a heritage, his sister Francis returned to London. She set herself up there and he tried to entice her back by writing about his loves, in hopes of making her jealous. In reality, he had more women than even he could satisfy. About one woman he wrote to his sister, ''She told me I did it so well she spent twice.'' About another, ''She is the best piece I ever fucked.''

In the meantime Byron's mother was teaching him something about feminine inconsistency by showering him with love and the best in clothes money could buy, but during angry spells she called him a damn lame brat and assured him he was just like his worthless father. It's unsurprising that Byron was soon known for his own unbridled rages.

In France Jack was assailed by creditors who took his every possession to pay his debts. He had also been coughing up blood. Perhaps luckily for everyone concerned, including Jack, he died at age 36, the same age as Byron who inherited all his vices, down to incest, all except Mad Jack's gambling. Jack had been a man who had lived the lives of a dozen men, just as his son would, who would die while still in beauty, biting lustily into life until his last breath.

Catherine's maid put little Bryon on the path of his father at age 9, in 1799. In her bed she masturbated him while doing herself, then gave herself freely to coachmen, while beating the boy mercilessly when she felt like it. He later wrote that his sexual awakening had come so early that no one would believe it, but was sorrowful because it was combined with the beatings and the inconsistency of the maid who abandoned him for other lovers.

Mad Jack nonetheless left his son his heritage: One day he would become the 5th Lord of Byron.

He entered Harrow at age 12 and it was paradise. The headmaster, Dr. Joseph Drury, immediately recognized the boy's terrible self-consciousness due to his leg in irons, but like everyone who would meet him, he fell in love with his charm and beauty. From then on Byron would use his leg as an arm to initiate sympathy and protection, his charm and beauty would do the rest. Although not at first. At first the heathen brutality of boys made him the target of the cruelest allusions to his deformity.

It was during summer vacation from Harrow that he first met his half-sister Augusta, 17, she with whom he would repeat his father's incest.

Back at Harrow after the summer holidays, Byron became popular by helping new first year students, some of whom became dedicated to him in thanks. He would write, "My school friendships were *with me passions*," his italics. One of his passions was 11-year-old John Fitzgibbon, Earl of Clare, about whom he wrote, 18 years later, "I never hear the word '*Clare*' without a beating of the heart--even now." He left Harrow at the age of 16.

Cambridge

He entered Cambridge at the age of 17. Cambridge was of little educational value. Yet he had picked up his knowledge somewhere, most probably at Harrow and with private tutors before entering Harrow, as his mother was set on him having the best in every domain. The more she denied her husband, the more she gave to her boy. Byron was reading at age 3, and his years in Cambridge were certainly not entirely worthless, although intellectually shallow. He went to brothels, the price being venereal disease that the doctors treated with leeches to bring down the swelling. One of his lovers was a choir boy of 15, John Edleston, for whom Byron, 17, was a man of the world. (It appears that for university students choir boys were redolent of dancehall girls for adults; it was good form for each boy to have sexual access to at least one.) "I *love* him more than any human being," Byron wrote to a friend. It would be a deep and long-lasting love for Edleston.

As I wrote, an education at Cambridge at that period was notoriously lamentable. Getting in was everything, because afterwards nothing was demanded. There were few lessons and few hours of study. Everything was based on money, money that paid for his clothes, his meals, his servant, the women who made him ill and the doctors that cured him with middle-ages efficiency. His money and title perhaps played a part in his seduction of Edleston. Certainly not his phsique. At age 18 he weighed over 200 pounds for a height of 5' 8". He wasn't chubby, he was fat, an inheritance from his mother who was fat all her life, having attracted Byron's father by her castle and fortune, and even then she was open and accepting of any man who would deign accept her largesse for a little bodily warmth.

He wrote to his Harrow love Claire and they exchanged letters on the cures they were taking for venereal diseases, Claire, as mentioned, treated with leeches, Byron with a powder, most probably mercury for syphilis. The illness went on for several months, which nonetheless ended (or went into remission) with his losing a great deal of weight, a temporary benefit for a boy who would be remembered as a poetic Don Juan. Between bouts of venereal disease, which made him often ill, he would literally fuck his brains out with whatever came to hand. It seems that the end of the fever always brought on a period of intense sexual activity, acting as a kind of aphrodisiac.

After Edleston came the gifted son of a butcher, John Cowell, whom he helped to enter Eton. The boy's parents, flattered by Byron's nobility, allowed their 15-year-old boy to spend long weekends with Byron. Cowell did so well in school that he won a scholarship to university. Later he wrote Byron to express his gratitude. From his letter it is obvious that Byron was and would rest the most important influence in the boy's life.

At age 21 Byron took his seat in the House of Lords. A new lord who took on a new page and lover, Robert Rushton, 17, but flew into a rage when his valet, William Fletcher, took the boy to a whorehouse for his very first prostitute.

It's easy to imagine these young boys, a lad who sings in a choir, another saved from cutting up pigs by the intervention of a veritable lord, falling under the sway of this tubby boy who had began his apprenticeship of life so young that he had by now personally known every minor earthly corruption, stunning in his lace, bowed to by his valet, offering fine dinners among spiritual friends, all of whom possessed to a perfection that special way of speaking known to the nobility, those like Byron whose only thought was to fill their stomachs and empty their scrotums.

Greece

He left London for Greece with some pals under terrible auspices, having had a fight with his mother over money, as that was her interest to Byron as it had been to his father. She had apparently told him his mind was as twisted as his body.

He went to Falmouth and saw boys of such beauty that he was hoping he would have, during his travels, intercourse to his heart's content (*coitum plenum & optabilem*, the words he used in a letter to a friend).

Byron was offered rooms by the British consul. He visited archeological sites, guided by Giovanni Lusieri, responsible for depriving the Parthenon of its façade, the Elgin Marbles now in the British Museum. He and his friends visited bordellos, one of the friends noting the number of climaxes he achieved. Byron had already met Lusieri's brother-in-law Nicolo Giraud who became Byron's favorite and whom Byron seemed to have taught as much as he could of the arts of sexual pleasure, as Nicolo was very young. But the boy wouldn't give himself as completely as Byron wished, as Byron complained that there was as yet no *pl & opt C* (complete and fulfilling intercourse). He nonetheless wrote that he personally was an attraction to boys, and that he had found himself in a boy heaven.

He came down with a fever so terrible it was feared he would die, but afterwards he noted something that would prove always true for him, as already noted, an enormous regain in sexual ardor which pushed him to enter into 200 *pl & opt C*.

Byron

Childe Harold

Childe Harold, his book of poems, was published at a time when even Boccaccio was considered as obscene. It was at first rejected. At that same moment he learned of his mother's death. He had to borrow the money to return home where his grief, certainly sincere, was overwhelming. He realized that he had lost, at age 46 (from undisclosed causes) the only person who had ever loved him for himself. He was now truly alone, and although he would be encumbered by a plethora of willing bodies to come, alone he would remain until the end of his life.

Byron at his most beautiful.

It was now that he met Caroline Lamb, married to an older husband, William Lamb, whom she had genuinely loved, but now wanted Byron more. Their sexual relationship was heated for both, but eventually petered out, perhaps due in part to the scandals Caroline wrought wherever she went. Byron went to see William Lamb's mother for advice, Lady Melbourne, known as the Spider, a spider in every domain of social congress, especially sexual. The 62-year-old woman was highly flattered by Byron's attentions, attentions which would soon have him probing her inners with his dick. She decided that the best way out of his problems with Caroline would be for Bryon to marry. Byron agreed, as long as the future wife was wealthy enough to care for his needs, exactly the reason his father had had for marrying Byron's mother. She found him Annabella Milbanke, the daughter of her brother Sir Ralph Milbanke, and her financial prospects were glorious. His life seemed unenviable because now he had to juggle his relationship with three women, old Lady Melbourne, rich Annabella Milbanke, and Caroline in order to keep her from more scandalous behavior, although he may still have cared for her sexually, especially as she was still young and eminently boyish. If this were not enough, he then took as mistress Lady Oxford, age 40, who had many lovers as well as a husband, but Byron seemed to find this natural as she had little time for seduction left to her. The height of horrors came when Lady Oxford found him trying to force an entry into her 11-year-old daughter.

Byron in Albanian splendor.

Caroline capped this all off by stabbing herself with scissors in public, careful to do minimal damage. The whole pathetic mess, fake suicides, effeminate Greeks lovers, sex with matrons, with children, with hysterical mistresses, with his sister, with choir boys, was so lamentable that one finishes by pitying the poet. He made his sister pregnant. She would eventually give him a girl he was surprised to find physically normal as children of incest were supposed to have been born deformed (and he didn't seem to care, one way or the other).

Newstead Abbey, Byron's manor

His presence was required at the marriage of the Earl of Portsmouth. Portsmouth was said to have been insane but wasn't committed to an asylum because of his nobility. He was tricked into the marriage, arriving in dirty clothes that the girl's father--a lawyer who oversaw Portsmouth's estate and was aware, therefore, of his wealth and his inclination to beating all around him, from servants to animal--exchanged for formal marriage attire. Byron walked the girl down the isle; she supposedly giggled as he reminded her that as a schoolboy he had been the first to fuck her. Years later the marriage was annulled; the girl had by then three children, one named Byron; and then she vanished from the face of the earth.

Byron, in tandem with his sister, chose Annabella Milbanke for wife, once assured of a stupendous dowry of £20,000 and a heritage that would assure many thousand more. She was deliriously happy and he, by necessity, fucked her that night on the couch, after the wedding, bloodied because she had been a virgin. He then told here they would have separate bedrooms as he never slept in the same bed with his women. Byron would later have his memoirs destroyed, but the man who did so wrote that that night Byron had awoken and had cried out, God I am in Hell! Even more unbelievably, Annabella had convinced herself that her only true friend in the world was Augusta, to whom she confided the despair of her marriage. Augusta immediately relayed every word to Byron. Annabella finished by accepting whatever scraps he left her. He continued to fuck Augusta and only turned to his wife when Augusta wasn't available.

No matter how much Annabella brought in, Byron spent more, and eventually a bailiff came to seize the furniture. Byron kept on running up debts and began to drink heavily. When he learned that Annabella was pregnant, he became wild, smashing what furniture was left, firing his pistol within his home, and shouted that he hoped both Annabella and the child in her womb would both perish. Augusta was now in control of the household, trying to bring sincere succor to both Annabella and Byron. Days before the birth of his and Annabella's child he forced her to have sex with him, but when this continued right up to the delivery, she refused and he ended up raping her. From that moment on her maid kept her rooms locked, and physically barred the entrance to Byron. It is actually believed that he tried to kill the unborn child by frightening Annabella to death. Four weeks after the baby's birth he ordered both out of the house. She left and *Byron would never see either again*.

He continued drinking, he became ill, he had memory loses, weeping jags, bouts of depression and violence. The problem for Byron was how to keep his sanity. The problem for Annabella was how to keep her child, for in Victorian England the husband had total and absolute rights to it. He could have taken it whenever he wished, and given the nature of the animal, he could have taken its virginity at any time too. The only way out for Annabella was to construct a case so damning against him that the courts would deprive him of his rights to the little girl. Annabella--and here there is no doubt possible--had truly loved the man. But from now on he ceased to exist as a human being in her eyes. Yet she held her head high. She was only a woman against him and against nearly every man in society who realized that if she won they would be open to any form of female aggression. Their survival as the ruling class was Byron's survival. How pitiful it was that later, in Greece, he would be unable to hold his own head high, as high as she could now, when brought low by a lad of 15, groveling at the feet of a lad of 15, begging for a few moments of shared warmth with a lad of 15.

Caroline Lamb then weighed in in favor of Annabella, informing the world that Byron was homosexual (Byron had told her about his relations with his valet Robert Rushton). Byron immediately realized that a divorce would be long and drawn out and *public*, that his homosexuality would be revealed in the newspapers and perhaps even his incest (and what if Lady Oxford came forward with his attempted rape of her 11-year-old daughter?). Only a legal separation was therefore possible, one that Annabella would agree to only if she could retain her child. Augusta was amazingly evenhanded, and its clear that she truly felt for Annabella, while hoping to do nothing that would harm her brother and lover. She knew about Byron's homosexuality and she knew too that if even a whiff of it hit the public he would be utterly destroyed. Then Annabella released a bomb. She told Byron's lawyers that she knew about his incest with Augusta. In reality she couldn't *not* have known, because they were doing it downstairs while she was upstairs in her rooms; indeed, she had heard everything for months. (The flooring was so thin that when Byron was working downstairs he would ask Annabella to stop walking about, as it disturbed his concentration.)

Byron still hesitated because he was hoping to milk Annabella for as much money as he could suck from the marrow of her bones (no exaggeration, as Augusta was shocked, during a visit to Annabella, to find her reduced to skin and bones by her effort to save her child). Then Annabella dropped the *atomic* bomb: Byron had raped her during the final days of her pregnancy, attested to by her maid and his valet (who were man and wife--the husband being Robert Rushton), by *sodomizing* her, the absolute in scandals.

Byron signed the civil separation, locked up his rooms, and fled to Europe.

Missolonghi

Byron traveled on the Greece where he took up residence in various locals, hiring pages that the Greeks knew to be synonyms to boys sexually available. The last one was Lukas Chalandrutsanos, age 15, before whom he groveled until fever carried him away.

Byron's outlandish reputation is based on his being a dissolute and ever-randy bisexual master of orgies, on his staged portraits (painted only after fevers when his weight had dropped) in which he is the personification of male splendor, and his publications, that I must leave entirely to the reader's judgment. Like the very young and the very old, he lived outside the circle of life. He made his own laws and rules; life owed him every favor to compensate for his infirmity; and the planets had obligingly aligned to give birth to this, their most unique creation. I have no idea if he succeeded his life, but I know that he succeeded his afterlife, because he will remain in our imaginations until the end of time. At age 36 he left the stage a little late, as he had not escaped the mutilation and humiliation of old age. He had known horrendous ups-and-downs, a rollercoaster that is the very definition of life. (6)

THE BLOOMSBURY SET

To understand the Bloomsbury Set one must understand the French expression *panier de crabes*, a basket of crabs, crawling over and through each other, fucking, yes, but also biting, their claws fully deployed.

A perfect example of this was Duncan Grant's relationship with Vanessa Bell. Duncan, a painter and a homosexual who had had exclusively homosexual encounters in boarding schools since puberty, decided to live with Vanessa who was nonetheless married but whose husband was off elsewhere with mistresses. Vanessa (the sister of Virginia Wolfe) badly wanted a child from the supremely handsome Duncan who agreed to move in with her for the time needed to get her pregnant, and immediately afterwards sexual relations ceased between the two while awaiting the birth of their little girl, Angelica, who was given Bell's name, Bell who pretended to be her father.

Duncan Grant

Duncan stayed on with Vanessa, which in no way inhibited his taking numerous lovers, for 40 years, until her death. One of his lovers was David Garnett who later married Angelica. Garnett was thusly fucking the father *and* the father's daughter! (although, perhaps, not at the same time).

David Garnett by Duncan.

Maynard Keynes said Duncan Grant had been the love of his life. From his youth Duncan had been one of Lytton Strachey's lovers, Strachey who was also his cousin. He was also the lover of Arthur Hobhouse. Hobhouse entered Eton at age 11 and then Balliol College, Oxford, seven years later. He had his own law practice, was on the board of a charity commission, worked as a law member for the council of the Governor-General of India, and was on the Judicial Committee of the Privy Council when he returned from India to London. He received a peerage as Baron Hobhouse, married and died without children.

Duncan Grant with Keynes and picture of Hobhouse, age 35.

Duncan was kept during his later life by Paul Roche and it was on Roche's estate that he died.

Roche by Duncan Grant.

Duncan was born in 1885, just six months before the passing of the Criminal Law Act that criminalized male homosexual acts in England, regardless of consent, an act used to convict Oscar Wilde in 1895. It was also dubbed the blackmailer's act because it was profitably used by hundreds of blackmailers afterwards. The fear of discovery was such that even later writers on Greek love, such as A.L. Rowse and Kenneth Dover, claimed to have been happily married, which, conceivably, could have been true.

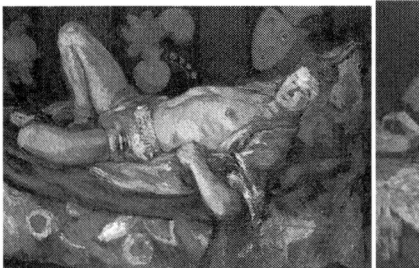

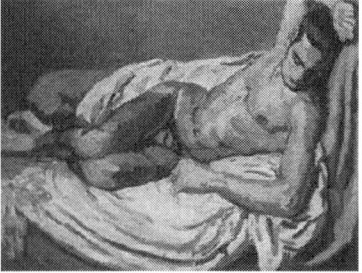

Paul Roche by Duncan.

Duncan went to prep schools in Rugby and London before entering the Westminster School of Art at age 17.

Hyllus by Duncan.

What seems incredible, at least to me, is that men like Grant were having sex with some of the homeliest men living then. Of course I'll be accused of being shallow, but a man does have to get hard to have good sex, and how can one do so in the presence of men like Keynes and Garnett?

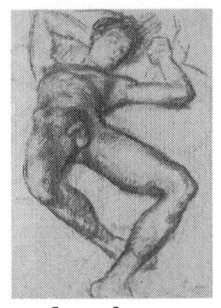

Paul Roche and perhaps an example of boarding-school fun, by Duncan Grant.

Paintings by Duncan are innumerable, and I've included a number here for the pleasure of the senses.

Leigh Farnell, one of Duncan's very first boarding-school friends, with whom he remained close all his life.

Duncan was unanimously described as being a good person and those who cared for him at the end of his life found him "impishly benign", with great personal charm. He admired the philosopher G. E. Moore and told the boys who gave access to his old hands that he owed all of his moral philosophy to Moore, "which possibly does not amount to much," probably among the truest words he ever spoke!

Duncan Grant of himself.

Another of his daughter's lovers, who had also been *his* lover, was George Bergen:

George Bergen

David Garnett, Grant's lover and Angelica's husband, was called Bunny since his childhood due to a rabbit cloak given to him then. When he married Angelica her parents were said to have been scandalized (although *which* parents, Vanessa and Bell or Vanessa and Grant, is not known). Garnett was an author, founded the Nonesuch Press and ran a bookshop. From a first wife he had had two sons and with Angelica four daughters before they separated. He died in France in 1981 at age 89.

Paul Roche was a novelist, poet and Greek and Latin translator, and was associated with the Bloomsbury Set. He was an ordained priest and married twice, fathering five children. Although Roche's last wife was against his taking in his lover, Duncan was imposed on the household but was said to have cooled things down out of respect for Roche's wife although, of course, men always succeed in getting what they want, in one secret place or another, so the cooling was most probably due to a greater desire to have sex with others than themselves.

Grant and David Garnett.

Duncan Grant died in 1978 at age 93 and Roche at age 91 in 2007. They had been together 32 years.

Paul Roche

Roche and Duncan's love had been the closest, the deepest, the truest of friendships, and Roche closes the chapter on their lives in this way: "I could see that he was in a very bad way, breathing heavily.... Dr Cooper said to me, 'I can't save him this time, he's too far gone, and it's much better to let him go'. So I agreed to that. Duncan lay on the bed.... I came up to him the night before he died... This is what I think I said, or the gist of it.... 'Duncan, you have nothing to worry about, whatever you have done in life that you are sorry for, God loves you, whatever you've done, He loves you. You don't have to worry about anything. You're in His hands, and so you can sleep peacefully and everything is ok.... Don't think that God is angry with anything.... He's not, He loves you.' Duncan was incapable of speaking ... so I quietly left the room.... When I came back in the morning ... I realised Duncan was dead. That was an enormous shock to me.... I went to Firle to be at the funeral, but I suddenly found that I couldn't stand, every time I stood up I simply collapsed onto the floor."

Duncan Grant's *The Bathers*.

One of the characteristics of the Bloomsbury Set, besides the fact that most lived so long, was that many ended up spending the last of their lives with women, as did Lytton Strachey and Maynard Keynes.

The Set was against what Roger Fry (who had been Vanessa Bell's lover) called Post-Impressionists, although Fry, an artist and art critic, defended it. Loved by many Bloomsbury members, male and female, he seems to have been heterosexual. His list of Post-Impressionists includes Cézanne, Gauguin, van Gogh and Seurat, to which he later added Rousseau and Toulouse-Lautrec. Many of the Set thought the Post-Impressionists were trivial in their art, reducing objects to basic shapes, while Seurat even painted tiny dots that some called Scientific-Impressionism. Van Gogh used lavish brush strokes to convey his feelings and state of mind, and Cézanne tried to bring purity in his art by reducing objects to basic shapes.

Roger Fry

Lytton Strachey, one of the founders of the Bloomsbury Set, seduced them all, and although he was presentable when very young, I have no idea how he did it later on, especially when he grew the beard he was so proud of, but that most others found ridiculous.

One of 13 children, Lytton is the 3rd from the left.

Perhaps Roy Campbell, a poet and satirist, had him in mind when he said that the Set was a group of "sexless folk whose sexes intersect." Some, happily, were far from being sexless. Duncan Grant was gorgeous, and when Strachey had intercourse with him he said that he felt joy because Grant was so moved and that what he loved "more than the consummation of my own poor pleasure ... was that for the first time I loved his soul," a need by the Set to introduce Plato somewhere in their sexual musical chairs. As a lad Strachey justified sex by saying that "I may be sinning, but I am doing it in the company of Greece" in reference to Socrates and other texts on Hellenic love. Strachey goes on and on about the ideal love, the meeting of the minds, but Roger Senhouse, a student of Eton and Oxford University and owner of the publishing house that published Colette, Orwell and Günter Grass, said his relationship with Strachey had been sadomasochistic. In the same way that Plato went on about Platonic love, stating that "evil is the vulgar lover who loves the body rather than the soul," Plato and Socrates had nonetheless special permission to attend the athletic preparation of boys, where adults were banned by law, to enjoy the beauty of youthful dicks with their first pubic down, and hairless asses.

Strachey: He was proud of the reddish hue of his beard.

Strachey wrote his book *Ermyntrude and Esmeralda* in 1913, published in 1969, long after his death, in which two innocent girls titter about the "absurd little things that men have in statues between their legs." When the girls asked a priest what love is, he replies "the sanctification of something", unless the object is a member of the same sex. A father banishes his son for having sex with his tutor, but the son claims that he was only doing what the Athenians did and, anyway, his father "had done the same when he was a boy in school but had forgotten about it."

Strachey's school was Trinity College, Cambridge, where he had sexual relations with Clive Bell who married Vanessa who would have sexual relations with Duncan Grant who would have sexual relations with Strachey and David Garnett, Garnett who would have sexual relations with Duncan Grant and, later, Grant's daughter Angelica, as reported.

Strachey was a member of the Apostles and the founder of the Bloomsbury Set. Bloomsbury was a location in central London encompassing Gordon and Fitzroy Squares. The aim of Bloomsbury was "to get a maximum of pleasure out of their personal relations. If this meant triangles or more complicated geographical figures, well then, one accepted that too." The Apostles was a discussion group that met weekly over coffee and "whales" (sardines on toast) to discuss a topic later thrown open to discussion. Former members were Angels, new members Embryos. The bond between them all was life-long. The spies Burgess, MacLean and Philby were members.

Strachey's hallmark was biography, combining psychology with sympathy for the subject, irreverence and wit. He wrote *Queen Victoria, Eminent Victorians* and *Elizabeth and Essex.* An example of his wit: He described Florence Nightingale as employing soldiers' wives to clean her laundry. When Strachey, a pacifist, was asked what he would do if a Hun tried to rape his sister, he answered: "I would insert my body between them." While others seduced by making girls laugh, he did so through spell-binding eloquence (maintained his admirers).

In another of those strange Bloomsbury multi-cornered sexual relationships, Strachey lived with Dora Carrington who adored him and she married *his* lover Ralph Partridge, not for love, but to bring Strachey closer to her. At the same time he was seeing other men, one of whom was Roger Senhouse, with whom he had his sadomasochistic arrangement, one that went so far as to include mock crucifixions. Strachey paid for the marriage between Carrington and Partridge and, naturally, accompanied them on their honeymoon to Venice. Carrington had a boy's haircut and appreciated girls, while her new husband was said to have genuinely loved her. Strachey bought the newly weds a house. Partridge left her for another woman and she became pregnant by another man who asked her to leave Strachey. She chose instead to abort. Around this time Aldous Huxley fell in love with her, "Her short hair, clipped like a page's.... She had large blue china eyes ... of puzzled earnestness."

Carrington and Strachey, Huxley and Senhouse.

The plot thickens: Ralph Partridge had left both Carrington and Strachey for another woman, Frances Marshall, who took up with Ralph because she knew he was Strachey's lover, and as she loved Strachey she thought her proximity with Ralph would bring her closer to Strachey.

Strachey and Partridge.

When Strachey died in 1932 at age 51 from stomach cancer, Carrington committed suicide.

Strachey must have been a force of nature because he was a character in nearly all the books his friends wrote before and after his death.

The intrigue doesn't end here: The painter Mark Gertler adored Carrington to the point of obsession. Incapable of understanding why she preferred a homosexual to him, he bought a revolver and threatened to kill himself when she married Strachey's lover Ralph Partridge. Gertler did finally commit suicide in 1939 at age 48. Today his paintings are worth millions.

Mark Gertler, said to have been a beauty.

In her diary Virginia Woolf wrote that she was glad to be alive and couldn't imagine why Carrington had killed herself. Ten years later, in 1941, Virginia did the same, by drowning.

E.M. Forester was above all a humanist, acknowledged as such when named President of Cambridge Humanists in 1959 and a member of the British Humanist Association from 1963 until his death in 1970 at age 81. A great aunt left him £800,000 in today's money, which freed him from any form of servitude. He was an on-the-fringe member of Bloomsbury, and a Kings College, Cambridge, student. His name is associated with several men, among them Isherwood and Benjamin Britten.

His travels took him throughout Europe, especially Italy, which inspired two books, *Where Angels Fear to Tread* and *A Room with a View*. He was secretary to a maharaja and several visits to India inspired his most read book, *A Passage to India*.

Among what is called his ''loving relationships'' was a very long one with a married policeman.

He was nominated for the Nobel Prize 13 times! He wrote his last book at age 35.

Forster

The problem with E.M. Forster's book *Maurice* was that it had a happy ending. Maurice meets a gamekeeper, they fall in love, decide to remain with each other throughout life, *and do so*. Had the book ended in the usual homosexual tragedy Forster might have decided to have it published, as then everyone could plainly see the consequences of immoral love.

The book begins with prep-school boarding-school love and goes on to university love (Greek texts encouraged by horny tutors), the whole apparently based on the true lives of Edward Carpenter and his lover George Merrill. It was finally published in 1971, a year after his death, 60 years after its creation.

Interestingly, Maurice tries to cure himself through hypnotism before deciding to be of service to the working class by running a boxing gym, the compensation being the naked lads under the showers.

A humanist like Forster, Edward Carpenter chose to aid the lower classes, as well as finding his sexual companions among them: ''the grimy and oil-besmeared figure of a stoker'' or ''the thick-thighed hot course-fleshed young bricklayer with a strap around his waist.'' He also doted on Parisian rent-boys.

He decried the industrial smog of Sheffield that was killing thousands and realized that only a strong socialist movement had the potential of putting things right.

Educated at Brighton College and Trinity Hall, Cambridge, at his father's death he inherited enough to become financially independent. He bought a farm that he worked, while writing his book of poems, *Towards Democracy*.

He met George Merrill, a working-class man without a formal education, in 1891 at age 47, and they lived together 27 years despite the hysteria due to the Oscar Wilde trial and the Criminal Law Bill that outlawed all forms of homosexual contact. Concerning Merrill he wrote, in his *Intermediate Sex*: "Eros is a great leveller. Perhaps the true Democracy rests, more firmly than anywhere else, on a sentiment which easily passes the bounds of class and caste, and unites in the closest affection the most estranged ranks of society. It is noticeable how often [homosexuals] of good position and breeding are drawn to rougher types, as of manual workers, and frequently very permanent alliances grow up in this way, which although not publicly acknowledged have a decided influence on social institutions, customs and political tendencies." The book was the foundation of the LGBT movement (lesbian, gay, bisexual and transgender).

Merrill and Carpenter.

Carpenter's last years were devoted to homosexual rights, as well as the protection of the environment and animals, the benefits of a vegetarian diet and the necessity of pacifism. George Orwell attacked him as representing "every fruit-juice drinker, nudist, sandal wearer and sex maniac" in the Socialist movement.

Merrill died in 1928, bringing on a stroke that kept Carpenter paralyzed until his own death in 1929.

Merrill and Carpenter's tombs.

Forster became a close friend of both men, as did John Addington Symonds.

Forster's tombstone.

Edward Carpenter did what he could when writing *The Intermediate*

Sex, given the homophobia of the times, the existing laws, and fears that his friends would be open to calumny. The book is very thin and so the copy sent to me, a reprint, is in such huge type that it's difficult to read! Here are the salient parts:

Carpenter begins by saying that all women have a dash of men in them and vice-versa, which means that today both sexes are drawing nearer, both appreciating music, art and bicycling.

The intermediate sex is a man like any other, healthy, well-developed, muscular, with a powerful brain and a high standard of conduct--Carpenter is describing, of course, his conception of himself. They do not necessarily force themselves to marry and have children, and if they do marry it is often platonically (as several Bloomsbury men did).

Those who realize what they are have serious inner struggles, particularly because they share the emotional soul-nature of women, even though, he stresses again, they are every bit as masculine as other men in body and mind.

Men who take to them are lucky "as they walk on roses without ever having to fear the thorns [because the intermediates are so sweet] and there is no better nurse when one is ill."

Carpenter offers a list of exceptional intermediates, including Michelangelo, Shakespeare, Marlow, Alexander the Great and Caesar.

He cites the Greeks, briefly mentioning Cleomachus who, when preparing to leave for war, was kissed by his beloved who tenderly placed Cleomachus' helmet on his head.

He invokes Melville [a homosexual] who spoke about the "extravagant" friendships between Polynesian males, and naturally Patrocles and Achilles, Alexander and Hephaestion came up, as well as quoting a Persian poem, "Bitter and sweet is the parting kiss on the lips of a friend."

Plato comes in with a quote from the *Symposium*, "I know not any greater blessing to a young man beginning life than a virtuous lover, or to the lover than a beloved youth."

Carpenter goes on to say that many intermediates marry for "ethical" and "social consideration," and form friendships with females that nonetheless are "of no avail to overcome the distaste on the part of one to sexual intercourse."

He elliptically uses expressions such as "the love in which we are dealing," and nearly never the word homosexual.

Concerning the subject of this book, boarding-school homosexuality, Carpenter says this of school friendships: "...between the young thing and its teacher, its importance in the educational sense can hardly be overrated." A 16-year-old says this about his tutor: "I would have died for him ten times over. My plan to meet him (to come across him casually, as it were) was that of a lad for his sweetheart, and when I saw him my heart beat so violently that it caught my breath, and I could not speak. We met in ___, and for the weeks that he stayed there I thought of nothing else--thought of him night and day--and when he returned to London I used to write him weekly letters, veritable love-letters of many sheets in length.''

''Anyone who has had experience of schoolboys knows well enough that they are capable of forming these romantic and devoted attachment,'' writes Carpenter.

He brings up Crete as an example of ''true friendship'', that receives the approbation of the boy's father. But the reality of Crete is this, an excerpt taken from my book *Greek Homosexuality*: ''In Crete a boy seems to have been abducted by a lover who, in concord with the boy's friends, takes the lad into the countryside where they spend two idyllic months hunting, feasting and sexually exhausting their young bodies. The belovèd is then returned home with the symbolic gifts of military dress, an ox and a drinking cup (and whatever else the man might wish him to have, gifts the expense of which would depend on the man's resources). Interestingly, the boy was then known by a Greek word meaning ''he who stands ready,'' perhaps signifying Ganymede who, after being abducted by Zeus, stood ready, at the god's side, to serve him food and drink. It's interesting too to note that the boy's father was kept informed of each stage of his son's abduction and, indeed, his great wish was to have a son who would be handsome enough to attract a suitable suitor--one influential enough to give the boy a boost into the better classes, knowing full well that his boy would be the object of sexual passion, as the father had himself been as a boy.''

Carpenter wrote that there was no sex education in British schools, and as a consequence a boy's desire for knowledge is filled in by his comrades: ''Contraband information is smuggled in ... smut takes the place of decent explanations; unhealthy practices follow; the sacredness of sex goes its way, never to return.'' I'd like to quote again Symonds, around the same age as Carpenter, both having shared identical educations: ''The talk in the dormitories and studies was of the grossest character, with repulsive scenes of onanism, mutual masturbation and obscene orgies of naked boys in bed together. There was no refinement, just animal lust.''

He states that ''boys and youths must be trusted to form decent and loving friendships ... considerably more important than friendship.'' ''Boys and youths'' perpetuate the Greek ideal of boys always having older friends (lovers for the Greeks), the idea being that one instructs the other. This was exactly the goldmine Byron fell upon. Because of his clubfoot he was mocked in college and his first year was a disaster. So the idea came, when he was in his second year, to show the new boys around and help them, warmly, to get to know the ropes. He never had a lonely night again.

Carpenter adds a footnote about the wisdom of sending boys 10 to 14 to boarding schools, hinting that the 15 to 18-year-olds will have their sexual will on them, which was exactly what took place.

He wrote that ''the capacity of a man to devote himself to the welfare of boys and youths ought not to go wasted.'' And later states: ''That capacity for sincere affection which causes an elder man to care so deeply for the welfare of a youth or boy is met and responded to by a similar capacity in the young thing of devotion to an elder man. This fact is not always recognized; but I have known cases of boys and even young men who would feel the most romantic attachments to quite mature men, sometimes as much as forty or fifty years of age, and only for them.'' This is, naturally, every older man's wet dream. One wonders at Carpenter's naivety in thinking that the boy would love a much older man for himself rather than what he was in a position to do for the boy--although, who knows?, this may have taken place.

AUDEN – ISHERWOOD – SPENDERS - KALLMAN

A greater eclecticist than W. H. Auden rarely existed, as shown through his work and travels. I'm going to combine his life with those of Christopher Isherwood, Stephen Spenders and Chester Kallman because the first three were an inseparable homosexual trio, and the last the great love of Auden's life. All four came out, at puberty, in boarding schools.

Auden, Spender and Isherwood

Boarding school began for Auden at age 8 at Repton, where he first met Isherwood; at 13 he went to Norfolk and at 18 to Christ Church, Oxford, where he studied English and became Isherwood's off-and-on lover, if not before. At age 21, in 1928, he went to Weimar Berlin, with its 170 boy whorehouses, a favorite haunt for Isherwood too, where both boys would return until the war, and where every form of existent sex could be found for a few pfennig. Auden could be stomped on, as appears to have been his preference, a sad defiling of the human body, even if Auden's had never been particularly comely. (Tut-tut.) He found a way of reconciliating his deep religiosity with his need to be degraded, which never ceases to amaze me. At the end of the segment on Auden's life I'll include a ''poem'' Auden refused to recognize as his, but is proof that he knew his subject intimately, even if anyone who has ever sunk to his knees to open a buttoned fly and give pleasure to its possessor knows as much, lacking only the ''fame'' of an Auden.

Auden, Isherwood and Spender's bar hopping in Berlin affords us a chance to have a look at sex through recent history in general, and in Berlin in particular.

What is amazing in the history of love among males was that after the Renaissance there followed an age darker than the Middle Ages which had preceded the Renaissance. Love between males during the Renaissance could be punished by death, but in reality under Lorenzo *Il Magnifico* de' Medici one got off with a simple slap on the hand. No one was punished because everyone was doing it, sharing, at some point in their lives, an orgasm with another male. As girls were worth their weight in gold thanks to advantageous marriages that would enrich their husbands, they were kept locked away. Unlike a boy who could offer himself to a hundred passing hands or mouths or anuses and still claim innocence, a girl had one chance, after which the fruit was eternally spoiled.

After the Renaissance we stepped back into the dark, where lads, in the 1800s, could not comprehend their attraction to lads, those they had seen swimming in rivers and lakes, naked and so beautiful the boys dreaming of them inundated their own bellies in equally wondrous rivers and lakes. Till then, men were thought (by some) to have become homosexuals because they were so insatiable sexually that they simply turned to men as an alternative to women who now bored them. To keep boys on the right track laws were harsh, although thankfully the death penalty had been dropped, except, in one of life's never-ending paradoxes, in Berlin--until 1868. It was felt that men who cared for other men were in reality women trapped in a man's body, which would not only account for their searching out other men, but would account too for those like Auden who were effeminate. The woman within was seeking an outlet for her femininity.

Men who were lucky, mostly educated men who emigrated to places like Berlin, could find sexual satisfaction in the garrison city of 400,000 where soldiers padded their pay by selling themselves, and that for generations. The unlucky ones, the vast majority, may have felt that they and their sexuality were alone in the world, that no others shared their dreams and lust. These would live and die alone. Following the French Revolution laws against sodomy were abolished in France in 1791. Under

French influence they were abolished also in Spain, Belgium, the Netherlands and Italy. Certain parts of Germany followed. In Bavaria, for example, only those who raped other men or who had sex with boys under 12 were prosecuted. But in all parts of Germany men could be imprisoned if they did something against public decency, a seemingly normal demand since having sex, for example, in the middle of a public street (homosexual or heterosexual sex), struck everyone as bad form. The law, in reality however, was diverted to cover whatever the police wanted it to cover. An example: a boy who related to another boy how he had been fucked--but well paid--in a park, was overheard by a woman who was shocked, a public act of indecency because the boys had spoken in public. The boy was found and jailed. But even this liberalism was revoked following several horrendous rapes of minors, and in 1871 laws were again reenacted in Germany against sodomy.

The population of Berlin exploded, from the 400,000 to 4 million in 1920. Berlin went from a city of open sewers to the first city ever electrified, with, in 1800, electric streetcars and lighting. It went from a city of open sewers to one of public toilets and baths, from the filthiest to the cleanest city in the world, infinitely more hygienic than London, Paris and N.Y. At the end of the 1400s in Florence the Office of the Night was formed to put an end to sodomy. The penalty was death but, as stated above, everyone got off with a slap on the wrist, except those who forced children to have sex. In 1885, Berlin established the Department of Homosexuals, proof of the growing number of gays. The police collected information and mug shots of homosexuals, and encouraged doctors and educators to study Berlin's unique sexual subculture, thanks to which reams of information concerning the sexuality of the times have come to us. In 1896 the name of the Department of Homosexuals was changed to Department of Homosexuals and Blackmailers. More money could be gained by pimps putting 14-year-old boys on the streets and then blackmailing the clients. In 1902 Friedrich Alfred Krupp, the Cannon King, committed suicide when blackmail led to the publication of his preference for Italian boys. For such a rich, powerful man to end his own life so young spoke volumes about being branded a homosexual, about the prevalence of blackmail and about the availability of underage lads. The department store magnate Hermann Israel killed himself on his yacht at age 40 when his companion blackmailed him. Before dying Israel turned the boy's threatening letters over to the police. The lad was sentences to two months imprisonment. Victims of blackmail numbered in the hundreds, two of whom were well-known jurists, one who shot his blackmailer when he literally didn't have a cent left to pay him off. In 1902 a 28-year-old ophthalmologist committed suicide when his card was found in a boy's jacket and the ophthalmologist was threatened with a trial. At the time, it was established that a third of Berlin's homosexuals were being blackmailed. But as Berlin's reputation for male prostitution bloomed, johns from all over Europe flocked to the world's greatest center of boys.

Kiosks were literally flooded with dozens of publications, and the kiosk owners didn't hesitate to have some pinned open, showing nude males. In 1930 Berlin had 280,000 tourists a year, among which were 40,000 Americans. There were believed to have been 100,000 rent-boys, all out for money to live on or pocket change, 1/3rd were believed to have been heterosexual. And they were cheap, especially soldiers going for 50 pfennig. Thomas Mann discovered Berlin at age 17. Isherwood refused to pay more than 10 marks, dinner and a few drinks for his boys (although this was outrageously overpaying), W.H. Auden, in his diary, detailed all sexual encounters, and the architect Philip Johnson claimed to have learned German through the horizontal method.

Isherwood and Don Bachardy.

Neither minors nor anyone badly dressed were admitted to the clubs in west Berlin. In the east everyone could enter. The sex was wildly tame compared to today's backrooms (although no-holds-barred was the rule in boy whorehouses). At the urinals boys showed their wares, and at tables boys allowed johns to put their hands through their pockets, which had been cut away inside to allow seizure of the boys' dicks. Isherwood was said to have had 500. Today, boys can do that in a year, easily, but here we're talking about quantity. Quality is a completely different story. Scotty Bowers in his fascinating book *Full Service* relates that heterosexuals who requested his services rarely asked for more than a redhead or big tits, while homosexuals were extremely demanding. And it's true. That was the problem in Berlin. The beautiful boys were in private clubs and in private hands, wealthy hands, hands that could offer far more than Isherwood's ten marks, even if ten marks were extremely generous for what was available. The boys who went with Isherwood thought he was fabulously rich because they were fabulously lacking in the attributes that would place them in an entirely different class.

Boys of quality in pre-W.W. I Berlin were in private hands,
not Auden and Isherwood's.

Then, as today, coke was ubiquitous, except that it had just been invented, by Albert Niemann, and was not only fully accepted, it was recommended by Freud to his patients.

With the arrival of the Nazis and the destruction of Röhm things came to an instant halt. 100,000 men were found guilty of homosexual crimes and between 5,000 to 15,000 died in camps, terrible but far fewer than I had imagined.

Today the legal age of consent is 16 in Germany, which strikes me as imminently justifiable.

In Berlin Auden, Isherwood and Spender spent their time in the Furbinger Strasse, the gay area with its nearly 200 male brothels, and where Auden could count on his favorite boy, Pieps, to beat him up.

It is said that Auden suffered from two major life failings, the first when he went to Spain to help in its Civil War and was rejected because he hadn't his card to the Communist Party (and certainly, too, because of his milquetoast appearance), and the second when Chester Kallman refused to be faithful to him, a demand that simply does not exist in Sodom where the promise within each new levis crotch is to die for, sight unseen. Kallman, aged 18 to Auden's 32, had apparently thrown himself at Auden during a poetry reading, offering his body--an offer that would continue to the end of Auden's life because they would never leave each other, even if sex soon stopped and Kallman went on sowing his wild oats where he wished.

Kallman and Auden.

Auden never stopped working: poems; film scripts; essays; reviews; more poems, some book length; along with travel--a trip to China with Isherwood--a travel book *Letters from Iceland* with Louis MacNeice; a *mariage blanc* with Erika Mann so she could become a British citizen; and stays in America where he took American citizenship, causing a scandal that reached the floor of parliament. For a while he lived in Brooklyn with Carson McCullers and Benjamin Britten, whose *Billy Bud* is the only opera without a single woman. Summers in Ischia (British gays, again, have historically craved Italian boys--and rightly so) and the first home he ever owned, in Austria. He taught English in Britain and America where he wrote for *The New Yorker* and *The New York Review of Books*. He wrote plays with Isherwood and the libretto for Stravinsky's opera *The Rakes Progress* with Kallman, and one of his poems was read aloud in the film *Four Weddings and a Funeral*. An anthology of all his work would fill thousands of pages. How much remains is for the reader to decide.

Kallman inherited the entirety of Auden's estate and died in Athens at age 54, intestate, his and Auden's heritage going to Kallman's eighty-year-old father.

Auden was said to have been extremely knowledgeable, funny, kind and generous. He once stated that pornography excited him more than a living person, and this was certainly true in his case.

Auden died in 1973 at age 66.

I'll end with his 1948 poem, title unknown. Why? Just for the hell of it.

It was a spring day, a day for a lay, when the air
Smelled like a locker-room, a day to blow or get blown;
Returning from lunch I turned my corner and there
On a near-by stoop I saw him standing alone.
I glanced as I advanced. The clean white T-shirt outlined
A forceful torso, the light-blue denims divulged
Much. I observed the snug curves where they hugged the behind,
I watched the crotch where the cloth intriguingly bulged.

Our eyes met. I felt sick. My knees turned weak.
I couldn't move. I didn't know what to say.
In a blur I heard words, myself like a stranger speak
"Will you come to my room?" Then a husky voice, "O.K."
I produced some beer and we talked. Like a little boy
He told me his story. Present address: next door.
Half Polish, half Irish. The youngest. From Illinois.
Profession: mechanic. Name: Bud. Age: twenty-four.
He put down his glass and stretched his bare arms along
The back of my sofa. The afternoon sunlight struck
The blond hairs on the wrist near my head. His chin was strong.
His mouth sucky. I could hardly believe my luck.
And here he was sitting beside me, legs apart.
I could bear it no longer. I touched the inside of his thigh.
His reply was to move closer. I trembled, my heart
Thumped and jumped as my fingers went to his fly.
I opened a gap in the flap. I went in there.
I sought for a slit in the gripper shorts that had charge
Of the basket I asked for. I came to warm flesh then to hair.
I went on. I found what I hoped. I groped. It was large.
He responded to my fondling in a charming, disarming way:
Without a word he unbuckled his belt while I felt.
And lolled back, stretching his legs. His pants fell away.
Carefully drawing it out, I beheld what I held.
The circumcised head was a work of mastercraft
With perfectly beveled rim of unusual weight
And the friendliest red. Even relaxed, the shaft
Was of noble dimensions with the wrinkles that indicate
Singular powers of extension. For a second or two,
It lay there inert, then suddenly stirred in my hand,
Then paused as if frightened or doubtful of what to do.
And then with a violent jerk began to expand.
By soundless bounds it extended and distended, by quick
Great leaps it rose, it flushed, it rushed to its full size.
Nearly nine inches long and three inches thick,
A royal column, ineffably solemn and wise.
I tested its length and strength with a manual squeeze.
I bunched my fingers and twirled them about the knob.
I stroked it from top to bottom. I got on my knees.
I lowered my head. I opened my mouth for the job.
But he pushed me gently away. He bent down. He unlaced
His shoes. He removed his socks. Stood up. Shed
His pants altogether. Muscles in arms and waist

Rippled as he whipped his T-shirt over his head.
I scanned his tan, enjoyed the contrast of brown
Trunk against white shorts taut around small
Hips. With a dig and a wriggle he peeled them down.
I tore off my clothes. He faced me, smiling. I saw all.
The gorgeous organ stood stiffly and straightly out
With a slight flare upwards. At each beat of his heart it threw
An odd little nod my way. From the slot of the spout
Exuded a drop of transparent viscous goo.
The lair of hair was fair, the grove of a young man,
A tangle of curls and whorls, luxuriant but couth.
Except for a spur of golden hairs that fan
To the neat navel, the rest of the belly was smooth.
Well hung, slung from the fork of the muscular legs,
The firm vase of his sperm, like a bulging pear,
Cradling its handsome glands, two herculean eggs,
Swung as he came towards me, shameless, bare.
We aligned mouths. We entwined. All act was clutch,
All fact contact, the attack and the interlock
Of tongues, the charms of arms. I shook at the touch
Of his fresh flesh, I rocked at the shock of his cock.
Straddling my legs a little I inserted his divine
Person between and closed on it tight as I could.
The upright warmth of his belly lay all along mine.
Nude, glued together for a minute, we stood.
I stroked the lobes of his ears, the back of his head
And the broad shoulders. I took bold hold of the compact
Globes of his bottom. We tottered. He fell on the bed.
Lips parted, eyes closed, he lay there, ripe for the act.
Mad to be had, to be felt and smelled. My lips
Explored the adorable masculine tits. My eyes
Assessed the chest. I caressed the athletic hips
And the slim limbs. I approved the grooves of the thighs.
I hugged, I snuggled into an armpit. I sniffed
The subtle whiff of its tuft. I lapped up the taste
Of its hot hollow. My fingers began to drift
On a trek of inspection, a leisurely tour of the waist.
Downward in narrowing circles they playfully strayed.
Encroached on his privates like poachers, approached the prick,
But teasingly swerved, retreated from meeting. It betrayed
Its pleading need by a pretty imploring kick.
"Shall I rim you?" I whispered. He shifted his limbs in assent.
Turned on his side and opened his legs, let me pass

To the dark parts behind. I kissed as I went
The great thick cord that ran back from his balls to his arse.
Prying the buttocks aside, I nosed my way in
Down the shaggy slopes. I came to the puckered goal.
It was quick to my licking. He pressed his crotch to my chin.
His thighs squirmed as my tongue wormed in his hole.
His sensations yearned for consummation. He untucked
His legs and lay panting, hot as a teen-age boy.
Naked, enlarged, charged, aching to get sucked,
Clawing the sheet, all his pores open to joy.
I inspected his erection. I surveyed his parts with a stare
From scrotum level. Sighting along the underside
Of his cock, I looked through the forest of pubic hair
To the range of the chest beyond rising lofty and wide.
I admired the texture, the delicate wrinkles and the neat
Sutures of the capacious bag. I adored the grace
Of the male genitalia. I raised the delicious meat
Up to my mouth, brought the face of its hard-on to my face.
Slipping my lips round the Byzantine dome of the head,
With the tip of my tongue I caressed the sensitive groove.
He thrilled to the trill. "That's lovely!" he hoarsely said.
"Go on! Go on!" Very slowly I started to move.
Gently, intently, I slid to the massive base
Of his tower of power, paused there a moment down
In the warm moist thicket, then began to retrace
Inch by inch the smooth way to the throbbing crown.
Indwelling excitements swelled at delights to come
As I descended and ascended those thick distended walls.
I grasped his root between left forefinger and thumb
And with my right hand tickled his heavy voluminous balls.
I plunged with a rhythmical lunge steady and slow,
And at every stroke made a corkscrew roll with my tongue.
His soul reeled in the feeling. He whimpered "Oh!"
As I tongued and squeezed and rolled and tickled and swung.
Then I pressed on the spot where the groin is joined to the cock,
Slipped a finger into his arse and massaged him from inside.
The secret sluices of his juices began to unlock.
He melted into what he felt. "O Jesus!" he cried.
Waves of immeasurable pleasures mounted his member in quick
Spasms. I lay still in the notch of his crotch inhaling his sweat.
His ring convulsed round my finger. Into me, rich and thick,
His hot spunk spouted in gouts, spurted in jet after jet.

Stephen Spender went to University College, Oxford, where he knew both Isherwood and Auden intimately, and even hand-reprinted Auden's first poems. He was well acquainted with the Bloomsbury Set as well as Berlin at the sides of Auden and Isherwood. He started a novel about the Weimar Republic and the pre-war openness of Germany (meaning easy access to lads), a novel called *The Temple* that he finished in 1988, at age 79 with still 7 years to live.

Spender and one of his boys.

Highly disturbed when Russia joined forces with Germany, Spender wrote an essay about his disillusionment in a book of other essays, *The God that Failed.* He taught in both America and England, poetry and rhetoric. Around age 30 he had homosexual relation with Lucian Freud, a teenager, Sigmund's grandson, although Lucian, an artist, went on to father 14 children he acknowledged and 25 he didn't, while Spender went on to marry twice (having as one of his many lovers Michael Redgrave, Vanessa's father.) Spender's letters to Lucian were put up for sale by his son Matthew Spender, age 70, and went for £35,000.

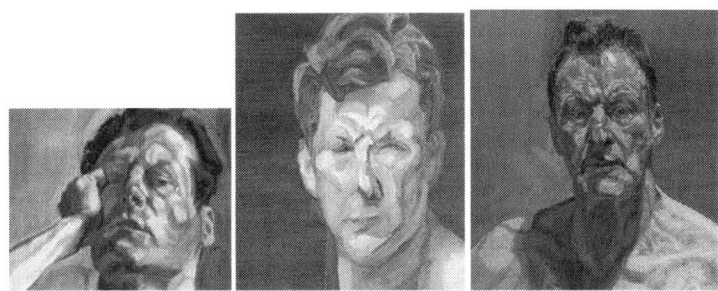

Lucian Freud by himself.

Isherwood had first met Auden at Repton School and as a young man was the lover of the violinist André Mangeot. Isherwood was a tutor in Berlin as in *Cabaret*, the 1972 film version of his book *Goodbye to Berlin*. It was in Berlin that he met the first love of his life, Heinz Neddermeyer, 17, who traveled widely with Isherwood but was imprisoned in Germany for 1½ years for mutual masturbation, plus 2 years of compulsory military service. Heinz later married and had a son, Christian.

Isherwood wrote plays with Auden, one of which was *The Dog Beneath the Skin*, about a man searching for a missing heir, accompanied by a dog that was the heir himself in disguise. Another was *The Ascent of F6,* about a man who accepted an offer by the British press to climb a mountain, F6, ahead of native climbers, but in his haste was killed. Benjamin Britten, with whom Isherwood had lived, wrote the music for the play.

Mangeot on the left.

In California he took in Truman Capote, a boy everyone wanted to have before he destroyed himself physically, for me the best writer who has ever lived, but as he didn't go to a boarding school he won't, alas, be included here. He nonetheless had plenty of sex, although nothing can replace pagan boarding-school orgies. At any rate, Gerald Clarke's biography of Capote can't be excelled by anyone living on the planet Earth.

Isherwood produced a book of photographs with texts with photographer and lover Bill Caskey in 1949.

Bill Caskey

The 48-year-old Isherwood met the 18-year-old Don Bachardy on a beach of Santa Monica and spent the rest of his life with the boy, along with

156

the usual ups-and-downs and multiple infidelities on both sides. A film about their lives, *Chris & Don: A Love Story* was released in 2008. Bachardy became an accomplished artist who painted numerous pictures of Isherwood, especially near the end, too sad to be reproduced here. During this time Isherwood taught English at the Los Angeles State College.

Isherwood wrote that he did to his lovers what all lovers do, "sucking, fucking and rimming". With that truism in mind we can close the chapter on the foursome, Auden, Isherwood, Spender and Kallman.

RUPERT BROOKE
1887 – 1915
MAYNARD KEYNES – DENIS BROWNE

In dealing with the life of Rupert Brooke one is threatened with every possible exaction--short of, perhaps, death by torture--if any copyrighted aspect of his existence is revealed. I will therefore simply allude to the letter he wrote concerning his plan to seduce a young friend. At any rate, the letter is cold and calculating, and once he did get the lad's shorts down, one cares little for the lack of passion that followed. This was supposedly Brooke's first attempt at losing his burdensome virginity, homosexually speaking, as he had apparently "known" girls for some time. I personally don't believe a word of a delayed loss of his cherry. He was so startlingly good-looking that he was certainly prey from his earliest years, and because sex is what took place in boarding schools, days and especially night, and given the nature of adolescent lust, and the fact that lads at the time took their sex very seriously, the boy he said he'd seduced in his letter was certainly far from the first.

Rupert Brooke

The problem evaluating Brooke's work is that one can't see the forest for the trees, the trees here being his beauty. He was president of the

Cambridge Fabian Society and a founder of the Marlowe Society, a drama club in which he acted in its plays. How many students were members thanks to their literary appeal and how many were there--boys and girls--drawn by Brooke's beauty can't be known. Born in Rugby, in 1887, he is reputed for his First World War poetry, appeals for young men to engage in the services and commit mass suicide, his most celebrated poem being this:

>If I should die, think only this of me:
>That there's some corner of a foreign field
>That is forever England. There shall be
>In that rich earth a richer dust concealed;
>A dust whom England bore, shaped, made aware,
>Gave, once, her flowers to love, her ways to roam,
>A body of England's, breathing English air,
>Washed by the rivers, blest by suns of home.

He was bisexual, having perhaps fathered a daughter on a visit to Tahiti. He was part of the Bloomsbury Set, with homosexuals E.M. Forster and John Maynard Keynes, a genius on economics who is daily cited somewhere in this world to our own day. Keynes' father was a professor of economics at Cambridge. Keynes' life was one brilliant exploit after another, during his college days and afterwards, in economics although his chief interest was philosophy. He represented the British Treasury at Versailles in 1918 and when he couldn't protect the German people from financial catastrophe, he resigned. Keynes was open about his homosexuality. His diaries were heavily encoded but he had an obsession with numbers since childhood and noted everything. He wrote having sex with ''a 16-year-old under Etna'' and ''the liftboy of Vauxhall''. In 1911, as one example, he had 16 C's, 4 A's and 5 W's. Enciphers guess that the A's were ass-contacts, the C's cocksucking and the W's wanks (jerking off) with boys/men. He married a ballerina in Diaghilev's Ballets Russes in 1925, a marriage that lasted 20 years. He died of a heart attack in 1946.

Rupert Brook

Brooke had numerous lovers and friends, one of whom caught the ear of Winston Churchill who commissioned Brooke into the Royal Naval Volunteer Reserve, an honor Brooke accepted on the condition that his friend Denis Browne, a composer, be commissioned to. It was in Denis's arms on the island of Skyros that Brooke ... well, let Denis tell it: "At 4 o'clock he became weaker, and at 4:46 he died, with the sun shining all round his cabin, and the cool sea-breeze blowing through the door and the shaded windows. No one could have wished for a quieter or a calmer end than in that lovely boy, shielded by the mountains and fragrant with sage and thyme." No one was luckier too to have a friend like Denis Browne.

Brooke died from a simple mosquito bite that had become infected. Denis died in battle at Gallipoli. His last letter was found in his wallet, that he'd put there knowing he hadn't long to live: "I'm luckier than Rupert because I've fought. But there's no one to bury me as I buried him, so perhaps he's best off in the long run."

Facing a Nazi firing squad Willem Arondeus had cried out: "Let it be known that homosexuals are not cowards!" Such was the case of Denis Browne.

LAWRENCE OF ARABIA
1888 – 1935
Damascus - 1918

I loved you, so I drew these tides of men into my hands
and wrote my will across the sky in stars
To earn you Freedom, the seven-pillared worthy house,
that your eyes might be shining for me
when we came.
Lawrence's gift to Selim Ahmed--Dahoum

Lawrence is our Everest, and I have no desire whatsoever to scale its heights. Yet the fact remains that he was a hero, and for those who share my preference, he was, in part, *our* hero. We know for certain he loved a boy, Dahoum (Selim Ahmed), perhaps the unique joy of his life. If the relationship went beyond friendship cannot be known. How Dahoum felt about Lawrence cannot be known either, as what Dahoum felt was an inextricable tangle of many sentiments: the pride of being in the service of an Englishman, his gratitude for the education that Lawrence offered him, wide travel at the side of his mentor, and freedom from even the shadow of want, as Lawrence cared for his every need. For both it was adventure and shared harmony, a moment more exhilarating than any temporary sharing of desire, even if there is no greater happiness than that found in the arms of one's belovèd.

Lawrence was 5' 5", a small size easily compensated for by a wonderful brain and the willpower of other hugely great Brits that I've had the privilege and temerity of including in my book *Homosexual Heroes*: Stanley, Speke, Burton among many. Lawrence was fearless, as were the men just cited, and in some portraits and some photos he was stunning.

Lawrence by Augustus John.

Lawrence began his career in Cairo as a cartographer, and it was Ronald Storrs, a Foreign Office official, who got him permission to visit Faisel, one of the sons of Hussein, the powerful Sharif of Mecca, so powerful in fact that Hussein demanded, for his aid in ridding the region of Turks, that he be made king over not only today's Saudi Arabia, but also Palestine, Syria, Lebanon and Iraq. The British agreed, but specified that the details would be decided during a conference to take place after the war. In reality, the British and the French had already divided the Arab world between themselves in a treaty between the British Parliamentarian Mark Sykes and the French diplomat François George-Picot, giving, in grossly general terms, today's Saudi Arabia and Iraq to England, and today's Syria and Lebanon to the French where they had roots dating back to the Crusades. (Even then the English and the French had been entwined, through the love affair between Richard Coeur de Lion and Philippe II.)

Lawrence had a great deal in common with Storrs, literature, interests in art and archeology, even music, and both would remain friends until Lawrence's death. But whereas Storrs appreciated the finer things in life, Lawrence neither smoked nor drank, he dressed carelessly, didn't like meat (although, apparently, he wasn't a vegetarian), and he never fit in, which is the case for many if not most homosexuals, especially those who love their recruits but would rather die than show it, like Jack Nicholson in India (see my book *John (Jack) Nicholson*). Storrs on the other hand was cut out for high society. Lawrence ate only to fuel his body, he was ascetic, decided, certain of his destiny, and as usual when one's destiny is accomplished, he detested every minute that followed his success. In fact, his success would destroy him.

He met Hussein's son Feisal at Wadi Safra. If it were not love at first sight for Lawrence, it certainly resembled it. As Lawrence wrote in his book, Feisal was tall, slim, with a perfectly trimmed black beard, drooping eyes, and hands that continually fidgeted with a dagger at his waist. In age Lawrence was 28, Feisal 33. Lawrence immediately knew that this was the man, and decided that from then on he would do anything in his power to see Feisal to Damascus where he would declare himself ruler, thusly shattering the Sykes-Picot Treaty. Feisal asked Lawrence how he found the encampment, and Lawrence answered, "too far from Damascus," which earned him Feisal's loyalty from then on, because Feisal correctly read the love for the Arabs in Lawrence's face.

Feisal

And there had to be love in order to overcome Arab failing. They stole whatever wasn't nailed down, from friends as well as foe. They fought exclusively for gold, the idea of a nation being foreign to them. Their nation was their family, clan and tribe, even if they continually wreaked vengeance through incessant blood feuds within the very same family, clan and tribe. They were supreme slave owners--black slaves that cared for their fields of dates, prepared their bread, freeing Arab wives to care for the goat herds while the men made war.

The Turks were disciplined, something the Arabs never ever were. The Turks, too, were barbaric to a point that shocked the Arabs who would never harm a woman or a child, while a Turk pasha would sit back in comfort while an Arab encampment was slaughtered to the last man, woman and baby, after raping or while raping the women. The encampment would be set on fire and the bodies caste into the flames.

It was then, too, that Lawrence met the enormously powerful and enormously dangerous chieftain Auda Abu Tayi, a warrior who fought against his own Arabs, cutting out the still-beating hearts of his enemies and biting into the throbbing flesh. He had wives and sons without number and was in the pay of the Turks because they hadn't been able to kill him. Hawk-nosed, his beard as pointed as Feisal's own, his eyes flashing, he was like Lawrence, fearless and a charismatic leader of men.

Auda Abu Tayi

Lawrence and Auda decided to blow up Turkish trains and rails. In one incident they came across a Circassians goatherd. Circassians were a Caucasian people who had sought exile from the Russians--who had conquered Caucasia in 1864--by seeking refuge in Turkey. Blue-eyed and fair skinned, their women were known for their beauty and got top price for Ottoman harems, and their boys were no less handsome. As the Arabs systematically slit the throat and robbed the clothes of whomever they came across, Lawrence wanted to save the boy but he couldn't tie him up because he would have died of thirst, yet had he freed the lad, he would have warned the Turks. So Lawrence had the soles of his feet cut with a dagger, obliging him to crawl home, where his feet would eventually heal.

It was Feisal who suggested that Lawrence dress as an Arab.

The Bedouins gorged themselves on the boy's herds, and once again Lawrence recognized how different they were from him. They didn't put meat aside for later, and indeed had trained their camels to eat it when available. The same was true with water that they would drink until bloated, with no thought of rationing it for future use. They wasted ammunition by announcing their arrival by firing in the air. They would be friendly to Lawrence but he would never be accepted as one of them, and could never, either, totally accept their ways, their heartless slitting of captives' throats, the filth of their jokes and personal habits. On the other hand, he appreciated their "voluntary and affectionate" sexual relations among themselves, which Lawrence found preferable to their visiting prostitutes and bestiality with animals, he later wrote. At the same time, the treachery of his own people towards the Arabs, as in the Sykes-Picot Treaty, distanced him forever from his native land.

All of which meant that he was exiled in his mind, from his own country, and that since his youth. The tragedy is that he found no replacement. The tragedy is that he had nonetheless returned "home". The tragedy is that one can't go back. He should have exiled himself elsewhere, free from the humiliation of home and Arabia both.

Lawrence's father was Sir Thomas Chapman, an Englishman living in Ireland, the father of four girls whose governess was Sarah Lawrence, the woman he loved and who would give him five illegitimate sons, concrete proof of an erotic attachment. It was her name that T. E. Lawrence, her second son, adopted. Of strict morals, she was one of life's paradoxes, a deeply religious woman, herself illegitimate, who produced five bastards, a term of no import during the Renaissance but shameful in Victorian Britain. In fact, had his father had the means of sending his boys to his own school, Eton, they would have been prevented from entering by their illegitimacy, one of life's countless injustices. Sarah seems to have consoled herself by repeating that God hated the sin but loved the sinner. Called Ned by the family, born in Wales, he would only learn of his illegitimacy later in his youth.

It is an incontestable fact that homosexuals disdain collective sports, favoring the individuality of swimming, athletics and bicycling--and as a boy Lawrence lived for his bicycle. His brothers Frank and Will, tall and of extreme beauty, preferred team sports, rugby and cricket, which made them popular, unlike Ned, the eternal loner. He seems to have been a practical joker and, as determined and inflexible as his mother, was often in opposition to her, earning him whippings, as it was she the family disciplinarian, perhaps why he himself, later in life, allowed himself to be beaten by boys he rigorously chose for the punishments. His brother

Arnold said, later, that she had tried to break Ned's will. As his father had money, the boys were looked after by nannies, and despite the discipline, the boys were said to have loved both parents, and were deeply loved in return. Lawrence was sent to a local Oxford school, close enough so that he and his brothers could sleep at home, thusly avoiding the bullying, arrogance and sexual slavery of boarding schools, something his father was obviously familiar with. Ned was said to have spoken French fluently at age 6 and had started Latin at age 5, both of which claims could possibly have been true. His father seems to have been an ideal companion, fulfilling his sons' needs, giving Ned, for example, his first bike and then accompanying him on long rides. Ned joined the army on a sudden impulse at age 16, disliked it, and was bought his freedom--apparently possible at the time--by his father. At age 18 his father had a cottage built for him so that he could be on his own, an immeasurable gift of love and understanding. At also 18 he cycled through the north of France, and studied French medieval fortifications, making drawings and taking pictures. He then returned to go to Oxford University.

An Oxford education is extraordinary to American eyes. After exams and an interview, one is accepted or not. A student has rooms, usually a sitting room and a separate bedroom, he can be served breakfast, lunch and dinner, there is someone, a kind of valet, to see to his needs, the luxury of which, or lack of luxury, depending on the students' parents' wealth. A student is assigned a tutor for a weekly hour who directs his studies, a man with whom he may remain in close contact throughout his entire life. The best minds taught at Oxford, men of immense experience, authors of renown. But as in all institutions, everywhere, some intellectually weak ones got through, stodgy old pussies it was a student's bad luck to draw. He had a best friend, Vyvyan Richards who himself claimed he loved Lawrence at first sight, something Lawrence didn't see or pretended not to see, even when Richards made his dedication to Lawrence obvious. Richards wrote that Lawrence was either sexless or unaware of sex. Michael Korda, in his wonderful book *Hero--The Life and Legend of Lawrence of Arabia*, writes that Lawrence was not so much sexless ''as armored against sexual temptation,'' and Korda feels, as did Lawrence's brother Arnold, that '' Lawrence died a virgin.'' There was an Officer Training Corps at Oxford that Lawrence joined, spending a great deal of time practicing with his pistol. Richards claims that he went swimming in winter, breaking the ice, which suggests to some that he was attempting to control his sexual urges (proof to girls reading this of the incredible pressure of said urges in adolescent boys).

In 1909 Lawrence set out to explore the Middle East, a harrowing journey fraught with dangers, as he could have been disposed of anywhere along the route he traveled and his money and pistol (he carried one with him) stolen. Even his clothes, stripped from his dead body would have been taken, as was the custom then. He studied Arabic in preparation for the trip, did the necessary reading, talked with those who knew the region (and at Oxford scholars in the know were numerous and available). His father gave him a huge $10,000 in today's money. He sailed to Port Said and then to Beirut, from which he took the train or walked--a total of 1,000 miles-- staying with inhabitants, Arabs honor-bound to welcome him, but once he left their tents he became game for robbers. He also stayed in missions. In Palestine he noted the wonderful farms of the Jews and hoped that more would come to perpetuate agriculture there. His letters home, especially to his mother, were warm-hearted, optimistic, wonderfully young in their enthusiasm, showing no fear because he was an absolutely fearless boy. His letters were so fresh and clean that one wishes to end the story of his life here, as far as possible from the deceptions, intrigues, murders, massacres and masochistic self-imposed suffering on the horizon.

He was often ill and could have died from cholera and malaria that he had already contracted. The heat was in the 120s and body lice ubiquitous. He was shot at, and a newspaper even claimed he had been murdered; he had his camera stolen and was beaten over the head by a man who stole his remaining possessions and would have shot Lawrence had his pistol not refused to fire. As Korda so perfectly puts it: to a hero ''a life-threatening encounter is merely a challenge to be overcome, a step forward in his apprenticeship--the more frightening and the more physically punishing the better, provided he survives.''

He handed in his thesis on Middle Eastern archeology and won a First Class. One easily understands why Richards loved such a boy.

He went off on another bicycle trip around France, this time with his brother Frank. They did 50 miles a day, and Lawrence read, read and read, writing his mother that it was his way to ''go beyond one's miserable self.'' Truer words never spoken.

Before taking this excursion into his childhood, we left Lawrence blowing up trains with Auda. There was a garrison a few miles from Aqaba that Lawrence and Auda stormed. Auda led the attack and Lawrence, either through excitement or by accident, shot his own camel through the head. He was thrown to the ground and knocked out. When he awoke 300 Turks lay dead, 160 wounded, with the loss of 2 Arabs. The bodies were stripped naked and the clothes and other valuables retained by the Arabs. In the full moon that followed Lawrence described the young Turks as ''wonderfully beautiful'' in the moonlight that softened ''them into new ivory.'' The Turkish garrison at Aqaba, harassed by local tribes that Lawrence had contacted in advance, surrendered when promised their lives. It was thus that Lawrence rode to the sleepy shore and lapping sea of Aqaba, gateway to Damascus.

Lawrence vitally needed to get word to Cairo about the victory. He also needed food for the Arabs and prisoners. The only way was for him to cross 150 miles of desert to the Suez Canal, which he did with 6 men. This they accomplished in a forced march of 49 hours. A telephone was found at an abandoned outpost and a boat ordered. Once on the other side Lawrence was offered lodging, a hot bath, ice tea and food. The 6 Arabs were sent to a camp where they were fed and bedded with their kind.

In Cairo Lawrence met Allenby, the only general who ever awed him. Lawrence showed up wearing robes, whether to impress Allenby or not (because Lawrence had had time to change into a uniform) is not known. Allenby apparently shrugged it off as a boy gone native. It's for certain that the British, largely thanks to their boarding-school loves, accepted a great deal of fantasy from their sons and from boys in general, accepting, before the rest of Europe, phenomenon like boys sporting earrings and dyed hair. Lawrence told Allenby what he needed in supplies to keep Aqaba from starving to death--guns, cannon and ammunition--as well as 20,000,000 of today's dollars per month, all of which would keep the Arab revolt on the rails.

Lawrence received the Victoria Cross, the highest existent, made from Russian cannon captured at Sebastopol during the Crimean War. Soon he would be immortal.

After winning a brilliant First in archeology at Oxford, Lawrence went on a three-year-long dig to the Hittite site at Carchemish. There were two water-boys present, one being the love of his life, Dahoum, a boy aged 14 to Lawrence's 21. The boy was both handsome and well built, good natured and intelligent, and could read a little Arabic. His real name may have been Salim Ahmed. He certainly genuinely appreciated Lawrence who took him back to London for a short visit to meet the family. They traveled to Aqaba where together they bathed in the sea. One wonders if Lawrence had a premonition that in a few years he would become master of the entire region, that he would take Aqaba at the head of Auda's bandits. Lawrence was at the dig for three years, an enormous length of time with the boy he loved. How intimate was their friendship cannot, of course, be known. That Lawrence repressed his urges seems possible. The poem at the beginning of this chapter was for Dahoum, the promise and deliverance of independence, but from the beginning of his relationship with Dahoum Lawrence had tried to help Dahoum's people. At the Carchemish site Lawrence had received advice from his doctor-brother Bob in how to vaccinate the Arabs against smallpox, a horrible plague then, one of the world's greatest mass murderers, and he cared for those with cholera, which killed 90% of its victims, another plague that could have killed Lawrence too, one he tried to treat while he himself suffered from bouts of malaria.

Dahoum by Francis Dodd.

Then came Aqaba at the head of his troops and, as I wrote, immortality.

The plan now was to get Feisal to Damascus, all the while raiding the Turk railway, 800 miles of line, which would oblige them to dedicate huge forces in its protection. At the same time news arrived that Auda was in contact with the Turks, the result of which would have meant the loss of Aqaba. Lawrence went to Aqaba to meet Auda, surprising him at dinner. After the usual show of pretended love, Lawrence accused him of complicity with the enemy, forcing Auda into howls of laughter. The truth was that someone in Auda's camp had written to the Turks offering them Aqaba in exchange for gold. The Turks had complied, but Auda discovered the plot and had waylaid and stolen the gold. Lawrence pretended to believe the story, but immediately understood that before armaments and munitions, what counted to the likes of Auda was gold, which determined Lawrence to supply it in advance of every military action to follow. It was perhaps around this time that Lawrence made his way to Mecca to buy the gold dagger he would never be without from then on. How he survived in the city forbidden to infidels goes unexplained, as he was blond, blue-eyed and his Arabic was supposedly not that good.

As stated, Lawrence decided that he could best bring victory by striking at the Turkish railway, which he did, aiming especially at bridges from which trains would fall and be destroyed. His success was complete. The Arabs got their loot and fulfilled their blood lust by slaughtering nearly every living thing on the trains, women and children excluded--those that hadn't perished in the train's fall. As winter set in, and bored, he decided to visit the garrison town of Deraa, a known rail center he planned to destroy in better weather, a decision that would mark him for the rest of his life. The rape of women is horrifying, and I in no way mean to lessen it by saying that for a man it is a life-ending experience, a destruction so complete that only suicide can put an end to his suffering, physical first and then, to the last day of his time on earth, mental. In Deraa Lawrence would be raped multiple times by multiple rapists.

He had set off for Deraa with a single companion who had killed a score of Turks and who had such a price on his head that he was forced to leave Lawrence on the outskirts. Dressed in dirty Arab robes, Lawrence entered alone. Seeking information that would help with an attack on the town, he made his way to what looked like an airfield. There he was stopped by soldiers who were indifferent to his story of his being a Circassian. He was taken to a room and ordered to clean himself, and await the orders of the Bey. Later he was taken to a room where a sweaty fat man had him stripped naked and began to caress him. Lawrence kneed him in the groin and the Bey, the moment the pain had sufficiently subsided, took one of the soldier's bayonets and plunged it into Lawrence's side. Lawrence was then dragged to a room and stretched over a bench where he was whipped, the torturers claiming that after 10 blows he would cry for mercy, after 20 he would plead for the Bey's caresses. The pain was indescribable, and at times they would pull his hair and head back so he could see the damage, his back covered with blood. He did cry out for mercy, and when finally they righted him, they whipped him too over his groin, buckling him again in pain. They then spread his legs and, as he himself wrote, "rode me like a horse." Lawrence admitted to feeling "a delicious warmth, probably sexual, was swelling through me." He erected and the men, seeing it, hit him again across the groin with the whip. They splashed him with water and pulled him back to the Bey's bedroom where the Bey called them fools for thinking he would want to touch a bloody mess. He was taken from the bedroom, where one of the youngest, handsomest of the guards was ordered to remain. He was pulled through the streets to an Armenian's house where the Armenian was ordered to clean and bandage him. The soldiers left, one inexplicably whispering in his ear that the door to the house was not locked. From somewhere he found clothes and made his escape, to the indifference of those he passed. There was no explanation as to why he hadn't been killed when the Bey bayoneted him.

This was his first sadomasochistic experience and he had enjoyed it, certainly a revelation to himself. Why he would write about it is a mystery. Why he chose to talk about the incident, later, to Bernard Shaw's wife Charlotte Shaw is strange too in that she had entered into a *mariage blanc* with her husband, refusing penetration.

During this time Allenby took Jerusalem and gave orders for Lawrence to join him. It was in Jerusalem that Lawrence was reunited with Storrs and where Storrs presented him to the man who would make him world famous, Lowell Thomas.

Thomas was a story in himself. A former gold miner, now a newspaper man with a master's degree from Princeton whose former president, Woodrow Wilson, asked him to make a film that would make the war popular to the American public. Later Thomas' lectures showing dashing Bedouins and camels became the talk of America. He took over the Madison Square Gardens for weeks and, combined with his book *With Lawrence in Arabia* he made millions. When someone asked him about Lawrence's purported modesty, Thomas answered, ''Lawrence had a genius for backing *into* the limelight.''

What happened six weeks later was, in my mind, nearly as disgusting as Lawrence's being sodomized. It must be noted that Lawrence had written in his book that prostitution was so immoral for him that he preferred the Bedouins to have sex among themselves, as mentioned. He forbad the English troops he was responsible for from seeking relief with whores. One of them, a young boy, was caught having intercourse with an Arab lad and the lad was ordered to receive, by his peers, 100 lashes that Lawrence reduced to 50. Lawrence decided to turn the British boy over to his captain who was away at the moment. A certain Corporal Driver, responsible for the British boy, begged Lawrence to keep the affair quiet but Lawrence refused. The corporal then had the boy given 60 lashes, 10 more than the Arab, and brought Lawrence, unaware of the punishment, to see the result. Lawrence wrote that he ''was inclined to laugh'' at the bloody mess before his eyes. The boy was forgiven and later proved valiant in battle. This story reminds me of other disgusting incidents: The first concerned the explorer Stanley, as sexually repressed as Lawrence, who got the permission from the English parents of a 14-year-old boy to accompany him to the Middle East where, in front of Stanley, the boy was sodomized by three Arabs (see the chapter on Stanley in my book *Homosexual Heroes*). Afterwards Stanley and Noe, the boy, were taken to prison where the guard hit Noe in the stomach, doubling him over. And, wrote Stanley, he (Stanley) laughed. The second incident concerned Cellini when he was in Paris executing a commission for King François I. The king just happened to visit Cellini's workshop the moment Cellini kicked a helper and lover, age 13, in the balls, doubling the boy up. Both François and Cellini broke out in laughter. (3)

Naturally, by that time Lawrence had seen and experienced, on nearly a daily level, so much death and violence--beginning with his own physical suffering--that he was inured in a way civilized men today cannot even have a notion of. His descent into barbarity was nonetheless heartbreaking.

Heartbreaking too were the deaths of two of his servants, two boys intensely in love with each other. They were inseparable, their hands always intertwined, ''for the happiness of feeling one another,'' Lawrence wrote. One was Daud, and he froze to death one night during a campaign, the other was Farraj who received a bullet in the spine, and because he was unmovable Lawrence drew his pistol to his head, "Daud will be angry with you," said Farraj, his last words before Lawrence pulled the trigger. "Salute him for me." Heartbreaking, intolerable pain impossible to imagine. It was said that only with these two boys and Dahoum could Lawrence be himself. Dahoum seems he have remained at the dig at Carchemish where he died of typhus in 1916.

From here on Lawrence was alone and bereft of love, and would remain so to his death.

As all of my stories evoke the wondrous sharing of knowledge, adventure and physical meshing of males among themselves, from here on I will go faster because there was no more love for Lawrence, just corporal pain and, bluntly, later in civil life, sadomasochistic ejaculation.

Next came the massacre of Tafa, a village slaughtered by 2,000 Turks. I won't go into the abominations except to mention that what struck the Arabs was the number of bayoneted babies strewn seemingly everywhere, the women, their thighs spread and one, heavily pregnant, who had been pinned to a wall upside down, by bayonets. Another child came stumbling towards them, blood gushing from the throat. One of Lawrence's men jumped from his camel and ran towards the child who screamed out, "Don't hit me, Baba!" A child from the man's own family, he took it in his arms where it expired. The man mounted his camel and charged at the retreating 2,000. Lawrence made to stop him but Auda prevented him with his hand. He rode towards the troops who watched him coming, in total silence, as were the Arabs too. Only when he was nearly on them did they open up with machine guns, killing him and his horse. Lawrence gave the *No prisoners* order and the slaughter began. Lawrence wrote that the Turks fought magnificently and that the Arabs were repulsed several times, but in the end "we killed and killed" bashing "in the heads of the fallen and of the animals, as though their death and running blood could slake the agony in our brains." Some of Lawrence's men had not heard the *No prisoners* order and 200 Turks were found roped together. We cannot know what Lawrence would have done had an Arab not been found next to them, taken prisoner during the fighting and despite a wound that would have eventually killed him, he had been pinned "out like a collected insect." "Who did it?" Lawrence asked. The man looked towards the prisoners. As the Arabs opened fire, slaughtering the 200, the man died.

Lawrence and the Arabs were brothers as never before, and as such they moved towards Damascus. On the way they went through Deraa where Lawrence had been sodomized. Most of the Turks had fled but those left had their throats slit, down to those in the Turk infirmary.

His entry into Damascus was met with cheers and crying. The assembly of Arabs that followed was perfect chaos, throwing of chairs,

Lawrence separating Auda from a Druse who tried to kill him, Auda just stopping a man who tried to put a dagger into Lawrence. Lawrence had decided to keep Feisal outside of Damascus for his safety, and Allenby had decided to keep his troops clear of Damascus too, but Lieutenant-General Chauvel, at the head of an Australian army, had entered the day before, so it was technically he the first to liberate Damascus. Lawrence wrote that he did what he could to help those in hospitals, but some patients had been dead so long that their bodies had to be scraped from the floors with shovels. When the commanding doctor screamed his indignation at Lawrence, Lawrence broke into laughter, a tick he had in times of extreme crises, he wrote, and received a slap on the face. It was true that since leaving Deraa he had had three hours of sleep.

This and the slaughter that preceded it, and his eventual failure to give the Arabs the freedom he had promised, made him, Korda so justly relates, an unclean being in his own eyes, something so soiled that no amount of scrubbing would ever cleanse him again.

Allenby arrived the next day. Feisal too, who learned that the Sykes-Picot agreement would be enacted. Lawrence returned to Oxford.

For the love of a boy he would bring freedom to the boy's people, he had written. The reader is encouraged to read more about this unique son of man, as well as his end, if the reader can stomach it. I can't. (8)

JACQUES D'ADELSWÄRD-FERSEN
1880 - 1923

During the time of Jacques d'Adelswärd-Fersen (whom I'll call Fersen from hereon), rich boys often turned to writing poetry to justify their existence, something Byron did. It is extremely difficult to judge their works because in modern times we need a Rosetta Stone to understand what they were trying to reveal to us. The basis for the obscurity were the laws of the land, so severe that one could be pilloried--caged in public, splattered with shit if one were lucky, one's eyes gouged out or throat pierced if one were not--or hanged by the neck until dead--or both, an excellent reason to encipher one's thoughts and lusts. In comparison, the texts from Ancient Greece, 2000 years earlier, are as clear as sparkling Spartan mountain cascades. Fersen was lucky in that France had given up burning boy-lovers since 1791, following the French Revolution, but one was nonetheless forbidden to incite boys to debauch or to debauch minors. There were also laws against public indecency. The police in Paris used this provision of the law as an excuse to raid taverns, brothels, parks, and other hangouts of sexual adventure. Scandal was an ever-hazardous threat, and nobody, absolutely nobody, wanted to be accused of vile sodomy, especially not when one was a noble, or the head of a family, or the father of children, or the director of a factory or enterprise.

Fersen

In the case of Fersen, as for Byron, his taste for boys dated back to boarding-school dormitories, and the remembrance of fresh, young, often virgin bodies, a taste that frequently increased as one aged. While anything was permissible in schools among students, having sex was as illegal then as it is today when adults are involved. In Renaissance Florence boys were bought on the street from age 9, which was also against the law but so prevalent that the adult offender got off with a fine (unless the boy was forced, in which case men could be--and at times were--burned alive).

Born in Paris in 1880, Fersen's grandfather, a Swedish count, founded a steel industry at Longwy in the east of France, which Fersen inherited at age 22, his father having died at age 40, perhaps of yellow fever contracted in Panama, when Fersen was seven. Fersen had a brother, Renold, who died young. Both father and brother were greatly loved by Fersen, if one can judge from the characters in his books, often named Axel after his father, and Renold. Fersen went to Science-Po in Paris, its best school then as today, and the University of Geneva. His literary reputation resides on his oeuvre, ten collections of poems, three novels and the creation of a literary review called *Akademos*.

Fersen

His best friend and lover was Hans de Warren, a school chum with whom he would pickup boys, often directly as they left their *lycées*, at times in parks. The lads were invited home to Fersen's wealthy residence near the Arc de Triomphe after a joyride in the family royal-blue Darracq, driven by a liveried chauffeur. There the boys would be offered cakes and wine, shown Fersen and Warren's extensive collection of pornography, and, thus excited, they would be masturbated and blown. There is no record of anal sex, but the subject would have been avoided even by later police investigators, or referred to in such general terms as to make denial easy, to the relief of the offenders and the questioners. One of the boys confessed that Fersen drew a picture of his penis, and he measured that of another, hard. A third lad said that after inhaling ether and ingesting morphine, Fersen, misty-eyed, proposed that they both go to Venice where he would give the boy half his fortune, and where they would die in a suicide pact.

All of this came out after the incident that brought both Fersen and Warren to trial. Both boys, in their early twenties, organized living tableaux that they put on in front of an audience. The actors in the tableaux were all young boys, from age 7 to 17, the average age being 14. The seven-year-old had an extremely early sexual awakening, thanks to his brothers who were participants, and whose talk and nightly masturbation filled him in on adolescent sex. During the tableaux the boys took poses while poetry was read. The boys, as well as the audience, were made up of the crème of Parisian society, the boys coming from the very best families and schools, the audience being formed of men--but some women--estimated as 70% pederastic. During the tableaux one of the boys would always be naked, his privates covered by gauze if seen frontally, his buttock *au naturel* if lying on a couch or the floor. Afterwards they would retire to the bathroom to clean up. Aroused by their performance, they gratefully allowed the two older boys to masturbate and blow them. Fersen and Warren would also allow themselves to be manipulated until ejaculation.

The séances went on twice a week, Thursdays and Sundays, until the father of the seven-year-old found out and demanded that the police arrest Fersen and Warren, threatening, when they hesitated because of the families involved, to go public if they didn't. They did, but he went public anyway, and the resultant scandal was horrendous. The seven-year-old and his two brothers must have gone through hell at the hand of their daddy, but of this we know nothing.

Fersen was examined by three psychiatrists, one of which *purportedly* diagnosed him with inherited insanity, alcoholism and epilepsy. A physician, Doctor Socquet, found he had scabies (a contagious skin infection caused by mites) and gonorrhea, and the judge questioning him, as well as his clerk, were said to have gone to public baths after each interrogation to avoid contamination (private bathrooms in one's apartment were still rare at the time).

A fictional account of the tableaux, called Black Masses in the press, came out in 1904, written by the pornographer Alphonse Gallais, *Les Mémoires du Baron Jacques*, in which Baron Jacque's mother takes his virginity at an early age (Byron lost his to a maid at age 9). Baron Jacques goes on to deflower his own young boys, copulating with them on his mother's skeleton!

For Fersen's times what he did was highly titillating, and because minors were involved he was sentenced to five months in prison. As he was no longer welcome by family and friends, he exchanged Paris' cloudy skies for sunny Capri. But before we get to his exploits there, perhaps a word on his oeuvre.

In 1902 he published a collection of poems called *L'Hymnaire d'Adonis*, in which we find the poem *Treize Ans*: At age 13, blond with precocious eyes full of desire and emotion, his lips already streetwise, he's in the study hall where all the boys are reading, bent over their books, while only he, in a corner, is going through randy poems by Musset. As the supervisor goes by he hides what he's doing and pretends to be hard at work, but when the coast's clear he brings out his book and, turning into the shadows so as not to be seen, he slips his hand into his pocket where a hole leads to his toy that, lost in licentious thoughts, he fondles for a long, long time. (*Treize ans, blondin aux yeux précoces, Qui disent le désir et l'émoi, Lèvres, ayant je ne sais quoi De mutin, de vicieux, de gosse. Il lit; dans la salle ils sont Tous penchés à écrire un thème, Lui seul dans un coin lit quand même, Des vers de Musset, polissons; Le pion passe, vite il se cache, Semblant travailler avec feu, À quelque devoir nébuleux, Très propre, soigné et sans tache, Puis calmé, le moment d'après, Reprend tout rose sa lecture, Se met à changer de posture, Pour être de l'ombre plus près; Coule ses mains, sans qu'on devine, Dans sa poche percée d'un trou, Et là longuement fait joujou, Rêveur de voluptés félines!*)

Sex was a daily and nightly pastime in boarding schools. Besides his school experiences, Fersen is known to have loved a young British boy from Eton during a summer holiday on the island of Jersey.

In 1904 he wrote a novel entitled *Lord Lillian*, which is about his trial and is dedicated to the judge that collected the information (in France a single judge collects facts for-and-against a person accused of a crime, and is supposed to present the facts, neutrally, to the court. This neutrality rarely takes place and is the cause of hundreds of years of injustice, but the power of the judiciary is such that a new system cannot be adopted).

The main character in Fersen's book is Renold, Lord Lyllian (named after his brother), who lost his adulterous mother and beloved father before the age of 17. He falls into the hands of a certain Skilde (Oscar Wilde), the author of *The Portrait of Miriam Green* (*Dorian Grey*). Skilde farms the boy out to take care of the sexual needs of Skilde's clients but following the suicide of a member of one of Skilde's orgies he flees, while Skilde is imprisoned and condemned to hard labor.

Renold tours the world, going from lover to lover until he meets a Swedish poet Axel Ansen (Axel from his father's name) who unfortunately dies young. Renold goes to Paris where he creates Black Masses with naked choirboys, one of which dies. Fersen has Renold proclaim that the Masses were simply to excite the boys so that they would find shared love among themselves (which is certainly what happened in the case of Fersen in his real life in Paris). Fersen is thought to have put himself into four of his characters, all of whom make love together at some point in the novel, and of course his greatest sexual partner was the poet Axel.

Renold decides to give up boy-love and marries a girl. In real life Fersen had been on the verge of marrying a very rich young lady who, despite his begging to see her, refused him following his trial.

His book *Youth* was dedicated to his very young lover Nino Cesarini, "More beautiful than the light of Rome."

It concerns the painter Robert, age 23, who is in love with Nino, a 16-year-old seminary student. But a priest is also in love with Nino *and* a girl, a girl Nino is in love with. Finally, the girl dies and Nino himself becomes a priest.

He wrote a poem entitled *So Sang Marsyas* which related the true story of his belovèd Nino who, in Venice, met and appreciated a girl, Alexandrine, who liked him so much she followed him to Capri where he bedded her. In the poem Fersen asked, "How many tears must I shed to wash away her kisses?"

In 1909 he published 12 editions of a cultural magazine called *Akademos*, a total of 2,000 pages, that was said to have been about 10% homosexual. It failed after a year.

Le baiser de Narcisse, The Kiss of Narcissus: Again, due to the times, one was cautious in what one wrote, especially if one wished a wide audience. In this book the most daring sentence evokes the hero coming upon a group of youths, whose tunics of transparent linen revealed their young and muscular forms. "Extremely young, he undid his tunic that he let fall to the ground, and in a pose equal to that of a god, he remained still, while the sun spread its golden rays over the mother-of-pearl forms of his flesh. His muscular legs rose like two columns of alabaster to his flat stomach and his precocious virility. He then sang and danced, in his glorious nudity."

The boy in question was Milès, born in Bithynia, the birthplace of Antinous. As a child he was already so beautiful that people turned to watch him pass, "for in those times the people knew how to appreciate beauty and a boy's splendid forms, a time before Antinous, born to please an emperor, and they all exclaimed, This boy is for Zeus, for they knew of the gods' love for earthlings."

The boy is taken as a slave to Athens by the architect Scopas who falls in love with him and frees him but is not given the boy's love in return, and so he dies of despair. The lad, by then 15, poses for the painter Ictinos for a fresco of Ganymede, Zeus' love mate. Milès then travels until he comes to a pond into which he finally sees a boy as beautiful as he. He leans over to kiss the image, his fingers slip ... and the book ends.

Now back to Fersen's life.

Rich but rejected, he withdrew to Capri, noted for being a homosexual refuge since Tiberius withdrew there 2000 years previously. Fersen built a palace, the Villa Lysis, facing Tiberius' Villa Jovis, a neoclassical affair of Ionic columns, an entrance with an atrium, and bedrooms with wondrous views of the palace gardens, the distant sea and Mount Vesuvius. There he surrounded himself with island boys until he was requested to leave when he brought in boys from elsewhere, in competition with the homegrown crop, a loss of income for the lads and their families. The Caprian boys in question have been immortalized by a succession of photographers and painters, their bodies caressed by generations of financially fortunate lovers of boys.

A basement apartment, called the Chinese Room, was dedicated to opium smoking, where Fersen contented himself with up to 40 pipes a day, a huge but supposedly not unheard of quantity for addicts. Opium depresses the urge to have sex, although it can be used to postpone an orgasm, allowing more enjoyment before eventual ejaculation. Taking 40 pipes meant he was having no orgasms at all. It was in the Chinese Room that, in 1923, at age 43, his health failing, he drank a mortal cocktail of cocaine and champagne, certainly entering eternity with an ecstatic Wow!

But we haven't quite reached that point in his life story.

The villa completed, Fersen went off on one of several trips to India and China from where he returned with his baggage full of opium and his head imbued with Hinduism. Because he had been ostracized from Capri, he went to Rome where he met the 14-year-old Nino Casarini, the love of his life, whom he worshipped, as did Hadrian with Antinous, by having the boy immortalized in paintings, sculptures and photos by the greatest homosexual artists of the times, Umberto Brunelleschi, Francesco Ierace, Guglielmo Plüschow and Paul Höcker. With Nino in tow, he returned to the Orient.

Nino

He was able to return to Capri, perhaps because he took on more Caprian boys to care for his villa and grounds, but immediately earned a second ostracism when he published, in 1909, *And the Fire was Extinguished by the Sea*, a tell-all about the mores and quirks of the inhabitants, who recognized themselves. But thanks to his sister, who had married into Roman nobility, he was able to return where, like Tiberius, there were said to have been nightly orgies in his villa and in local grottos. He was again requested to leave, this time from Italy itself.

Nino

Back in Paris he began the magazine *Akademos*, already described. He and Nino became habitués of Parisian gay clubs, which, I can assure the reader from my own experience, had absolutely nothing of the excitement that went on, later in N.Y., at Studio 54. In 1910 Nino, drunk, grievously hurt a young cyclist at the wheel of Fersen's automobile. Both then left for Nice and Porquerolles, a nice town and a beautiful island. Nino was obliged to do his military service, after which he returned to Capri where he and Fersen were still again admitted. Fersen spent a great deal of his time in what a newspaper called his Opiarium. In 1920 he met 15-year-old Corrado Annicelli, the son of a notary on vacation on the island.

Nino

It's true that life is an eternal recommencement, varying only in details, and here too Fersen was lead by the nose by a boy, exactly as Byron

178

had surrendered, at the end of his life, to a 15-year-old Greek lad. Fersen's boy is said to have extracted every gift he could wish for from Fersen, but in the end the boy seems to have genuinely grown to love the man, a lucky break Byron was not to know. The boy certainly had little sexual contact with Fersen, impotent from his opium and cocaine, and Fersen most probably contented himself with gazing at the lad's nudity.

The part played by Nino at the time is not known, although he was there, chauffering man and boy, and he even went to Naples to bring Fersen back to Capri, accompanied by Corrado, when Fersen was too sick to return unaided.

Perhaps Corrado

There he committed suicide, a gold coin was placed on his tongue to pay Charon for his passage over the River Styx, and he was cremated.

Corrado went on to become an appreciated Italian actor (alas, I cannot vouch for the accompanying photo as being of him). He died in 1984.

Nino received shares in the Longwy steel mills, the money Fersen had in his bank accounts, and any money found in the Villa Lysis. Nino had the right to live in the villa until his death. Instead, he went to Rome where he bought a kiosk and opened a bar. He died in 1943.

THE PRINCETON RUB (OR THE FIRST-YEAR-PRINCETON)

DEFINITION

The Oxford English Dictionary came out with this definition of the Princeton Rub, a.k.a. the Princeton-First-Year:

Designating a form of male homosexual activity in which the penis is rubbed against the thighs or stomach of a partner.

This was picked up by the University Press Club. This is what the Club says about itself (I haven't asked for permission, but in my bones I feel these guys are cool): "The University Press Club is a highly selective group of undergraduate students who write professionally for numerous newspapers, magazines and wire services in the northeast. The club was founded in 1900, making it one of the oldest student organizations at Princeton University. Members are chosen through a three-month application process and typically write for a number of papers during their three or four years with the club, filing stories with publications from the *Princeton Packet* to the *New York Times*."

The Club wrote this article, that I'm reproducing in its entirety:

What… is going on? The world's been shaken, and I don't know quite where to begin.

The Oxford English Dictionary, one of the world's renowned comprehensive English dictionaries, has an entry for "Princeton."

And it's really, really, really surprising and erotic and graphic and scaring like walking in on your parents and forever changes "Princeton" in a mind and where did it *come* from?

What am I on about? This:

Princeton, n.

Designating a form of male homosexual activity in which the penis is rubbed against the thighs or stomach of a partner.

Yeah. I don't… No, I don't know what to say. And even more outrageous, the etymologies:

1965 S. FRIEDMAN Totempole *265, I should have known..it would be the Princeton rub or nothing. 1969 W. H. AUDEN in N.Y. Rev. Bks. 27 Mar. 3/4 My guess is that at the back of his mind, lay a daydream of an innocent Eden where children play 'Doctor', so that the acts he really preferred were the most 'brotherly', Plain-Sewing and Princeton-First-Year. 1972 B. RODGERS* Queens' Vernacular *154 Princeton style,..fucking the thighs. 1980* Times Lit. Suppl. *21 Mar. 324/5 'Princeton-First-Year' is a more condescending version of the term 'Princeton Rub'; that is,* coitus contra ventrem. *2004 D. BERGMAN* Violet Hour *iii. 105 He arrives there still a virgin, without even the benefit of the 'Princeton rub'.*

Wait, what's that, Patrick Bateman from *American Psycho*?

MORE ABOUT THE PRINCETON RUB

The Princeton Rub is also daubed the Ivy League Rub, a form of mutual masturbation which is highly enjoyable because the nerve endings of the frenulum just under the glans are stimulated through friction, while the participants are in a position to kiss, in the knowledge that there is no risk at all of the transmission of disease, all the while relieving sexual pressure, a physiological need imposed on the body by millions of years of evolution, the aim being the reproduction of the species, even if, in this case, that aspect is sidestepped. Indeed, other primates like the bonobos regularly have recourse to what is also called frottage, cock rub, sword-fighting, the Princeton-First-Year and the Oxford Style or Oxford Rub. It is an alternative to anal sex and is commonly available to boys who may prefer the warm, enjoyable welcome of the vagina, but without the bother, expense and time needed to convince women to let them take their pleasure. Between males no explanation and no financial expenditures are required, just blissful discharge of accumulated semen.

Princeton, the world's 7th greatest university.

GG-rubbing (genital-to-genital) was popular in Oxford and Cambridge during the last two centuries too, with a great deal of mutual masturbation, less fellatio, but more anal intercourse, as *young* buttocks have been considered more penis-accommodating than those of older men, a belief held since the early Greeks.

Those wishing to encourage phallus-to-phallus sex maintain that it is mutual in the sense that one boy is not ''passive'' (effeminate and degraded), a bottom to the more virile male who is the top. No matter how one wishes to dismiss it, a bottom will always be feminized, the reason why many boys who love anal sex insist on flip-flopping, one cuming in his partner, and then the partner cuming in him. Friction against the prostate is said to offer intense pleasure to some boys, and even *some* heterosexual rent-boys love being fucked for this reason when their johns insist on anal penetration. As in vaginal intercourse, nothing will replace anal sex as the most intimate way possible of becoming close to one's partner. The ultimate step following mutual masturbation, frottage, fellatio and rimming, anal sex is becoming more prevalent today thanks to Internet which shows boys exactly how it's done and the intense pleasure it can procure.

TODAY

In the times in which we live no one will ever know the incidence of homosexuality in today's boarding schools, and no one really cares because the acts are between consenting boys of the same age. The acts may also only be *sexuality* and not *homo*sexuality in the sense that they are merely a discovery of sex itself, or a discovery of how much one is attracted to those of one's sex, or not attracted, or slightly, or what-have-you.

If two lads do agree to share a joint orgasm, the Princeton Rub is the best form because the enjoyment engendered is more fulfilling than staying in one's own corner, ejaculating into airy nothingness. It's exciting because it's sexual, which is always an adventure.

The boys, naked *de préférence*, can perform in dozens of ways, one lying on his partner, stomach against stomach, the glans always wondrously sensitive, rubbing against each other. The shaft can be inserted between the thighs, or one boy can mount the reclined back, his chest just below the shoulder blades of his friend, his penis inserted between the ass cheeks, but with no anal penetration. He can lean over and kiss the boy who is grinding his own cock into the sheets, or the boy above can make a sheath with his hand for the boy under him to fuck, or he can jerk off the boy's cock for him, or they can lie side by side, etc., etc., etc.

Once they know each other in such a way they can masturbate together or separately in each other's presence. They can share girls together or both a single girl, encouraging each other on by gently fondling the other's ass or balls.

The best advice concerning homosexuality, heterosexuality or omnisexual comes from Marlon Brando who said that one must simply follow one's erect cock, going in whatever direction its pointing to. It *never* makes a mistake.

Nature pushes us to sexual release. It is a gift to be shared, the body's gift to the boy it houses. A miracle to be called upon *without* moderation. When it's had enough, the body will let its user know. Feed your body well, exercise it well, educated its brain, and let its intimate parts help you to make new friends.

To you all, many, many *pl & opt C.*

SOURCES

(1) See my book *TROY*.
(2) Much more in my book *Greek Homosexuality*.
(3) For much more, see my book *Cellini*.
(4) Much more in my book *Caravaggio*.
(5) Much more in my book *Roman Homosexuality*.
(6) More can be found in my book *Gay Genius*.
(7) Much more in my book *Renaissance Homosexuality*.
(8) See my book *Homosexual Heroes*.

The major sources for the Greek segment of this book are the following:

<u>Aelianus</u> was a Roman author and teacher of rhetoric who spoke and wrote in Greek.

<u>Aeschylus</u>, of whom 7 out of perhaps 90 plays have survived. His gravestone celebrated his heroism during the victory against the Persians at Marathon and *not his plays*, proof of the extraordinary importance of Greek survival against the barbarians (sadly, he lost his brother at Marathon). He is said to have been a deeply religious person, dedicated to Zeus. As a boy he worked in a vineyard until Dionysus visited him in a dream and directed him to write plays. One of his plays supposedly divulged too much about the Eleusinian Mysteries and he was nearly stoned to death by the audience. He had to stand trial but pleaded ignorance. He got off when the judges learned of the death of his brother at Marathon and when Aeschylus showed the wounds he and a second brother had received at Marathon too, the second brother left with but a stump in place of his hand. In one of his later plays, Pericles was part of the chorus. The subjects of his plays often concerned Troy and the Persian Wars, Marathon, Salamis and Xerxes (Xerxes is accused of losing the war due to hubris; his building of the bridge over the Hellespont was a show of arrogance the gods found unacceptable). In *Seven against Thebes* he too tells about Oedipus' two sons. This time the boys agree to become kings of Thebes on alternate years. Naturally, when the time comes for them to change places the king in place refuses, which leads to both boys killing each other. *Agamemnon* is an excellent retelling of the Trojan War, as Agamemnon sails home to be murdered by his wife Clytemnestra. In *The Libation Bearers* Agamemnon's boy Orestes returns home to destroy his father's assassins, Clytemnestra and her lover Aegisthus. In *The Eumenides* (the Kindly Spirits) Orestes is chased by the Furies for having killed his mother. He takes shelter with Apollo who decides, with Athena, to try the boy before a court. The vote is a

tie, but Athena, preaching the importance of reason and understanding, acquits him. She then changes the terrible Furies into sweet Eumenides.

<u>Anacreon</u> was born in 582 B.C. and was known for his drinking songs.

<u>Andocides</u> was implicated in the Hermes scandal and saved his skin by turning against Alcibiades in a speech that has come down to us called, what else?, *Against Alcibiades*.

<u>Aristophanes</u>, my preferred playwright, is, naturally, the father of comedy. He wrote perhaps 40 plays of which 11 remain. He was feared by all: Plato states that it was his play *The Clouds* the root of the trial that cost Socrates his life. Nearly nothing is known about him other than what he himself revealed in his works. Playwrights were obliged to be conservative because part of each play was funded by a wealthy citizen, an honor for the citizen and a caveat for the author. He was an exponent of make-love-not-war who saw his country go from its wonderful defeat of the Persians to its end at the hands of the Spartans. Along with Alcibiades and Socrates, Aristophanes is featured in Plato's *The Symposium* in which he is gently mocked, proof that he was considered, even by those he poked fun at, as affable. *The Acharnians* highlights the troubles the Athenians went through after the death of Pericles and their defeat at the hands of Sparta. *The Peace* focuses on the Peace of Nicias. *Lysistrata* tells about the plight of women trying to bring about peace in order to prevent the sacrifice of their sons during war, occasioning the world's first sex strike. When Athens lost its freedom to Sparta, Aristophanes stopped writing plays.

<u>Athenaeus</u> lived in the times of Marcus Aurelius. His *Deipnosopistae* is a banquet conversation *à la Platon* during which conversations on every possible subject took place, filling fifteen books that have come down to us.

<u>Bion</u> was a Greek philosopher known for his diatribes, satires and attacks on religion. He lived around 300 B.C.

<u>Cicero</u> was born in 106 B.C. and murdered by Mark Antony in 43 B.C. Michael Grant said it all when he wrote, ''the influence of Cicero upon the history of European literature and ideas greatly exceeds that of any other prose writer in any language.''

<u>Cornelius Nepos</u> was a Roman friend of Cicero. Most of what he wrote was lost, so what we know comes through passages of his works in the books of other historians.

<u>Ctesias</u> was a Greek historian from Anatolian Caria, and the physican of Artaxerxes, whom he accompanied in his war against his brother Cyrus the Younger. He wrote a book on India, *Indica* and Persia, *Persica*. The fragments we have of his writing come to us through Diodorus Siculus and Plutarch.

<u>Diodorus Siculus</u> lived around 50 B.C. and wrote *Historical Library*, consisting of forty volumes.

Diogenes of Sinope (aka Diogenes the Cynic) comes to use through extracts of his writing passed on by others, as nothing he wrote has survived. He had a truly remarkable life, at first imprisoned for debasing the coins his father, a banker, minted. Afterwards he pled poverty, sleeping in a huge ceramic jar, walking the streets of Athens during the day with a lighted lamp, saying he was in search of an honest man, and teasing Plato by noisily eating through his lectures (later Plato claimed he was "a Socrates gone mad".) On a voyage he was captured and sold as a slave in Crete to a Corinthian who was so entranced by his intelligence that he made him his sons' teacher. It was in his master's household that he grew old and died. Plutarch tells us he met Alexander the Great while Diogenes was staring at a pile of bones. In answer to Alexander's question he said he was searching for the bones of Alexander's father, but could not distinguish them from those of a slave. To which Alexander supposedly said that if he couldn't be Alexander he would choose to be Diogenes. He was the first man ever to claim to be "a citizen of the world." He urinated on people, defecated where he would and masturbated in public, about which he said, "If only I could banish hunger by rubbing my belly." The word cynic meant dog-like, and when someone questioned him about it he said he too was dog-like because he licked those who helped him, barked at those who didn't, and bit his enemies. Rogers and Hart wrote these lyrics about him: There was an old zany/who lived in a tub; he had so many flea-bites/he didn't know where to rub.

Eupolis lived around 430 B.C. An Athenian poet who wrote during the Peloponnesian Wars.

Euripides may have written 90 plays of which 18 survive. His approach was a study of the inner lives of his personages, the predecessor of Shakespeare. Due to his stance on certain subjects, he thought it best to leave Athens voluntarily rather than suffer an end similar to that of Socrates. An example: "I would prefer to stand three times to confront my enemies in battle rather than bear a single child!" He was born on the island of Salamis, of Persian-War fame; in fact he was born on the very day of the battle. His youth was spent in athletics and dance. Due to bad marriages with unfaithful wives, he withdrew to Salamis where he wrote while contemplating sea and sky. When Sparta defeated Athens in war, it did not destroy the city-state: Plutarch states that this was thanks to one of Euripides' plays, *Electra*, put on for the Spartans in Athens, a play they found so wonderful that they proclaimed that it would be barbarous to destroy a city capable of engendering men of the quality of Euripides. (The real reason was to preserve the city that had twice saved Greece from Persian victory.) Euripides was known for his love of Agathon, a youth praised for his beauty as well as for his culture, and would later become a playwright. Aristophanes mocked Euripides for loving Agathon long after he had left his boyhood behind him. (Remember, not everyone followed boy-love to the letter. The idea of men loving boys until they grew whiskers did not always hold true. Boys grown "old" could shave their chins and butts; some men just preferred other men, hairy or not; most men impregnated boys but other men adored being penetrated.) Plato says that Agathon had polished manners, wealth, wisdom and dispensed hospitality with ease and refinement.

Herodotus was also contemporary to the events that interest us here. Cicero called him the Father of History, while Plutarch wrote that he was the Father of Lies. His masterpiece is *The Histories*, considered a chef-d'oeuvre, a work that the gods have preserved intact right up to our own day, a divine intervention that would not have surprised a believer like Herodotus (it's also a book I reread every year). Part of his work may have been derived from other sources (what historian's work isn't?) and the facts rearranged in an effort to give them dramatic force and please an audience. Much of what he did was based on oral histories, many of which themselves were based on early folk tales, highly suspect, naturally, in all their details. Aristophanes made fun of segments of his work and Thucydides called Herodotus a storyteller. Surprisingly little is known about his own life. For example, he writes lovingly about Samos, leading some to believe that he may have spent his youth there. Born near Ionia, he wrote in that dialect, learning it perhaps on Samos. He was his own best publicist, taking his works to festivals and games, such as the Olympic Games, and reading them to the spectators. As I've said, many people doubt that he actually went where he said he went and saw what he said he saw. But the same was true of Marco Polo who causes disbelief to this day simply because he never mentioned eating noodles in China or seeing the Great Wall or even drinking Chinese tea. But no historian, then as now, can write a book on ancient occurrences without referring to Herodotus' observations. An amusing example of recent discoveries that give credence to Herodotus is this: Herodotus wrote about a kind of giant ant, the size of a fox, living in India, in the desert, that dug up gold. This was ridiculed until the French ethnologist Peissel came upon a marmot living in today's Pakistan that burrows in the sand and has for generations brought wealth to the region by bringing up gold from its burrows. Peissel suggests that the original confusion came from the fact that the Persian word for marmot was similar to the word for mountain ant.

Isocrate was a student of Socrates who wrote a speech in the defense of Alcibiades during a trial that took place after his death.

Lysias was extremely wealthy and contemporary with Alcibiades. He founded a new profession, logographer, which consisted of writing speeches delivered in law courts. One of his speeches was *Against Andocides*, another was *Against Alcibiades*.

<u>Mimnermus</u> was born in Ionian Smyrna around 630 B.C. He wrote short love poems suitable for performance at drinking parties.

<u>Myron of Priene</u> is the author of a historical account of the First Messenian War.

<u>Pausanias</u>, a Greek historian and geographer, famous for his *Description of Greece*. He was contemporary with Hadrian and Marcus Aurelius. He's noted as being someone interested in everything, careful in his writing and scrupulously honest.

<u>Phanocles</u> lived during the time of Alexander the Great. He was the author of a poem on boy-love that described the love of Orpheus for Calais, and his death at the hands of Thracian women.

<u>Philemon</u> lived to be a hundred but alas only fragments of his works remain. He must have been very popular as he won numerous victories as a poet and playwright.

<u>Pindar</u>'s great love was Theoxenus of Tenodos about whom he wrote: "Whosoever, once he has seen the rays flashing from the eyes of Theoxenus, and is not shattered by the waves of desire, has a black heart forged of a cold flame. Like wax of the sacred bees, I melt when I look at the young limbs of boys." He lived around 500 B.C. and celebrated the Greek victories against the Persians at Salamis and Plataea. His home in Thebes became a must for his devotees.

<u>Plato</u> was a major source for this book, along with Xenophon, Thucydides and Plutarch. Plato's most famous work is the Allegory of the Cave. Humans in the cave have no other reality than the shadows they see on the walls. If they looked around they could see what was casting the shadows and by doing so gain additional knowledge. If they left the cave they would discover the sun, analogous to truth. If those who saw the sun reentered the cave and told the others, they would not be believed. There are thusly different levels of reality that only the wisest are able to see; the others remain ignorant. It's basically thanks to Plato and Xenophon that we know what we do about Socrates. Plato's perfect republic is ruled by the best (an aristocracy), headed by a philosopher king who guides his people thanks to his wisdom and reason. An inferior form of government, one that comes after an aristocracy, is a timocracy, ruled by the honorable. A timocracy is in the hands of a warrior class. Plato has Sparta in mind, but it's unclear how he could have found this form of government better than, for example, a democracy. The problem may be that we know, in reality, so little about Sparta. Next comes an oligarchy based on wealth, followed by a democracy, rule by just anyone and everyone. This degenerates into a tyranny, meaning a government of oppression, because of the conflict between the rich and the poor in a democracy.

<u>Plutarch</u> was born near Delphi around 46 A.D. to a wealthy family. He was married, and a letter to his wife even exists to this day. He had sons, the

exact number unknown. He studied mathematics and philosophy in Athens and was known to have visited most of the major Greek sites mentioned in this book, as well as Rome. He personally knew the Emperors Trajan and Hadrian, and became a Roman citizen. He was a high priest at Delphi and his duty consisted of interpreting the auguries of the Pythoness (no mean task). He wrote the *Lives of the Emperors* but alas only two of the lesser emperors survive. Another verily monumental work was *Parallel Lives of Greeks and Romans* of which twenty-three exist. His interest was the destinies of his subjects, how they made their way through the meanders of life. I too have a passionate interest in how men strive their wholes lives for success, only to be crushed, like Alcibiades, like Pericles, at the end. In explanation of his oeuvre Plutarch wrote that what interested him was not history but lives, and the Jekyll/Hyde struggle of virtue versus vice. A small jest, he went on, often reveals more than battles during which thousands die. His writings on Sparta, alongside those of Xenophon, are nearly all we possess concerning that extraordinary city-state. His major biographies are the *Life of Alexander* and the *Life of Julius Caesar*. Amusingly, Plutarch wrote a scathing review of Herodotus' work in which he stated that the great historian was fanatically biased in favor of the Greeks who could do, according to Herodotus, no wrong.

No gratitude can ever be enough for what this man has given us, although in the case of the Greeks we must never forget that he was writing *500 years after the events*.

Polybius was a Greek historian born in Arcadia around 200 B.C. His work describes the rise of the Roman Republic and he is known for his ideas on the separation of powers in government.

Polyenus was a Macedonian known as a rhetorician and for his books on war strategies.

Simonides of Ceos was a Greek poet born about 550 B.C. Besides his poems, he added four letters to the Greek alphabet.

Sophocles was the author of 123 plays of which 7 remain, notably *Oedipus* and *Antigone*. An Athenian born to a rich family just before the Battle of Marathon, he was a firm supporter of Pericles. He fought alongside Pericles against Samos when the island attempted to become autonomous from Athens. He was elected as a magistrate during the Sicilian Expedition led by Alcibiades, and given for function the goal of finding out why the expedition had ended disastrously. Sophocles was always ready and willing to succumb to the charms of boys. Plutarch tells us that even at age 65 ''he led a handsome boy outside the city walls to have his way with him. He spread the boy's poor himation--a rectangular piece of cloth thrown over the left shoulder that drapes the body--upon the ground. To cover them both he spread his rich cloak. After Sophocles took his pleasure the boy took the cloak and left the himation for Sophocles. This misadventure was eventually known to all.'' He died at 90, some say while reciting a very long tirade from *Antigone* because he hadn't paused to take a breath. Another version has him choking on grapes, and a final one has him dying of happiness after winning the equivalent of our Oscar at a festival. The first of his trilogy--called the Theban plays--is *Oedipus the King*. Here the baby Oedipus--in a plot that goes back to Priam and Paris at the founding of Troy--is handed over to a servant to be killed in order to prevent the accomplishment of an oracle, an oracle stating that he will kill his father and marry his mother. He does both after solving the riddle of the sphinx (which creature becomes four-footed, then two-footed and finally three-footed?). His mother, when she finds out she's been bedding her own son, commits suicide and Oedipus blinds himself. In *Oedipus at Colonus* Oedipus dies and we learn more about his children Antigone, Polyneices and Eteocles. In *Antigone* Polyneices is accused of treason and killed. His body is thrown outside the city walls and the king forbids its burial, under pain of death. Antigone does so anyway and, faced with death, she commits suicide, followed by the king's son who was going to wed her, followed by the king's wife who couldn't face losing her precious son. (Whew!)

Theocritus was a Sicilian and lived around 270 B.C. In his 7th Idyll Aratus is passionately in love with a lad. His 12th Idyll refers to Diocles who died saving the life of Philolaus, the boy he loved, and in whose honor kissing contests were held every spring at his tomb. In his 23rd Idyll a lover commits suicide because of unrequited love, warning his belovèd that one day he too will burn and weep for a cruel boy. Before hanging himself the lover kissed the doorpost from which he would attach the noose. The boy treated the corpse with disdain and went off to the gymnasium for a swim where a statue of Eros fell on him, coloring the water with his blood. In his 29th Idyll a lover warns his belovèd that he too will age and his beauty will lose its freshness. He is therefore advised to show more kindness as ''you will one day be desperate for a beautiful young man's attentions.'' Although lads are often disappointing, it is impossible not to fall madly in love with them. In the 30th Idyll the poet states that when a man grows old he should keep a distance from boys, but in his heart he knows that the only alternative to loving a boy is simply to cease to exist.

Theognis was born around 550 B.C. His poems consist of maxims and advice as to how to live life. Fortunately, a great deal of his work has come down to us, most of which is dedicated to his belovèd, the handsome Cyrnus.

Thucydides was an Athenian general and historian, contemporary with the events he described. What he wrote was based on what actually happened; there was no extrapolating; no divine intervention on the part of the gods as was the case with Plutarch. An example of this was his observation that birds and animals that ate plague victims died as a result, leading him to conclude that the disease had a natural rather than supernatural cause. His description of the plague has never been equaled, the plague that he himself caught while participating in the Peloponnesian War. He is thought to have died in 411 B.C., the date at which his writing suddenly stops. He admired Pericles and democracy but not the radical form found in Athens.

Tyrtaeus, a rare Spartan writer, left us an account of the Second Messenian War. The purpose of his poetry was to inspire Spartan support of the Spartan state. Athenians claimed he was of Athenian birth. Pausanias maintained that the Athenians had sent him to Sparta as an insult, because he was both crazy, lame and had one eye. Herodotus wrote that he was only one of two foreigners to be given Spartan citizenship.

Xenophon, born near Athens in 430 B.C., was a historian and general. His masterpieces are *The Peloponnesian Wars* and *Anabasis*. He loved Sparta and served under Spartan generals during the Persian Wars. Like the Spartans, he believed in oligarchic rule, rule by the few, be they the most intelligent or wealthy or militarily acute. He spent a great deal of time in Persia alongside Cyrus the Younger who raised an army, among whom were Xenophon's 10,000 and other mercenaries (all of which is the subject of *Anabasis*). After Cyrus' death Xenophon and his ten thousand made their way back home, the breathtaking account of which ends his *Anabasis*. The Athenians exiled him when he fought with the Spartans against Athens but the Spartans offered him an estate where he wrote his works. His banishment may have been revoked thanks to his son Gryllus who brilliantly fought and died for Athens.

Other Sources for the book as well as sources for the Greek segment:
Abbott Jacob, *History of Pyrrhus*, 2009.
Ady, Cecilia, *A History of Milan under the Sforza*, 1907.
Aldrich and Wotherspoon, *Who's Who in Gay and Lesbian History*, 2001.
Aristophanes, Bantam Drama, 1962.
Baglione, *Caravaggio*, circa 1600.
Baker Simon, *Ancient Rome*, 2006.
Barber, Stanley, *Alexandros*, 2010.
Beachy, Robert, *Gay Berlin*, 2014. Marvelous.
Bellori, *Caravaggio*, circa 1600.
Bergreen, Laurence, *Over the Edge of the World. Magellan.* 2003.
Bicheno, Hugh, *Vendetta*, 2007.
Bramly, Serge, *Leonardo*, 1988. A wonderful book.
Bury and Meiggs, *A History of Greece*, 1975.
Calimach, Andrew, *Lover's Legends*, 2002.
Carpenter, Edward, *The Intermediate Sex*, 1912,
Cawthorne, Nigel, *Sex Lives of the Popes*, 1996.

Cellini, Benvenuto, *The Autobiography of Benvenuto Cellini*.
Ceram, C.W., *Gods, Graves and Scholars*, 1951.
Cooper, John, *The Queen's Agent*, 2011.
Crompton, Louis, *Byron and Greek Love*, 1985.
Curtis Cate, *Friedrich Nietzsche*, 2002.
Davidson, James, *Courtesans and Fishcakes*, 1998.
Davidson, James, *The Greeks and Greek Love*, 2007.
Davis, John Paul, *The Gothic King, Henry III*, 2013.
Dover K.J. *Greek Homosexuality*, 1978.
Duby, George, *William Marshal*, 1985.
Eisler, Benita, *BYRON Child of Passion, Fool of Fame*, 2000. Wonderful.
Everitt Anthony, *Augustus*, 2006.
Everitt Anthony, *Cicero*, 2001.
Everitt, Anthony, *Hadrian*, 2009.
Fagles, Robert, *The Iliad*, 1990.
Forellino, Antonio, *Michelangelo*, 2005. Beautiful reproductions.
Frieda, Leonie, *Catherine de Medici*, 2003. Wonderful.
Gathorne-Hardy, Jonathan, *The Public School Phenomenon*, 1977.
Gayford, Martin, *Michelangelo*, 2013. A beautiful book.
Gillingham, John, *Richard the Lionheart*, 1978.
Goldsworthy Adrian, *Caesar*, 2006
Goldsworthy Adrian, *The Fall of Carthage*, 2000.
Goodman Rob and Soni Jimmy, *Rome's Last Citizen*, 2012.
Graham-Dixon, Andrew, *Caravaggio* 2010. Fabulous.
Grant Michael, *History of Rome*, 1978.
Graves, Robert, *Greek Myths*, 1955.
Grazia, Sebastian de, *Machiavelli in Hell*, 1989.
Guicciardini, *Storie fiorentine (History of Florence)*, 1509. Essential.
Halperin David M. *One Hundred Years of Homosexuality*, 1990.
Harris Robert, *Imperium*, 2006.
Herodotus, *The Histories*, Penguin Classics.
Hesiod and Theognis, Penguin Classics, 1973.
Hibbert, Christopher, *Florence, the Biography of a City,* 1993.
Hibbert, Christopher, *The Borgias and Their Enemies*, 2009.
Hibbert, Christopher, *The Rise and Fall of the House of Medici*, 1974.
Hicks, Michael, *Richard III*, 2000.
Hine, Daryl, *Puerilities*, 2001.
Hochschild, Adam, *King Leopold's Ghost*, 1999.
Holland Tom, *Rubicon*, 2003.
Hughes Robert, *Rome*, 2011.
Hughes-Hallett, *Heroes*, 2004.
Hughes, Robert, *The Fatal Shore*, 1987.
Hutchinson, Robert, *Elizabeth's Spy Master*, 2006.

Hutchinson, Robert, *House of Treason*, 2009.
Hutchinson, Robert, *Thomas Cromwell*, 2007.
Jack Belinda, *Beatrice's Spell*, 2004.
Johnson, Marion, *The Borgias*, 1981.
Kanfer, Stefan, *Marlon Brando*, 2008.
Köhler, Joachim, *Zarathustra's Secret*, 1989.
Korda, Michael, *HERO The Life and Legend of Lawrence of Arabia*, 2010.
Lacey, Robert, *Henry VIII*, 1972.
Lacy, Robert, *Sir Walter Ralegh*, 1973.
Lambert, Gilles *Caravaggio*, 2007.
Landucci, Luca, *A Florentine Diary*, around 1500, a vital source.
Lev, Elizabeth, *The Tigress of Forli*, 2011. Wonderfully written.
Levy, Buddy, *Conquistador*, 2009.
Levy, Buddy, *River of Darkness*, 2011. Fabulous.
Lévy, *Edmond, Sparte, 1979.*
Lewis, Bernard, *The Assassins*, 1967.
Livy, *Rome and the Mediterranean*
Livy, *The War with Hannibal.*
Lubkin, Gregory, *A Renaissance Court*, 1994.
Lyons, Mathew, *The Favourite*, 2011.
Mackay, James, *In My End is My Beginning, Mary Queen of Scots*, 1999.
Mallett, Michael and Christine Shaw, *The Italian Wars 1494-1559.*
Malye, Jean, *La Véritable Histore d'Alcibiade*, 2009.
Manchester, William, *A World Lit Only By Fire*, 1993.
Mancini, *Caravaggio*, circa 1600.
Marchand, Leslie, *Byron*, 1971.
Martines, Lauro, *April Blood-Florence and the Plot against the Medici*, 2003.
Matyszak, Philip, *The Mithridates the Great*, 2008.
Maugham, Robin, *Escape from the Shadows*, 1972.
McLynn, Frank, *Richard and John, Kings of War*, 2007. Fabulous.
McLynn, *Marcus Aurelius*, 2009.
Meier, Christian, *Caesar*, 1996.
Meyer, G.J. *The Borgias, The Hidden History*, 2013.
Meyer, G.J. *The Tudors*, 2010.
Meyer, Jack, *Alcibiades*, 2009.
Miles Richard, *Ancient Worlds*, 2010.
Miles Richard, *Carthage Must be Destroyed*, 2010.
Miller, David, *Richard the Lionheart*, 2003.
Minichiello, Victor and John Scott, *Male Sex Work and Society*, 2014.
Moore Lucy, *Amphibious Thing*, 2000.
Mortimer, Ian, 1415, *Henry V's Year of Glory*, 2009.
Nicholl, Charles, *The Reckoning*, 2002.
Noel, Gerard, *The Renaissance Popes*, 2006.

Opper Thorsten, *Hadrian*, 2008.
Opper, Thorsten, *Hadrian, Empire and Conflict*, 2008.
Parker, Derek, *Cellini*, 2003, the book is beautifully written.
Payne, Robert and Nihita Romanoff, *Ivan the Terrible*, 2002.
Pernot, Michel, *Henri III, Le Roi Décrié*, 2013, Excellent book.
Peyrefitte, Roger, *Alexandre*, 1979.
Plutarch's Lives, Modern Library.
Pollard, .J., *Warwick the Kingmaker*, 2007.
Polybius, *The Histories*.
Read, Piers Paul, *The Templars*, 1999.
Reed, Jeremy, *The Dilly*, 2014.
Reid, B.L., *The Lives of Roger Casement*, 1976.
Renucci Pierre, *Caligula*, 2000.
Reston, James, *Warriors of God, Richard and the Crusades*, 2001.
Rice, Edward, *Captain Sir Richard Francis Burton*, 1990.
Ridley, Jasper, *The Tudor Age*, 1998.
Robb, Peter, M – *The Man Who Became Caravaggio*, 1998.
Robb, Peter, *Street Fight in Naples*, 2010.
Rocco, Antonio, *Alcibiade Enfant à l'Ecole*, 1630.
Rocke, Michael, *Forbidden Friendships*, 1996. Fabulous/indispensible.
Romans Grecs et Latin, Gallimard, 1958.
Ross, Charles, *Richard III*, 1981.
Rouse, W.H.D., Homer's *The Iliad*, 1938.
Royle, Trevor, *Fighting Mac, The Downfall of Sir Hector Macdonald*.
Ruggiero, Guido, *The Boundaries of Eros*, 1985.
Sabatini, Rafael, *The Life of Cesare Borgia*, 1920.
Saslow, James, *Ganymede in the Renaissance*, 1986.
Schiff, Stacy, *Cleopatra*, 2010.
Setz, Wolfram, *The Sins of the Cities of the Plain*, 1881.
Seward, Desmond, *Caravaggio – A Passionate Life*, 1998.
Simonetta, Marcello, *The Montefeltro Conspiracy*, 2008. Wonderful.
Skidmore, Chris, *Death and the Virgin*, 2010.
Soares, André, *The Life of Ramon Novarro*, 2010.
Solnon, Jean-Fançois, *Henry III*, 1996.
Stirling, Stuart, *Pizarro Conqueror of the Inca*, 2005.
Strathern, Paul, *The Medici, Godfathers of the Renaissance*, 2003. Superb.
Strauss Barry, *The Spartacus War*, 2009.
Stuart, Stirling, *Pizarro - Conqueror of the Inca*, 2005.
Suetonius, *The Twelve Caesar.s*
Tacitus, *The Annals of Imperial Rome*.
Tacitus, *The Histories*.
Terry, Paul, *In Search of Captain Moonlite*, 2013.
Thucydides, *The Peloponnesian War*, Penguin Classics.

Tibullus, *The Elegies of Tibullus*, translated by Theodore C. Williams
Turner, Ralph, *Eleanor of Aquitaine*, 2009.
Unger Miles, *Magnifico, The Brilliant Life and Violent Time.s*
Unger, Miles, *Machiavelli*, 2008.
Vasari, We would know next to nothing if it were not for him.
Vernant, Jean-Pierre, *Mortals and Immortals*, 1991.
Virgil, *The Aeneid*, Everyman's Library, Knopf, 1907.
Viroli, Maurizio, *Niccolo's Smile, A Biography of Machiavelli*, 1998.
Ward-Perkins Bryan, *The Fall of Rome*, 2005
Warren, W.L., *Henry II*, 1973.
Weir, Alison, *Eleanor of Aquitaine*, 1999. Weir is a fabulous writer.
Weir, Alison, *Mary, Queen of Scots*, 2003.
Weir, Alison, *The Wars of the Roses*, 1995.
Wheaton James, *Spartacus*, 2011.
Wikipedia: Research today is impossible without the aid of this monument.
Williams Craig A. *Roman Homosexuality*, 2010.
Williams John, *Augustus*, 1972.
Wilson, Derek, *The Uncrowned Kings of England*, 2005.
Worthington, Ian, *Philip II of Macedonia*, 2008.
Wright, Ed, *History's Greatest Scandals*, 2006.
Wroe, Ann, *Perkin, A Story of Deception*, 2003. Fabulous
Xenophon, *A History of My Time*s, Penguin Classics.
Xenophon, *The Persian Expedition*, 1949.

The major sources for the Roman segment of this book are the following:

<u>Appian</u>, who lived during the reigns of Trajan and Hadrian, was a Roman historian of Greek origin. He was a friend of Fronto, Marcus Aurelius' tutor and, perhaps, lover. He left his book, *Roman History*, which describes, among other events, the Roman civil wars.

<u>Ausonius</u> was a Latin poet and teacher of rhetoric, around 350 B.C.

<u>Cassius Dio</u>, 155 A.D. to 235 A.D., was a noted historian who wrote in Greek and published a history of Rome in 80 volumes, many of which have survived, giving modern historians a detailed look into his times.

<u>Diogenes of Sinope</u> was a Greek philosopher alive around 300 B.C. A totally exceptional personage, he was said to sleep in a large ceramic jar, to make a virtue of poverty, to having disputed everything Plato said about Socrates and to have mocked Alexander the Great who, meeting him, said ''If I had my life to live over, it would be as Diogenes.'' Diogenes answered, ''If I had my life to live over, it would be as Diogenes.'' Nothing of what he wrote survived, but we know about him thanks to others.

<u>Herodian</u> wrote a history of Greece entitled *History of the Empire from the Death of Marcus*, in eight books. Thanks to him we learn a great deal about Elagabalus.

Josephus, 37 A.D. to around 100 A.D., was a historian born in Jerusalem. He fought against the Romans and was captured by Vespasian who kept him as his interpreter and, later, Josephus even assumed the emperor's family name, becoming a citizen (Titus Flavius Josephus). A Jew, he turned against his people and helped Vespasian's son Titus to loot the Second Temple. His works include *The Jewish War* and *Antiquities of the Jews*.

Juvenal was a satirical poet who wrote *Satires*.

Lucan (Marcus Annaeus Lucanus) lived from 39 A.D. to 65 A.D., a short life due to his being ordered by Nero to commit suicide because of his role in the treasonous Piso conspiracy. In hopes of a pardon, he implicated his mother among others, all of whom followed him in death. He was a poet, a close friend of Nero until the emperor grew tired of him and his poetry, after which Lucan's writing became insulting, insults Nero was said to have ignored.

Memmius was an orator and poet, and friend of Pompey but eventually went over to Caesar.

Pliny the Elder was a Roman historian, philosopher and general, and a friend of Vespasian. He wrote *Naturalis Historia*. He died trying to rescue and friend and his family who were themselves trying to escape from the eruption of Vesuvius which destroyed their city, Herculaneum.

Pliny the Younger was the Elder's nephew. He too witnessed the explosion of Vesuvius. He was a lawyer and a letter writer, many of which remain, vital historical sources of the times. His letters concerning Trajan are of special importance. Under Trajan he worked side by side with Suetonius.

Polybius, around 200 B.C. to 118 B.C. was a Greek historian whose *The Histories* covered the period from 264 to 146 B.C. He was a friend of Scipio Africanus. He details the ascent to empire of Rome, and was present at the destruction of Carthage.

Sallust was a Roman historian and politician, 86 B.C. to about 35 B.C. One of his works concerned Catiline and he wrote *Histories* of which only fragments remain.

Suetonius (Gaius Suetonius Tranquillus) lived around 69 A.D. to 123 A.D. He was a truly great Roman historian known for his *Twelve Caesars*, his only extant work. Pliny the Younger says that he was studious and totally dedicated to writing. He was highly favored by both Trajan, under whom he served as his secretary, and Hadrian who fired him for having an affair with the Empress Vibia Sabina.

Seneca (Lucius Annaeus Seneca) lived around 4 B.C. to 65 A.D. He was the advisor of Caligula, Claudius and Nero who forced him to commit suicide for supposedly planning his overthrow. He is known for his philosophical essays, letters and tragedies.

<u>Tacitus</u>, around 56 A.D. to 117 A.D., was a historian who wrote *Annals* and *Histories*, concerning Tiberius, Claudius, Nero and the Year of the Four Emperors. He is known for his insights into the psychology of his subjects.

<u>Tibullus</u> died in 19 B.C. at the age of 36 but I've not learned how. He was a Latin poet who lost most of his estate to the confiscations of Marc Antony and Augustus. Why, I know not.

Other Sources for the roman segment:

Abbott Jacob, *History of Pyrrhus*, 2009
Baker Simon, *Ancient Rome*, 2006
Everitt Anthony, *Cicero*, 2001
Everitt Anthony, *Augustus*, 2006
Everitt Anthony, *Hadrian*, 2009
Goldsworthy Adrian, *The Fall of Carthage*, 2000
Goldsworthy Adrian, *Caesar*, 2006
Goodman Rob and Soni Jimmy, *Rome's Last Citizen*, 2012
Grant Michael, *History of Rome*, 1978
Harris Robert, *Imperium*, 2006
Holland Tom, *Rubicon*, 2003
Hughes Robert, *Rome*, 2011
Livy, *Rome and the Mediterranean*
Livy, *The War with Hannibal*
Matyszak Philip, *Mithridates the Great*, 2008
McLynn, *Marcus Aurelius*, 2009
Miles Richard, *Carthage Must be Destroyed*, 2010
Miles Richard, *Ancient Worlds*, 2010
Opper Thorsten, *Hadrian*, 2008
Polybius, *The Histories*
Renucci Pierre, *Caligula*, 2000
Schiff, Stacy, *Cleopatra*, 2010
Strauss Barry, *The Spartacus War*, 2009
Suetonius, *The Twelve Caesars*
Tacitus, *The Annals of Imperial Rome*
Tacitus, *The Histories*
Tibullus, The Elegies of Tibullus, translated by Theodore C. Williams
Ward-Perkins Bryan, *The Fall of Rome*, 2005
Wheaton James, *Spartacus*, 2011
Wikipedia: Research today is impossible without the aid of this monument.
Williams Craig A. *Roman Homosexuality*, 2010
Williams John, *Augustus*, 1972

All pictures are from Wikipedia.

Printed in Great Britain
by Amazon